SAMUEL BECKETT AND THE PHILOSOPHICAL IMAGE

Beckett often made use of images from the visual arts and readapted them, staging them in his plays, or using them in his fiction. Anthony Uhlmann sets out to explain how an image differs from other terms, like 'metaphor' or 'representation', and, in the process, to analyse Beckett's use of images borrowed from philosophy and aesthetics. This is the first study of Beckett's thoughts on the image in his literary works and of his extensive notes to the philosopher Arnold Geulincx. Uhlmann considers how images might allow one kind of interaction between philosophy and literature, and how Beckett makes use of images which are borrowed from, or drawn into dialogue with, philosophical images from Geulincx, Berkeley, Bergson and the Ancient Stoics. Uhlmann's reading of Beckett's aesthetic and philosophical interests provides a revolutionary new reading of the importance of the image in his work.

ANTHONY UHLMANN is Associate Professor in the School of Humanities at the University of Western Sydney, Australia.

D1331276

REFERENCE

KA 0357512 8

SAMUEL BECKETT AND THE PHILOSOPHICAL IMAGE

ANTHONY UHLMANN

University of Western Sydney

CAMBRIDGE UNIVERSITY PRESS
Cambridge, New York, Melbourne, Madrid, Cape Town, Singapore, São Paulo, Delhi

Cambridge University Press
The Edinburgh Building, Cambridge CB2 8RU, UK

Published in the United States of America by Cambridge University Press, New York

www.cambridge.org
Information on this title: www.cambridge.org/9780521120128

First published 2006
This digitally printed version 2009

A catalogue record for this publication is available from the British Library

ISBN 978-0-521-86520-3 hardback
ISBN 978-0-521-12012-8 paperback

*To Andrea
and our boys
Liam and Xavier*

Contents

Acknowledgements

I would like to acknowledge the generous support of the Australian Research Council, as this book is the fruit of an ARC Large Grant. I wish to acknowledge the Research Office, and the School of Humanities at the University of Western Sydney, who have supported this project from the beginning. I would also like to thank a number of people. Firstly, Professor Wayne McKenna, Dean of the College of Arts, Education and Social Sciences at the University of Western Sydney, and a distinguished Joyce scholar, for the support he has offered to a number of projects (including the 2003 Sydney Beckett conference) which contributed directly and indirectly to this work. Stephen McLaren for his insightful reading and thorough proofreading of the final version. Jay Johnston and Chris Conti for their intelligent conversation and assistance with the early parts of this project as research assistants. Martin Wilson and Han van Ruler, for their work on the translation of Arnold Geulincx's *Ethics* (which we hope to publish shortly), which contributed greatly to aspects of this work. The readers at Cambridge University Press for valuable criticisms and insights which allowed me to strengthen the book considerably, and the editor Ray Ryan for his faith and positive criticism. I wish to thank my wife Andrea Curr both for her moral support and for her invaluable research assistance, and our sons, Liam and Xavier, for their support. Parts of this book have appeared in different form, and with different points of emphasis, in the journals *Substance*, *Angelaki*, *Samuel Beckett Today/Aujourd'hui*, and some material which contextualises an otherwise quite different piece is repeated in my essay in the University Press of Florida book *Beckett after Beckett*, which I co-edited with S. E. Gontarski. The publishers of these works are gratefully acknowledged. I wish to thank the executor of Samuel Beckett's estate, Mr Edward Beckett, for permission to cite from unpublished materials, and the staff at the Beckett Archives of the Beckett International Foundation at the University of Reading and at the Archives of the Library at Trinity College Dublin for their assistance during my research.

Introduction

in relation to intelligence, the image is the condition of thought; 'there is no thought without an image,' because the image is the material through which intelligence contemplates the universal.[1]

Ever since people have written about Beckett it has been noticed that he is a writer who is, even more than usual, interested in images. A good deal of work has recently been done concerning Beckett's interest in, and use of, images from the visual arts.[2] Most famously, Beckett told Ruby Cohn that he had remembered a Casper David Friedrich painting, *Two Men Looking at the Moon*, which he had seen during his trip to Germany prior to World War Two and had adapted this image, staging it in *En Attendant Godot*.[3] Working from a diary Beckett made while travelling through Germany and visiting art galleries before World War Two, and directed by comments made by Beckett himself, James Knowlson has convincingly displayed how Beckett made use of images from paintings which had had a forceful impression on him and reconfigured them in developing his own striking images in later works. Might the same be claimed for Beckett's use of philosophy? That is, did he borrow images used by philosophers and reuse them in his texts? Furthermore, what, in effect, is an 'image'; what can it do, and what does Beckett make it do?

Certainly, Beckett would not have been the only artist to translate images from other media, or to use them as a point of departure for his own works. In his review of Lewis Lockwood's biography of Beethoven, Owen Jander quotes Beethoven's friend and pupil Carl Czerny, who states:

It is certain that in many of his finest works Beethoven was inspired by visions and images drawn either from reading or created by his own excited imagination, and that we should obtain the real key to his compositions and to their performance only through the thorough knowledge of these circumstances, if this were always practicable.[4]

Jander suggests that for the most part Beethoven hid these images and did not tell others about them, except in one or two cases: as for example,

String Quartet in F major, Op. 18 No. 1, a movement which Beethoven said was inspired by the tomb scene in Shakespeare's *Romeo and Juliet*.[5]

The image and the ways in which it might be used are clearly important to Beckett. Yet Beckett is also important to the image and our apprehension of it: aspects of his artistic practice develop an aesthetic logic which extends our understanding of what an image is and can do in literature, drama and audiovisual media.

The work of French philosopher Henri Bergson (1859–1941) is of key importance to Beckett's understanding of the image and its relation to thought. Beckett knew both Bergson's work and the ideas of the early modernist movement, including the 'Imagists'. This group, led by Ezra Pound, and T. E. Hulme, who translated Bergson's essay *Introduction to Metaphysics*[6] into English, developed theories of the image in broad sympathy with the understandings I will outline in chapter 1 below. Bergson's ideas in turn were adapted, developed and transformed by other modernists, including Marcel Proust, T. S. Eliot, William Faulkner, James Joyce, Wallace Stevens, Vladimir Nabokov and literary theorists, including Bakhtin and the Russian Formalists.[7] Indeed, such a series of creative responses to problems described by Bergson (and his understanding of duration, memory, intuition and the image among other things) inflect so much work of substance that Bergson's philosophical system continues to be of relevance to contemporary practice. This importance has been amplified by the work of French philosopher Gilles Deleuze. Deleuze, who dedicates two important essays to Beckett which discuss Beckett's use of the image,[8] turns to Bergson, and *Matter and Memory*[9] in particular, in developing his concept of the image in the *Cinema* books[10] and elsewhere.[11]

Beckett discusses the 'image' a number of times in *Disjecta*,[12] and in several places within his works Beckett uses the term 'image' in a manner which brings it into line with philosophical definitions of the term. His 'imagination' from *Imagination Dead Imagine*[13] and *All Strange Away*[14] strongly relates to the use made of the word by Spinoza, Descartes and other seventeenth-century Rationalists who understand it to include all sensations (what we see, hear, touch, smell and taste here and now as much as those images we project from memory or faculties of fancy). Beckett clearly also considers the 'image' to be something which can be projected (through art, memory, fancy or some other cognitive faculty). This is apparent in his use of the term in *The Image*[15] and *How It Is*[16] and in the processes of image production described in works such as ... *but the clouds* ...[17] and *Nacht und Träume*.[18] It also becomes apparent that the production of such images might be related to philosophy as much as the arts. In a letter to his friend Thomas MacGreevy of 1933, Beckett specifically identifies his own interest in philosophical images, even if these are divorced from the systems in which they are used: 'Leibniz a great cod, but full of splendid little pictures'.[19]

So, sights, sounds, smells, tastes and things touched all produce 'images' to the sense organs which are interpreted by the brain in line with processes described by Bergson in *Matter and Memory* (and discussed in detail in chapter 1 below). As images, firstly, they are 'something' which requires interpretation, secondly they are interpreted by the brain as meaningful sensations and brought into contact with sign systems, including language. The image interacts with processes of cognition or thought. Indeed, the image, as what is first sensed and secondly related to sense or made sense of, might be understood to be a key element within the cognitive process. Rather than creating or structuring thought, it induces thought. It also precedes thought and exceeds thought. It can be understood to be a sign but is not always or only a sign (that is, one can fail to understand an image, one can find multiple and shifting sense in an image, and the meaning of an image can exceed the meanings assigned to it by signifying systems).

Further, because the image precedes and exceeds thought, it is something which is of equal importance to (but made different use of by) literature and philosophy. It is one way, then, of understanding how literature and philosophy might interact. Images can pass between literary and philosophical discourse, no doubt being transformed in the process of translation, but also carrying with them something in common, a translatable component which inheres in the image which is put into circulation. This process can be, and is, two-way. That is, a philosopher might borrow an image from a writer of fiction, and vice versa. The consequences of the theories I am developing here, then, while they will be explored via the work of Samuel Beckett, are generally applicable to discussions of philosophy and literature.

The image, of course, is not the only element available to literature: the music of the interplay of the sounds of words and their rhythm, the power of the story and the worlds brought forth by the voices of characters and narrators are equally important elements, yet these fall outside the scope of this study.

This study has two parts. Firstly, I develop a reading of philosophical understandings of the image, drawing out the importance of the concepts of 'presentation' and 'representation', and relate this to Beckett's aesthetic theories of the image, and his artistic practice (chapters 1–3). Secondly, I turn to questions of how images might allow one kind of interaction between philosophy and literature, and how Beckett makes use of images which are borrowed from or drawn into dialogue with philosophical images (chapters 4–7).

At the outset it is necessary to define exactly what is meant by 'the image', the kind of thinking it allegedly induces and how this relates to sensation or affective understandings. Chapter 1 confronts these questions in relation to the philosophy of Bergson and the theory of the image (cinematic and otherwise) developed by Deleuze in dialogue with Bergson and Charles Sanders Peirce. Chapter 2 ties these theories to Beckett's own aesthetic statements. Chapter 3 considers how Beckett's artistic practice develops from one concerned with relation and allusion in his early writings to a form which makes use of strategies (including the image) to present an art of 'nonrelation'.

Chapters 4 and 5 draw upon materials which have only just become available to scholars: Beckett's detailed notes to Arnold Geulincx,[20] and the first English translation of Geulincx's *Ethics*.[21] These new materials enable the development of significantly new readings in this study. These sources also serve to illustrate how Beckett makes use of images drawn from philosophy.

Chapter 6 considers the use of Bergson's notion of intuition, and the image of the philosophical system which he describes in relation to Berkeley, and compares these with Beckett's adaptation of Berkeley's ideas in the ideogrammatic work *Film*.[22] Chapter 7 turns to Beckett's late works. I look to the Stoic understanding of the image, link it back to ideas developed in the early chapters of this work and explore how their particular understandings of bodies and incorporeals shed light on the strange late plays of Beckett. I take *What Where*[23] as an example and look at this play in some detail.

I conclude by drawing together the implications of the use of the image in Beckett, both in relation to his own work and as an ongoing provocation to the contemporary theory and practice of literature and art more generally. I then list the kinds of images I have outlined in this study.

CHAPTER I

Representation and presentation: Deleuze, Bergson, Peirce and 'the image'

images can never be anything but things, and thought is a movement.[1]

'IT'S DONE I'VE DONE THE IMAGE'[2]

In *Gilles Deleuze: An Apprenticeship in Philosophy*,[3] Michael Hardt describes how Deleuze develops themes which have a long history in the Western philosophical tradition, but which have 'remained suppressed and dormant'. Hardt places Spinoza, Nietzsche and Bergson within a minor tradition which Deleuze develops:

we cannot read Deleuze's work as thought 'outside' or 'beyond' the philosophical tradition, or even as an effective line of flight from that block; rather we must see it as the affirmation of a (discontinuous, but coherent) line of thought that has remained suppressed and dormant, but nonetheless deeply embedded within that same tradition.[4]

One might apply Hardt's idea to an understanding of the image that has emerged at various times within the Western philosophical tradition, and that has been both suggested by and answered by certain kinds of artistic practice within the Western aesthetic tradition. At times this idea has emerged with clarity and force, and at times the insights it claims to reveal have been surrounded, taunted, ridiculed.

This idea considers that the apprehension of the image (which emerges from the real and is impressed upon our senses like a 'signet ring in wax') is fundamental both to our understanding of what the world is and to how we know that world. The idea is apparent in the work of the Ancient Greek Stoics, with their concept of 'phantasia', and with 'the comprehensive image' which grounds truth; in the work of Roman rhetorician Quintillian, who speaks of an image which is so forceful that we immediately apprehend its truth; in Descartes, who, according to Stephen Gaukroger, draws his understanding of the 'clear and distinct' idea from

5

Quintillian[5] (though Descartes moves from here to an intense focus on epistemology which leaves behind and disparages the image once it has been used as a point of departure). It is apparent in Spinoza, who both works with certain Cartesian ideas and returns to ideas drawn from the Ancient Stoics in developing his understanding of the three kinds of knowledge. It is there at the end of the nineteenth century in the work of William James and Charles Sanders Peirce, and in the idea of the image developed by Henri Bergson in *Matter and Memory*. These ideas in turn are developed and transformed by an army of modernist writers and artists who answer Bergson and James.[6] The idea has recently returned again, in the work of Gilles Deleuze, who develops a theory of the image in art that draws heavily on the work of Peirce and Bergson in particular. It is most fully developed in his *Cinema* books, but is also an important element in his works on Francis Bacon and Samuel Beckett. This idea is also of key importance to our understanding of the image in Samuel Beckett, who knew the work of many of the thinkers mentioned above.

A few works have been dedicated to Deleuze's *Cinema* books, where the relation between Bergson and Deleuze has been discussed.[7] While there are inevitably points of overlap, this is a complex problem, and my point of focus differs from studies that have appeared so far. That is, nothing has yet been written concerning the pairing of the concepts of 'representation' and 'presentation' in relation to the image in Deleuze, yet this is crucial to an understanding of the nature of the image. The purpose of this chapter is to look at the role of the image, from a cognitive perspective, as an interaction between notions of 'presentation' and 'representation', and to use this distinction in order to begin to develop an understanding of how the image might work in art.

In the *Logic of Affect*, Paul Redding traces points of correspondence between eighteenth- and nineteenth-century German idealism and contemporary theories of cognition. Redding underlines how a key distinction, or point of contention, in both nineteenth- and twentieth-century debates about the nature of cognition, concerned the problem of whether sensations should be considered 'presentations' or 'representations'. 'Direct Realists', such as William James, and more recently J. J. Gibson, consider that 'worldly things are directly and primarily *presented to* the mind'.[8] Such presentations are understood to have being in their own right, and therefore one looks to ontology when considering their nature. Others, including idealists such as Fichte and Schelling, argue that what occurs in our experience of the world is the production of 'representations'. That is, they contend that the immediate process of sensation is always lost and out of reach and what remains is the interpretation of the sensation. It is these interpretations or *re*presentations which involve or produce knowledge, and so one looks to epistemology when considering their nature.[9] The distinction between the representation and the presentation (as understood by William James) is described by Redding as follows:

> For James, the notion of a psychic 'representation' could apply only *within* experience: one mental content, my thought say, of tigers in India, could only be said to represent some other experiential content such as an immediately perceived tiger encountered when my thought had played the appropriate role in leading me to that latter experience. A truly representational content was thus a 'substitution' for a direct perceptual encounter, and its cognitive value was dependent on that of direct perception. This meant that actual perceptual encounter could not itself be thought of as a 'representation' of a perceived object as in the traditional representative theory, but more as its direct *presentation*.[10]

What is at stake is the understanding of the process of perception: both the manner in which we sense or apprehend the world and the manner in which we interpret what we have sensed or apprehended. The thinkers who work within the minor tradition I have sketched above have in common that, like the Direct Realists, they consider the image itself to have real being, one that directly acts upon us. The word 'image' concerns all those materials that are presented to our nervous system via our senses. In being presented to us, these things literally touch us: the sound waves which vibrate the mechanisms of our inner ear; the bodies which touch ours; the molecules of other entities which are captured by our senses of smell and taste; the waves of light which pass into our eyes. In each case, following Bergson, the brain screens these images. Firstly, things project their images through our senses onto our brain. The brain itself (which, for Bergson, forms another image) then acts as a screen in two ways: images are screened upon it in the manner of a cinema screen, and it screens or filters these images in interpreting them. For Bergson, we consciously perceive by subtracting all those things from an image which are not of interest to us and focusing on those things which might either act upon us or upon which we might act.

BERGSON'S IMAGE AND DELEUZE'S IMAGE

While it is not possible to fully understand Deleuze's concept of the image, or more specifically the image as sign, through a straightforward comparison with Bergson, certain points of convergence and divergence between them are instructive.

Bergson's influential work of 1896, *Matter and Memory*, draws heavily upon the concept of 'the image', a term which already had a long history in philosophy tying it to inadequate modes of understanding.[11] Yet rather than the image being a secondary category, linked to the inferior kinds of understanding derived from the testimony of the senses, the image, in Bergson's system, is given a much more prominent place.

Matter, in our view, is an aggregate of "images." And by "image" we mean a certain existence which is more than that which the idealists call a representation, but less than that which the realist calls a thing – an existence placed halfway between the 'thing' and the 'representation'.[12]

What Bergson proposes is not, on the one hand, using the image to displace terms with a more aristocratic genealogy, such as 'the idea' or 'thought' – terms which were often set up against the image as superior mental processes, and both of which are implicit in the term 'representation' – or on the other hand as a means of dissolving the reality of 'things' external to one who perceives. Rather, he is proposing understanding 'the image' as a bridge between those objectively existing things and our thoughts. It is a bridge because the image exists both in the thing, which has or projects an image consistent with the nature of its own being, and in our minds, which receive the projected images in the manner of a screen. 'This is as much to say that there is for images merely a difference of degree, and not of kind, between being and being consciously perceived'.[13] Though perhaps not immediately clear, the ramifications of this are extraordinary. That is, the image partakes both of being and of knowing: it therefore offers a path through which we might directly know the thing in itself. This no doubt scandalous idea, which is clearly compatible with Bergson's concept of intuition (which, in turn might be compared with Spinoza's third kind of knowledge), is also quite close to the grounding of knowledge through a particular privileged image developed by the Ancient Stoics.

For Bergson, my body too is an image, though different to all others in that it is one that I perceive not only externally through perceptions but internally through my affections.[14] The body is an image that acts like all other images, receiving movement and giving back movement, 'with, perhaps, this difference only, that my body appears to choose, within certain limits, the manner in which it shall restore what it receives'.[15] That is:

if . . . all images are posited at the outset, my body will necessarily end by standing out in the midst of them as a distinct thing, since they change unceasingly, and it does not vary. The distinction between the inside and the outside will then be only a distinction between the part and the whole. There is, first of all, the aggregate of images; and, then, in this aggregate, there are 'centers of action,' from which the interesting images appear to be reflected: thus perceptions are born and actions made ready.[16]

So the brain is more than a screen that passively receives a projection from outside: it is a screen which in turn acts, and acts in two ways. It both analyses the images projected upon it and itself selects the movements it executes within its body: 'the brain appears to us to be an instrument of analysis in regard to the movement received and an instrument of selection with regard to the movement executed'.[17] The brain does not produce representations in the manner understood by idealism (bringing the world into being);[18] rather, it receives and acts upon images.[19]

Representations do occur, but they are not the result of our brain *adding* something to perceptions of images; rather, conscious perception, for Bergson, involves the process of realising representations by *subtracting* what does not interest us from an image (that is, the way in which it is linked to all other images, which comprises its real action) and concentrating on those aspects of it with which we might potentially interact (the virtual action).[20] Such a subtraction, focusing only on those elements of the image upon which we might act or which might act upon us, relates (and Deleuze underlines this point) to the motor-sensory circuit of perceiving and acting. That is, there is a stimulus, and then there is an action or reaction. This involves a selective causal chain, one based on a logic through which the effects one perceives are understood to be first causes.[21] In turn, we isolate these causes in considering what will act upon us and what we might act upon. This process provides the structure on which narrative (which develops through tracing selected causal chains) is built. The brain, then, is a screen in two senses: in one sense it is the repository for the images of things which it reflects in the manner of a cinema screen, in another it filters or sifts, screening out what is not able to be understood in terms of motor-sensory interest.

Our [brains, which are] 'zones of indetermination' play in some sort the part of the screen. They add nothing to what is there; they effect merely this: that the real action passes through, the virtual action remains.[22]

We begin to see, from what we have selected here, how Bergson's theories should have an effect on notions of representation, and it is worth attempting to trace these effects in Deleuze's work in order to better understand the nature of the 'image'.

CREATING THE WORK

If we assume a critical reading of this we must retrace these steps. If the world projects onto the screen of the brain, does the artist select or screen the real to reproject an already represented world onto the screen of the work? Would the work in turn be reprojected into the brain of the audience, who in turn would screen or filter it further? If so, how would this process not involve a dissolution or degradation of the image, when Bergson tells us the representation already involves the subtraction from the image of what does not interest us?

As Deleuze states in a number of places, art does not involve mimesis, the representation or mimicking of any other thing; rather, it is a form of creation, the creation of something new which affects us directly, rather than indirectly. It is worth emphasising a particular point, which is crucial to my argument. The term 'representation' is understood here in the cognitive sense discussed above. For Bergson, as we have seen, the interpretation or cognitive appraisal involved in developing a representation does not involve adding something, but, rather, examining what is presented and filtering it, concentrating only on those elements of the presentation which interest us. Conscious perception, then, for Bergson, is a process of selection, and this selection is already implicated in processes of interpretation. I see a tiger charging towards me and perceive it by focusing on it, isolating it from the mass of less important information being offered to my senses at that moment. This process is related to the sensory-motor circuit described above: you sense (danger, for example) by quickly recognising what you can act upon or what can act upon you and then you immediately react.

This process in turn can be related to art if the term 'representation' is always understood in this sense and not confused with the many other senses it has developed in being used to describe works of art. I understand representation in art, as in cognition, here, to involve this process of selection or screening (in its dual sense), a selection of what is of interest, which already involves interpretation. With cognition, this interpretation is single, as the perceiving individual creates a representation from a presentation.

In creative forms, when they involve representations, there can be a double process. On the one hand, some works are representations that already carry clear interpretations with them (which can only be accepted or rejected by an audience). Some of these works are representations of representations (drawing their form and content from previous works of representation rather than offering something new). In each of these cases, the interpretations available to an audience will be impoverished.

On the other hand, art does not have to represent something that has already been represented. Rather, it can create, and in creating, offers the audience a new image that they must interpret (with an effort of thought) rather than a pre-interpreted, represented, image.

Many works offer pre-interpreted, pre-digested images, so that the audience is called upon to recognise and react rather than to interpret and think. For Deleuze, however, at least in some works, the world is created, not represented. There is no imitation involved in such created images. Such created images do not send us back to the world in order to be authenticated; rather, they immediately form part of our world as we set the screen of our brain against the screen of the work.

REPRESENTATION AND PRESENTATION

Further light might be shed on this problem if we turn to one of the few passages in which Deleuze specifically mentions 'representation' in the *Cinema* books. Here we have an example of a submerged system, as Deleuze never seeks to appeal to the concept of representation in order to buttress the concepts related to the image. Yet, in looking back to Bergson and in examining one of the few occasions when Deleuze does use the term representation, it becomes clear that there is a distinction between a selected representation (a degraded interpretation of a real image) and the presentation of an image in its fullness (such as is possible within Deleuze's system in the 'crystal-image' but, perhaps, not only here), an image which requires interpretation and thus strikes us with its power.

In *Cinema 2*, Deleuze states that the movement-image provides a *representation* of time while the time-image provides a *presentation* of time:

By raising themselves to the indiscernibility of the real and the imaginary, the signs of the crystal go beyond all psychology of the recollection or dream, and all physics of action. What we see in the crystal is no longer the empirical progression of time as succession of presents, nor its indirect *representation* as interval or as whole; it is its direct *presentation*, its constitutive dividing in two into a present which is passing and a past which is preserved, the strict contemporaneity of the present with the past that it will be, of the past with the present that it has been ... the time-image has arisen through direct or transcendental *presentation*, as a new element in post-war cinema ...[23]

We need to keep in mind how Bergson has defined the representation as involving subtraction; as involving a selection from the image rather than the whole image; as being something less than the image. The movement-image *represents* time in that we arrive at an understanding of time not by being shown time directly but by being shown a line of action which necessarily involves the passage of time in its unfolding (an empirical progression). Following Bergson, this is a representation because it involves a process of subtraction from the image. We would be shown a man at the bottom of a staircase, for example, and then through the techniques of continuity editing, be shown the man at the top of the staircase, the passage of time taken to mount the staircase being *represented* through the subtractions involved in the codes of continuity editing. The time-image, on the other hand, *presents* the flow of time (which is not simply monodirectional from past to present but involves flux). Deleuze states, the cinema of the time-image is the cinema of the seer not the actor. The movement-image and the narrative form attached to it relates to sensory-motor links such as those described by Bergson, which result from selective perception: that is, the editing-out of material from the images received; the clear connections made between one represented image and another in a process of interpretation. This process includes the subtraction involved in forming representations of the real, which in turn allow us to act. The time-image, however, emerges in response to situations 'to which one can no longer react'.[24]

These are pure optical and sound situations, in which the character does not know how to respond . . . But he has gained in an ability to see what he has lost in action or reaction: he SEES so that the viewer's problem becomes 'What is there to see in the image?' (and not now 'What are we going to see in the next image?' . . . This is no longer a sensory-motor situation, but a purely optical and sound situation, where the seer has replaced the agent . . .[25]

We are given an image that requires us to see with the protagonist, which makes us look and directly experience time. The time-image, then, requires the movement of the viewer into the image in order that that viewer might directly experience seeing and the time involved in seeing. This is described as a 'presentation' because there is no process of subtraction involved.

CLICHÉ

Mediocre works partake of cliché. The cliché, insofar as it concerns images, only makes use of an image which is closely connected with a familiar idea: it is a well-worn metaphor, in short. Falling into cliché, for Deleuze, marks the crisis of the action-image, which is only fully overcome with the emergence of the time-image. With the cliché, the images used are not only familiar and pre-interpreted but complacently refer to earlier pre-interpreted images and seek to rely on those interpretations for their (reflected) power. In one sense it is simply a problem of the history of representation: the cliché is not so much a representation or interpretation of the real; rather, it is a representation of other representations. It refers to – in shorthand – and necessarily subtracts from, the store of metaphors that have been gathered in cultural history. Part of the burden of tradition is the problem of how to escape from cliché, how to avoid the danger of showing again what has been shown too often and has therefore lost its power to affect or even entertain. The representation of the representation is related to habit, while the image (the presentation) and the original metaphor (a non-clichéd representation) elude habit in forcing the viewer to participate in their understanding.[26] Clearly, the question of the relation of the image to repetition is begged here, and I will return to this below.

The problem becomes even more pronounced when one considers how cliché emerges not simply through the repetition of pre-interpreted images in works but through the imitation of elements of 'the real' that have themselves become clichéd. It is as if mediocre art has invaded life so that we sometimes (developing our real-life representations with processes of selection already contaminated by common expectations or cliché) play out hackneyed scenarios that are in turn re-represented by mediocre works. The crisis stems from the hardening of the image into a representation, and the hardening of our own perceptions (which, following Bergson, already involve representations) into cliché or habit. The problem today remains, as it has long been in literature, for Flaubert,[27] Shklovsky,[28] Proust[29] and Beckett[30] among others: how does one overcome cliché in art, how does one overcome habit in life? Deleuze asks:

if images have become clichés, internally as well as externally, how can an Image be extracted from all these clichés, 'just an image', an autonomous mental image? An image *must* emerge from the set of clichés ... With what politics and what consequences? What is an image which would not be a cliché? Where does the cliché end and the image begin?[31]

Deleuze seems to offer an answer that involves two kinds of image. Firstly, Deleuze describes an 'autonomous mental image' which 'had not to be content with weaving a set of relations, but had to form a new substance'.[32] One might seek to understand this kind of image with reference to Deleuze's essay on Francis Bacon, where he speaks of the process of creating an image through extraction, rather than abstraction, from the real.[33] Such an image is cut from the set of relations commonly offered and presented as an autonomous substance, a pure affect, and I will return to this idea in the following two chapters. Secondly, we have seen how Deleuze speaks, in the second *Cinema* book, of the time-image as presentation. That is, rather than showing us an image which has already passed through the screening process of perception, the time-image offers us an image which makes us see but does not allow us to act, an image in all its fullness.

The presentation is the image in its fullness: William James's 'blooming buzzing confusion'. The representation is an interpretation of the presentation, an interpretation which involves removing elements which are not of interest, and adding already formulated understandings of it, a process which, when the human is fully and properly functioning, proceeds by habit.

Habit, for the Bergson of *Matter and Memory*, is a state which we all should aspire to. He compares, for example, spontaneous or involuntary memory with voluntary memory. The properly functioning, mature human being represses involuntary memory, which emerges most forcefully among the ill-disciplined and not fully educated (children, for example) and makes use of voluntary memory to properly perform daily functions.[34] Marcel Proust responded to this idea by reversing the poles: involuntary memory, for Proust, is that which allows us access to a deeper meaning, whereas the world of habit is a dead world. You bite into the madeleine and you are taken back to plenitude: a full, involuntary memory, which transports you through time. It overwhelms you, you cannot control it. In this sense, the presented image of Proust's involuntary memory shares some of the attributes of the sublime, which was so important to the Romantic tradition of the previous century. Indeed, we also see this idea – the idea that we need to overcome habit – emerging in much of the artistic theory of the modernist movement. We see it in Ezra Pound's 'Make It New',[35] for example, and the Russian Formalist idea that one needs to 'defamiliarise' an object so as to break with habit, which stops us from seeing that object.[36] These ideas, then, even if in negative image, are linked to a Bergsonian theory of perception which has much in common with earlier systems developed by the Ancient Stoics, Spinoza and others.

The role of art for Proust, and many of the modernists, as well as for many of the Romantics who wished to convey the sublime that overwhelms our everyday experience, is to overcome our habits in approaching the thing in itself. In short, the role of art is to make us think, with thought here understood in an almost primal form, as our response to an environment or thing, a response that is felt and immediate and not an imitation of a former response, not an expected or taught response.

It is apparent, however, that the representation and the presentation can co-exist in a work. Asked in what sense he means that the cinematic image (the time-image) is not 'in the present', Deleuze states:

> it seems obvious to me that the image is not in the present. What the image 'represents' is in the present, but not the image itself. The image itself is an ensemble of time relations from the present which merely flows, either as a common multiple, or as the smallest divisor. Relations of time are never seen in ordinary perception, but they are in the image, as long as it is a creative one.[37]

The presentation can emerge out of the representation in some cases. On the other hand, there is the representation of the representation alone in the case of mediocre work. There is, therefore, a need to talk of the actualisation of the virtual in certain works: that is, the process of drawing out or entering into an image (which always carries with it a set of unrealised or not yet realised possibilities) which is in part undertaken by the viewer.

We find here, then, two interrelated elements toward a general definition of the image. Firstly, they involve the avoidance of, or the escape from clichés, as processes of creation. Secondly, they involve presentation, which might be understood as the necessary involvement of the audience in their interpretation, rather than the referral of the audience to ready-made or habitual responses. Further, the image as presentation has at least two possible forms: a) the extracted image, the autonomous mental image (in the manner of Francis Bacon), and b) the direct presentation, the non-represented image (in the manner of Proust).

One can compare this with the Stoic understanding, which we will encounter in chapter 7, and which strongly attracts Deleuze, who uses it extensively in *The Logic of Sense*. Emile Bréhier affirms that for the Stoics, the point of departure for knowledge is the 'image' (φαντασια, or 'phantasia').[38] Cicero, quoted in Bréhier, affirmed that the Ancient Stoic Zeno of Citium described how one moves through stages of knowledge as follows:

> He would raise his hand, spread out his fingers, and say: 'This is [image].' Then he would bend his fingers slightly and say: 'This is assent.' Then he would clinch his fist and say: 'This is perception.' Finally he would clasp his right fist to his left hand and say: 'This is wisdom which belongs only to the sage.'[39]

The 'image', then, belongs to a primal perceptual moment: in the Stoic system it is that which impresses itself upon us and asks us to respond, to understand.

CLICHÉ, IMAGE AND REPETITION

It is important to clarify how processes of repetition might interact with the ideas of the image and the cliché which are outlined here. Repetition, in and of itself, does not necessarily lead to an image becoming a cliché. Firstly, repetition, as has been admirably demonstrated by Steven Connor in particular in relation to Beckett's works, might add complexity rather than subtract from an image. One example of this is when the repeated image, rather than serving to underline or emphasise a given meaning, adds a new layer of uncertainty, a new element which requires further interpretation.[40]

Secondly, as I seek to demonstrate throughout this work, one might borrow an image from another source without that image inevitably becoming a cliché. It should also be noted that artists might conceivably work with cliché, but if the work is to rise above mediocrity, it will need to overturn or put into question the clear interpretation which rests at the heart of the cliché.

It is possible to illustrate what is at stake here by turning to examples from Beckett's early career as a playwright. Beckett's first play, which remained unpublished during his lifetime and still remains unperformed, is *Eleutheria*.[41] As is well known, Beckett makes strong use of cliché in this work: that is, he refers to images and situations which are well known from theatre history and, in particular, recent theatre history. To cite McMillan and Fehsenfeld:

As its Greek title suggests, *Eleuthéria* is the assertion of 'freedom' from the constraints of dramatic precedents reaching back into classical antiquity ... The play is, among other things, a very sophisticated and funny burlesque catalogue of particular plays or traditions ... The list is exhaustive. There are parodies or allusions from Sophocles, Shakespeare, Molière, Corneille, Shaw, Zola, Ibsen, Hauptmann, Pirandello, Yeats, Symbolism, Surrealism, Artaud, Jarry and Socialist Realism to name only the most evident. As the Glazier, who functions as a kind of stage manager, says near to the end of the play: '*Pour un tour d'horizon. C'est un tour d'horizon.*'[42]

Beckett, in effect making use of a technique which was itself to become well worn in postmodern aesthetic practice, draws our attention to these images, making it clear to the audience that they are being shown clichés, and that these clichés are being held up to ridicule. One might ask, however, as Deleuze does with regard to works by American filmmaker Robert Altman, whether it is enough to simply show how everything has become cliché. Deleuze answers that this is not enough, that rather than simply recognising an impasse and, as it were, throwing up one's hands, it remains necessary to *make* the image.[43] That is, the imperative remains to bore holes in the surfaces which enclose, to make an image which might elude this smug, self-satisfied, comforting recognition of the same; which might break with the impoverished pleasures of irony and lead us back to the uncomfortable need to think for ourselves, to interpret for ourselves. One might argue that Beckett considered *Eleutheria* unworthy for this reason: it remains mediocre because it functions through clichés which, even as it attempts to undermine them, it never manages to escape.

This work can be compared with *Waiting for Godot*,[44] which was written soon after *Eleutheria*. Rather than working through cliché, *Godot*, as is again well known, borrows images from domains which are distinct from (if not foreign to) highbrow theatre: the music-hall tradition, the comic tradition of silent cinema, for example. The images of the tramps, their hats, their slapstick routines, and so on, are apparently borrowed images. Yet, when this play was first performed, it struck its first audiences with its newness: the newness of the language as well as the newness of the visual representations. Yet neither of these elements could be considered to be new in and of themselves; rather, they were new to the medium of highbrow theatre. The language, rather than being invented, among other things borrows usages from everyday speech. The visual representations too borrow images from the mediums mentioned above. *Godot*, then, in making use of borrowed forms, does repeat images. It does not, however, repeat images which had already hardened into cliché within the medium of theatre; rather, it imports images from other mediums which at the time were not being brought into direct contact with the theatre. These images, then, were new to the theatre, and therefore needed to be understood, to be interpreted, for the first time by the first audiences of *Godot*. This offers a stark contrast with *Eleutheria*, where the borrowed images are well known within the theatre tradition and the audience is asked only to recognise that these images have occurred before, so that we can all agree that they are now unserviceable clichés. While this mutual process of recognition might lead us to share a knowing guffaw, it produces a work which remains mediocre. The identification of a borrowed image, however, an image borrowed from another medium not commonly related to the first, requires thought, as we are asked to try and understand how the first might relate to the second: that is, we are asked to find connections for ourselves rather than recognise already clearly established connections.

The reading of Bergson in Deleuze has taken us in a certain direction, and we are beginning to see the importance of the interaction between perception, the presentation and the representation. The process is not complete, however. More light can be shed on the problem and a clearer understanding might be uncovered by linking Bergson with Charles Sanders Peirce.

In developing his theory of the cinematic image in *Cinema 1* and *Cinema 2*, Deleuze turns not only to Bergson, but to the founder of semiotics, Charles Sanders Peirce. Deleuze is careful to differentiate between semiotics (the study of signs) and what he calls 'semiology' (the study of language-based sign systems). Deleuze considers that the semiologists (those theorists, highly influential in the twentieth-century French intellectual tradition, who build upon theories developed by Saussure) are wrong to use language as the privileged model for all semiotic systems, because this model is limited and unable to do justice to thought, which might work through image-signs (or other kinds of signs) just as readily as through human language. He prefers Peirce because Peirce does not privilege language; indeed, Peirce does not even privilege human systems of communication. Rather, Peirce considers that everything is a kind of sign. He defines a sign as: 'Anything which determines something else (its *interpretant*) to refer to an object to which itself refers (its *object*) in the same way, the interpretant becoming in turn a sign, and so on *ad infinitum*'.[45] For Peirce this is true of the world as a whole. That is, the human brain is not a prerequisite for thought or the existence and interaction of semiotic systems:

Thought is not necessarily connected with a brain. It appears in the work of bees, of crystals, and throughout the purely physical world; and one can no more deny that it is really there, than that the colors, the shapes, etc., of objects are really there. Consistently adhere to that unwarrantable denial, and you will be driven to some form of idealistic nominalism akin to Fichte's. Not only is thought in the organic world, but it develops there. But as there cannot be a General without Instances embodying it, so there cannot be thought without Signs. We must here give 'Sign' a very wide sense, no doubt, but not too wide a sense to come within our definition.[46]

We should note that Deleuze criticises Peirce for asserting, rather than deducing, the nature of the sign (that is, that it does not depend on language). This use of unargued assertion is dangerous, in Deleuze's view, because he considers that it does not provide the sufficiently strong impetus that would allow Peirce's system to resist the gravitational pull of linguistic systems. This is because, for Deleuze, Peirce still does tend, from time to time, to privilege 'knowledge' or the *interpretation* of signs, which in turn causes Peirce to fall too heavily under the influence of linguistic models of communication. As Deleuze states:

the sign's function must be said to 'make relations efficient': not that relations and laws lack actuality *qua* images, but they still lack that efficiency which makes them act 'when necessary', and that only knowledge gives them. But, on this basis, Peirce can sometimes find himself as much a linguist as the semiologists. For, if the sign elements still imply no privilege for language, this is no longer the case with the sign, and linguistic signs are perhaps the only ones to constitute a pure knowledge, that is, to absorb and reabsorb the whole content of the image as consciousness or appearance. They do not let any material that cannot be reduced to an utterance survive, and hence reintroduce a subordination of semiotics to a language system.[47]

Deleuze goes on to claim that his own theory of the image avoids this pitfall because he deduces the three types of images[48] rather than claiming them 'as fact'.[49]

In order to understand better the nature of the image, it is worth unpacking something of what is at stake here. Peirce develops three categories, the First, Second and Third:

The First is that whose being is simply in itself, not referring to anything nor lying behind anything. The Second is that which is what it is by force of something to which it is second. The Third is that which is what it is owing to things between which it mediates and which it brings into relation to each other.[50]

Although Peirce relates notions of First-, Second- and Thirdness to kinds of signs, the sign, in principle, is an expression of the Third: that is, 'A sign is an object [1] which stands for another [2] to some mind [or interpretant, 3]'[51] and for Peirce, as we have seen, everything is a sign, and the universe itself is a semiotic system.

How, then, could this be made to fit with the ideas of Bergson? This question is not directly posed by Deleuze, but its outlines can be traced in what we have laid out above. For Bergson, we will remember, an image is 'a certain existence which is more than that which the idealists call a representation, but less than that which the realist calls a thing – an existence placed halfway between the "thing" and the "representation"'.[52] It is possible, to a certain extent, to roughly line up these coordinates again with Peirce. The 'thing' of the realists would correspond with the First,[53] while the 'representation' of the idealists would be replaced by Peirce (who breaks definitively with idealist models) with the sign that is the Third. Half-way between the First and the Third is the Second, and I would argue that, at least to an extent, at least on some occasions, the image can correspond with the Second. That is, the image is second to the thing which projects an image, and again second to a brain which receives and screens that image.

That is, moving here in some senses between Peirce and Bergson and in some senses outside their systems, the image can appear in a work in an at least partially uninterpreted state. In such a state, it is an image that confronts another (for we are all images for Bergson). As a mind, I may move to understand the image which appears to the image that is my brain, and, insofar as I succeed in understanding that image, I might be said to interpret it, or constitute it, as a sign (moving from Zeno's open hand – the image – to the closed fist – perception). This might occur with some ease or with some difficulty. Insofar as the image is already integrated into a semiotic system with which I am familiar, the process will be easy, and the image might immediately be understood or recognised as a sign. It is a sign because it stands for something to me.[54] If, however, the image is not easily understood, one of two things will happen. I will either pass over the image as something upon which I cannot act and which cannot act upon me, screening it out as being without relevance. Or, having been forced to concede that the image might act upon me, or to believe I might act upon it, I will struggle to understand the image (and perhaps fail).

The power of the image, then, in part rests in the fact that it is that which I must move towards that I must actively interpret. Certain signs are understood passively: they belong to systems that have become familiar and to which one can respond through a kind of reflex or habit.[55] In art, these image-signs can become clichés. Those images that are not clichés, then, are those that require the interpretant to actively interpret, to move toward the unfamiliar. These images are not yet signs, but one has already assented to their significance (moving from Zeno's open hand to his slightly closed fingers), and it is the ungrasped significance that gives them their power. They are presentations that we are seeking to grasp as representations. One might bend Peirce's terms here and argue that this involves a movement between Secondness and Thirdness (and even on occasion, where the image is infinite, potentially back to Firstness, which is the apprehension of all being, the presentation in its pure form).

The First must ... be present and immediate, so as not to be second to a representation ... What the world was to Adam on the day he opened his eyes to it, before he had drawn any distinctions, or had become conscious of his own existence, – that is first, present, immediate, fresh, new, initiative, original, spontaneous, free, vivid, conscious, and evanescent. Only, remember, that every description of it must be false to it.[56]

Of course, not all images can aspire to dragging us back to this unfallen state (though I would suggest that on certain occasions, such as Proust's endeavour to express spontaneous memory, this is, at least, attempted). In effect, the image, as understood here, largely concerns a Secondness, or the recognition of meaningfulness and the imperative to understanding: the recognition of the need to interpret which is not yet complete and possibly impossible to complete.

Such interpretation, in effect, involves an effort to bridge the gap between the Second and the Third (or the First, Second and Third), between presentation and representation. It involves, then, genuine thinking, an active struggle that might even be overwhelming on occasion. It is, I would argue, one way in which one might begin to understand the difference between the affect of presentations in art and the affects of kinds of representation. Simple representation does not produce or require thought. Art, in whatever medium it might exist, stimulates thought in the interpretant, and one way in which it does this is by producing images that are on their way to being signs but are not yet or are no longer signs. The image both precedes and exceeds the sign.

BERGSON AND INTUITION[57]

In *Matter and Memory* Bergson states: 'images can never be anything but things, and thought is a movement'.[58] In developing a description of 'intuition' in his *Introduction to Metaphysics*, Bergson urges us to develop a kind of thinking that does justice to movement.[59] There are two kinds of knowledge, he claims: firstly, there is the relative, which is outside the object it seeks to describe. Such knowledge is relative because one views an object from a given position. Another will view it from a different perspective and so the truth of the observations will be relative to the given position from which one observes.[60]

The second kind of knowledge, however, is absolute. The understanding of movement, in such a case, is no longer relative because the observer is no longer outside the object; rather, the observer is within the object. Such absolute knowledge is achieved through an intuition that involves a being within a given object. In this way I have, at least potentially, insofar as I am able to achieve intuition, an absolute knowledge of my self, as the self is what I inhabit.

A representation taken from a certain point of view, a translation made with certain symbols, will always remain imperfect in comparison with the object of which a view has been taken, or which the symbols seek to express. But the absolute, which is the object and not its representation, the original and not its translation, is perfect, by being perfectly what it is.[61]

In illustrating this point Bergson turns to art, and specifically the novel. While claiming that such art (which he seems to understand as involving representations rather than presentations) will always fail to capture the absolute, and while describing the nature of this failure, he also posits an ideal art:

The author may multiply the traits of his hero's character, may make him speak and act as much as he pleases, but all this can never be equivalent to the simple and indivisible feeling which I should experience if I were able for an instant to identify myself with the person of the hero himself. Out of that indivisible feeling, as from a spring, all the words, gestures, and actions of the man would appear to me to flow naturally ... The character would be given to me all at once, in its entirety ... Description, history, and analysis leave me here in the relative. Coincidence with the person himself would alone give me the absolute.[62]

The 'absolute' here is another word for the pure, complete, presentation that it is no doubt impossible for any artform to completely achieve. It is the First, and 'every description of it must be false to it',[63] but at least, in taking us back to the Second, the image which requires interpretation does bring us as close as possible to this. To cite Bergson one last time:

Now the image has at least this advantage, that it keeps us in the concrete. No image can replace the intuition of duration, but many diverse images, borrowed from very different orders of things, may, by the convergence of their action, direct consciousness to the precise point where there is a certain intuition to be seized.[64]

If we are to accept these ideas, we might begin to see how two kinds of understanding differ. Insofar as I understand through habit (that is, insofar as I recognise a sign, acknowledge a representation) I am only able to achieve relative understanding. I am external to the object (1) which is a sign of something else (2) to my mind (3). If, however, the image is recognised as significant but not understood, if it urges me to struggle to understand, I need to move back toward the image in order to understand,

and this movement is, at least potentially, one which moves with the image object (that is, it moves towards, while never quite achieving, the absolute). If I ever grasp such an image I will do so through intuition (yet I will fail to represent this understanding when I turn to the kind of critical analysis one must necessarily adopt in discussing an object such as a work of literature).

CHAPTER 2

Beckett's aesthetic writings and 'the image'

Beckett's understanding of the image, and its importance to literature, as it is expressed in his occasional aesthetic writings, is formed around premises which closely relate to understandings which pass through the idea of the presentation. Beckett's interest in the image begins quite early in his career, and attention to his aesthetic writings makes it apparent that he holds consistently to certain of the conceptions he develops early on. This is not to claim that there are no developments or shifts in his understanding or practice, or that he is always able to adequately apply these ideas to his works. Rather, as we will see in examining Beckett's aesthetic practice in the next chapter, there are important shifts as well as points of apparent contradiction between his works and the aesthetic ideas he describes. In short, it takes Beckett some time before he is able to develop a form which is able to do justice to ideas whose outlines at least he seems to have perceived from the outset.

We have seen, through the reading of Bergson, Peirce and Deleuze, how, rather than being understood as relating to the Thirdness of the sign, which already involves interpretation, the image should be understood as involving the immediacy of Secondness, which is presented to us and requires interpretation. A similar understanding of the cognitive functioning of the image (which is immediate and requires interpretation), as opposed to the symbol (which exists as a relation and so already carries an intended interpretation) can be found in Beckett's own aesthetic writings. In a review of Jack Yeats's novel *The Amaranthers*, published in the *Dublin Magazine* of July–September 1936, Beckett states:

There is no symbol. The cream horse that carries Gilfoyle and the cream coach that carries Gilfoyle are related, not by rule of three, as two values to a third, but directly, as stages of an image.[1]

This short passage sheds light both on the well known 'no symbols where none intended' of *Watt*,[2] and the desire Beckett expressed for developing an art in the absence of relations: a nonrelational art whose outlines are traced in more detail in chapter 3. Such an absence of relations might be understood, in part, as involving the presentation of material that requires interpretation, rather than the representation of pre-interpreted signs or symbols, brought about by relating 'two values to a third'.

In 'Peintres de l'Empêchement', which was written in 1948, Beckett states that all works of art have involved the readjustment of the relation between subject and object,[3] a relation that he claims has now broken down. He announced this crisis over a decade before and prior to World War Two, in 1934, in another review: 'Recent Irish Poetry'.[4] The breakdown might be understood to have taken place because, on the one hand, the subject is no longer able to understand itself as a simple point of relation, and, on the other, the object is no longer something which is able to be simply represented, simply understood. For Beckett a good definition of modern painting would be, 'Le premier assaut donné à l'objet saisi, indépendamment de ses qualities, dans son indifférence, son inertie, sa latence'.[5] The modern painters Beckett discusses in 'Peintres de l'Empêchement' have in common that the 'objects' they paint are understood to have a kind of unity with one another in that, 'ils ne font qu'un en ceci, que ce sont des choses, la chose, la choseté'.[6] Such 'things' are directly presented to us, in an uninterpreted state.[7] A key problem with any attempt to represent (and therefore interpret) the object is that the interpretation, the representation, rather than revealing the object, simply adds another layer to it, one which serves to conceal it still more fully, 'Car que reste-t-il de représentable si l'essence de l'object est de se dérober à la représentation?'[8] This problem, whereby the thing itself is constantly eluding any attempt to be portrayed, is something Beckett attempts to approach, strategically, from different sides at different times. The use of the image, which serves to 'present' or create an object rather than represent one, is one strategy. In 'Peintres de l'Empêchement' Beckett answers his own question as follows: 'Il reste à réprésenter les conditions de cette dérobade'.[9] That is, another approach, which is related to the use of the image, is the attempt to reveal the process of hiding, to create the affect of the power of an object by occluding rather than attempting to represent the essential components of that object. This second process is something which also involves images, images which occlude, and we will examine this in chapters 4, 5 and 6 below. Beckett draws his argument together by indicating that there are two kinds of 'empêchement' or impediment to simple representation, with Greer and Bram van Velde being, in turn, examples of each kind. The first (Greer) says, 'Je ne peux voir l'objet, pour le

représenter, parce qu'il est ce qu'il est.'[10] That is, developing an interpretation based upon the materials we have treated thus far, the essential
components of the object cannot be seen, because the essential nature of
the object is to project images which elude representation. The second
(Bram) says, 'Je ne peux voir l'objet, pour le représenter, parce que je suis ce
que je suis.'[11] That is, the essential components of the object cannot be seen,
because the essential nature of the subject (the one who sees) is to screen or
interpret the images projected upon his brain by the object (and this
screening links the object to familiar contexts which enable ready interpretation or an habitual response).

Although his artistic practice, as we will see in the next chapter, continues to develop and change, we witness here a continuity in Beckett's
aesthetic thinking concerning the image from between the wars until after
World War Two, when his major works, along with the letter to Georges
Duthuit, which was written in 1949,[12] and other important aesthetic
writings were composed. Indeed, the suggestion that art should involve
presentation, or the creation of not yet interpreted material, instead of
offering pre-digested representations, is something which Beckett was
already stressing in his earliest piece of aesthetic writing, 'Dante ...
Bruno. Vico.. Joyce',[13] which appeared in 1929. Here Beckett outlines a
concept of 'direct expression' in writing, and claims that such direct
expression can be found in Joyce. Joyce's writing is not the kind of writing
that offers pre-digested representations:

And if you don't understand it, Ladies and Gentlemen, it is because you are too
decadent to receive it. You are not satisfied unless form is so strictly divorced from
content that you can comprehend the one almost without bothering to read the
other. The rapid skimming and absorption of the scant cream of sense is made
possible by what I may call a continuous process of copious intellectual salivation.
The form that is an arbitrary and independent phenomenon can fulfil no higher
function than that of stimulus for a tertiary or quartary conditioned reflex of
dribbling comprehension.[14]

The 'tertiary or quartary conditioned reflex' no doubt refers to the 'rule
of three', the rule of the symbol or sign as representation Beckett describes
in his review of Jack Yeats in 1936.[15] Joyce's writing, bringing to mind the
comments made by Bergson in the previous chapter,[16] on the other hand,
'is not about something; it is that something itself'.[17] This claim clearly
aligns Beckett's understanding with the distinction which Deleuze makes
between created works, which need to be directly interpreted by the reader,
and mediocre works, which represent what has already been shown,
and which we interpret through reflex or habit. Deleuze and Guattari

consistently refer to the production of works which escape mediocrity as
a process of creation, not as a process of representation – artists create and
present (rather than represent) affects, and draw us into the mix:

> In relation to the percepts or visions they give us, artists are presenters of affects,
> the inventors and creators of affects. They not only create them in their work, they
> give them to us and make us become with them, and they draw us into the
> compound.[18]

As Joyce has the narrator of *Stephen Hero* state: 'For Stephen art was
neither a copy nor an imitation of nature: the artistic process was a natural
process.'[19] This is not solely brought about through the use of images, as
'direct expression' is a concept developed, via Vico, with regard to language
and writing, but images are an important part of this process. Beckett
quotes Joyce to underline this point:

> Stephen says to Lynch: 'Temporal or spatial, the esthetic image is first luminously
> apprehended as selfbounded and selfcontained upon the immeasurable back-
> ground of space or time which it is not ... You apprehend[20] its wholeness'[21]

This idea is something we have already touched upon in the previous
chapter and seems very close to the notion of 'the autonomous mental
image' discussed below in relation to the painting of Francis Bacon. It is
also very close to comments Beckett makes in *Proust*.[22]

In 'Recent Irish Poetry', a review written for *The Bookman* in August
1934 under the pseudonym Andrew Belis, Beckett claims that certain
younger Irish poets 'evince awareness of the new thing that has happened,
or the old thing that has happened again, namely the breakdown of the
object, whether current, historical, mythical or spook'.[23] This claim might
be partly understood as beginning to develop the idea of art in the absence
of relation; an idea that I discuss further in chapter 3. The difficulties
involved, the problem of attempting expression under such conditions,
however, is also something that brings us into contact with Beckett's
understanding of the image. One of the younger Irish poets Beckett refers
to in this article is his friend Denis Devlin. In 1938, writing in the celebrated
modernist journal *transition* (number 27), Beckett reviewed *Intercessions*, a
book of poems by Devlin. Toward the end of this piece he seems to take
issue with another review which had recently appeared in the *Times Literary
Supplement*. Beckett replies:

> It is naturally in the image that this profound and abstruse self-consciousness first
> emerges with the least loss of integrity. To cavil at Mr Devlin's form as overimaged
> (the obvious polite cavil) is to cavil at the probity with which the creative act has

carried itself out, a probity in this case depending on a minimum of rational interference, and indeed to suggest that the creative act should burke its own conditions for the sake of clarity.[24]

The image, then, offers one way of examining the breakdown of the object/subject relation, one way of avoiding the rational interference of pre-digested interpretation. Rather than interpreting its object for us (representing it by cutting it from everything not considered useful to the conscious perception of that object), art presents us with material that we must struggle to understand. Art is not about making things clear or easy for us. On the contrary, for Beckett:

art has nothing to do with clarity, does not dabble in the clear and does not make clear, any more than the light of day (or night) makes the subsolar, -lunar and -stellar excrement. Art is the sun, moon and stars of the mind, the whole mind.[25]

Devlin, using his images as a means of developing his presentations, achieves 'the same totality' for Beckett, 'directly and with concreteness'.[26]

THE MODERNIST MILIEU

Beckett did not invent this terminology for himself. Rather, he finds himself, prior to World War Two, in any case, in a milieu in which terms such as 'the image', and 'apprehension' (as a kind of direct perception prior to interpretation; that is, the apprehension of a presentation) and 'concreteness' would be understood because they were in currency.

In the last two decades a good deal of work has been done establishing the extent to which Bergson's theories were well known to, and made use of by, key English-language modernist writers.[27] The list of names, which I have already touched upon is long and impressive: Joyce, T. S. Eliot, Pound, Stevens, Faulkner and Nabokov, to name the most prominent. Bergson, of course, was also important to French literature. The relationship of his ideas to those developed by Proust has been much discussed, and this example highlights how it is important to avoid simplifying the kinds of relationships developed between Bergson's ideas and creative responses to them.[28] That is, while Bergson offered concepts which opened ways for these writers, the writers never simply repeat or illustrate these ideas. Rather, he is a key point in a system of relays, like that described by Deleuze in the following quotation, one which, in this case, passes by important notions of the image, duration, consciousness and intuition. As Deleuze states:

The encounter between two disciplines doesn't take place when one begins to reflect on the other, but when one discipline realizes that it has to resolve, for itself and by its own means, a problem similar to one confronted by the other. One can imagine that similar problems confront the sciences, painting, music, philosophy, literature, and cinema at different moments, on different occasions, and under different circumstances. The same tremors occur on totally different terrains. The only true criticism is comparative ... because any work in a field is itself imbricated within other fields ... There is no work that doesn't have its beginning or end in other art forms ... All work is inserted in a system of relays.[29]

The artists who feed upon Bergson's works, then, enter into creative engagement with these concepts, which they ingest and transform into feelings. At times he is used as much as a negative influence as a positive one, as is the case with Proust, who, as we have seen, gave positive meaning to involuntary memory, which Bergson understands in negative terms in *Matter and Memory*. In speaking of 'influence', then, it is important to recognise the shifts of perspective that take place as ideas pass through the prism of the brain of the one who reads and responds to what has been read.

That Beckett knew of Bergson in general, and his understanding of intuition and its influence on French literature in particular, is incontestable. During the Michaelmas term of 1931 Beckett taught a course on Gide and Racine at Trinity College Dublin, and notes to these lectures, taken by Rachel Burrows, have survived. Parts of these explicitly touch upon Beckett's understanding of Bergson's concept of intuition, and its influence on art and literature in France.

conflict v. intelligence & intuition. Bergson – interested in this ... Suggests that intuition can achieve a total vision that intelligence can't. Philosophical visionary – position like ... – Rimbaud. Passionate justification of 'La vision intuitive' ... 'originalité, feuilleté [above this Burrows has written 'disorder'], imprevisibilitié', as artistic attributes. Flaubert had last. Taken up Symbolistes and Dadaists – last interested in his [Bergson's] idea of inadequacy of the word to translated impressions registered by instinct.[30]

.... Crisis for Gide to deal with – new incoherence – impatience with patient fabricated order of Romantics and Naturalists, Proust detached from Bergson's conception of time but interested in this opposition – instinct & conscious intelligence. Bergson insists on absolute time: Proust denied it. In Proust it's a function of too many things – local but not absolute reality.[31]

As well as being important to French aesthetic theory around the turn of the nineteenth and twentieth centuries, Bergson also had a major influence on early twentieth-century English-language modernism. T. E. Hulme, who was primarily responsible for the theoretical underpinnings of

'Imagism', a poetical movement which drew together numerous important figures including Ezra Pound, H. D., D. H. Lawrence, Richard Aldington (who helped publish Beckett's first published poem, *Whoroscope*) and, at a slightly greater distance, T. S. Eliot, translated Bergson's essay *Introduction to Metaphysics*. Beckett speaks approvingly of both Eliot and Pound in his review 'Recent Irish Poetry',[32] and indicates his knowledge of 'Imagism' and its goals in a review of Pound's *Make It New*, which appeared in *The Bookman* in 1934, where he notes that '"Stray Document" is a synopsis of "Imagism"'.[33] In 1953 T. S. Eliot stated that the 'starting-point of modern poetry is a group denominated "imagists" in London about 1910'.[34] In his biography of Hulme, Robert Ferguson quotes F. S. Flint as follows: 'Hulme was the ringleader. He insisted too on absolutely accurate presentation and no verbiage'.[35] Hulme's impact was not limited to circa 1910, as the greater part of his writing was not published until 1924, after which time his fame, and his ideas, spread considerably.

The three tenets of Imagism, formulated by Pound and Flint in close relation to their discussions with Hulme, were as follows:

1. Direct treatment of the 'thing', whether subjective or objective.
2. To use absolutely no word that does not contribute to the presentation.
3. As regarding rhythm: to compose in the sequence of the musical phrase, not in sequence of a metronome.[36]

Evidently, the first two of these tenets, and the insistence on the use of the word 'presentation', understood in the sense of the immediate presentation of a thing to the senses, are of immediate relevance to the discussion here.

Beckett, then, clearly knew of the genealogy of the concept of the image, and, via Bergson, its relationship with theories of cognition, and this explains how his own comments, with regard to the use of the image, are so closely aligned with the concepts sketched in the previous chapter, which also draw heavily on close readings of Bergson. Beckett, while developing a kind of image which would become his own in his art, was happy to make use of Bergson and others to help illustrate the kinds of aesthetic understandings necessary to taking into account how such an image might function. Writing to Thomas MacGreevy in 1938 about MacGreevy's recent book on the painting of Jack Yeats, Beckett states:

I understand your anxiety to clarify his pre and post 1916 painting politically and socially, and especially in what concerns the last pictures I think you have provided a clue that will be of great help to a lot of people, to the kind of people who in the phrase of Bergson can't be happy till they have 'solidified the flowing', i.e., to most people. I am inclined personally to think that the turning away from the local, not merely in his painting but in his writing (he has just sent me <u>The Charmed Life</u>), even if only in intention, results not so much from the break down of the local, of the local human anyway, as from a very characteristic and very general psychological mechanism, operative in young artists as a naiveté (or an instinct) and in old artists as a wisdom (or an instinct). I am sure I could illustrate this for you if I had the culture. You will always, as an historian, give more credit to circumstance than I, with my less than suilline interest and belief in the <u>fable convenue</u>, ever shall be able to.[37]

Making use of the image is not, of course, Beckett's only strategy. The above quotation bears witness to Beckett's ongoing interest in psychology and other theories of the self, and he explores this interest in the psychological largely by paying attention to voices and stories, rather than the image.

Beckett also draws a number of discussions of aesthetics into the narrative of *Dream of Fair to Middling Women*,[38] where a good deal of emphasis is given to the importance of music as a model for all the arts. Literature, like other art forms, can be made to adopt a 'musical' form, and an understanding of this process is crucial to an understanding of Beckett's works. This strategy, however, is beyond the scope of the present study.

DELEUZE AND THE IMAGE IN BECKETT

Deleuze has dedicated two major essays to Beckett, and in each concepts of 'the image' emerge. Further, in one of his most important writings on art, *Francis Bacon: Logique de la sensation*, he compares Beckett's aesthetic methods to those of the Irish painter Francis Bacon on several occasions, and these are connected in important ways to the idea of 'the image'.

For Deleuze, throughout his career Beckett was concerned with 'exhausting the possible'; with having done. In 'The Exhausted'[39] Deleuze identifies three kinds of 'language' in Beckett's works which all emerge in order to be exhausted. Beckett attempts to exhaust 'language I', a language of names, through permutations, such as those seen with Molloy's sucking stones, Murphy's biscuits or the movement of furniture in *Watt*. Beckett attempts to exhaust 'language II', a language of voices, by allowing the 'others' who speak to tell their stories to the point of exhaustion. Beckett exhausts these voices by working through an indefinite series: Murphy, Watt, Molloy, Malone, etc., before arriving at the aporia of an I, the Unnamable, which is somehow conflated with this indefinite series of others, and which continues to endeavour to exhaust these voices.[40]

'Language III', on the other hand, a language of images and spaces aligned to images, rather than simply being exhausted, is made in order to further exhaust the other two kinds of language. By making images ('it's done I've done the image'),[41] which are 'visual or aural refrains', energy can be released which might somehow allow an escape from the impasses we have been brought to by the other two languages. Images themselves are understood to appear and then dissipate in Beckett, emerging to tear holes in the word surface (in the manner Beckett describes in his letter to Axel Kaun)[42] and, according to Deleuze, loosening 'the grip of words', drying up 'the oozing of voices'.[43] Though created, at times, through language, the language of images and spaces is in effect an 'outside of language'.[44] The images 'compose and decompose themselves',[45] 'insinuate themselves, breaking the combination of words and the flow of voices'.[46] The image, then, for Deleuze, is the most effective means of exhaustion in Beckett.

The energy of the image is dissipative. The image quickly ends and dissipates because it is itself a means of having done with itself. It captures all of the possible in order to make it explode. When one says, 'I've done the image,' it is because this time it is finished, *there is no more possibility.*[47]

In 'The Greatest Irish Film',[48] Deleuze further examines the notion of exhaustion in Beckett, linking it with the terminology of the three kinds of image Deleuze develops in relation to the cinematic form: the action-image, which is related to the movement of the camera tracing movement in the film (the camera which tracks, pans, zooms and so on); the perception-image, which is related to notions of characters perceiving (the point of view) and being perceived (the shot reverse shot and other kinds of cross cutting) both by others in the film and the camera itself; and the affection-image (that image which captures or creates emotion via the face, through the close-up). Beckett, according to Deleuze, exhausts each of these types of image in turn in his only cinematic work, *Film*.

For our purposes, however, it is Deleuze's discussion of the image in relation to Francis Bacon (who in turn Deleuze often pairs or compares with Beckett) which sheds most light on the concept of the image and its role in art.[49] This in turn facilitates an understanding of how images might be being used in Beckett's works. On page 36 the tableaux of Beckett's characters and Bacon's Figures are compared, with Deleuze contending that the similarity derives from their partial genesis in the same Ireland. The two are closest, he suggests, in movement, the pauses or stops in movement which equate to levels of sensation[50] (just as Beckett states in the text for *Film* that the movement of the rocking chair in the final scene and its pauses are related to the heightening of sensation).[51] So too, the word '*dépeupleur*', which carries the flavour of Beckett (indeed this Beckett text is mentioned on more than one occasion by Deleuze),[52] is understood as referring to the process through which the Figure is cut from its natural milieu, the process of deterritorialisation.[53] '*Dépeupleur*' is not literally translated in the English version of this text, *The Lost Ones*;[54] rather, a literal translation would be something like, 'the depeopliser'. This, in turn, though Deleuze does not develop this point, would draw us back to certain of Beckett's aesthetic concerns in the letters to MacGreevy. Here, on more than one occasion Beckett discusses an ideal of art as something which can be non-anthropomorphic, both in relation to realms outside the human, such as the landscape,[55] and even in relation to the human realm itself.[56]

Deleuze begins by discussing Bacon's isolation of the Figure in a place, explaining how creating the Figure involves processes which are quite different to figuration or the figurative.

The relation of the Figure to its place defines a fact: the fact is ... that which takes place ... And the Figure isolated in this way becomes an Image, an Icon.[57]

Why does one need to isolate a Figure in this way? There are, Deleuze suggests, two ways of avoiding the figurative, the illustrative, in art: on the one hand there is abstraction and on the other extraction (or isolation). The figurative and illustrative involve representation: 'the figurative (representation) implies, in effect, the relation of an image to an object which it is supposed to illustrate'.[58] We have seen how such a break with representation might be considered necessary, and it is worth reflecting upon how the desire to break with the possible in art, with the simply representational, the relation of subject to object, is one of the most well-known aspects of Beckett's aesthetic of nonrelation.

For Bacon and Deleuze (who develops many of his concepts in this work from his understanding of Bacon's own aesthetic writings and notes) the function of art is to capture sensations, to render visible invisible forces, to make these immediately perceptible and to enable them to act directly on the nervous system of the viewer. Illustration prevents such direct responses from taking place because one is too distracted by the intended meaning of an illustration to apprehend the sensation. So too, in Beckett, one might be overly distracted by trying to understand the situation of May, for example, in *Footfalls*[59] and lift it out into the safety of a complete narrative form: yet reading the work in such a fashion would move one away from the direct sensations created in the situation we witness. It is this explanation which must be avoided, because the too neat understanding allowed by such illustrative explanations (cause and effect and their representation) kills sensation.[60]

For Bacon, modern painting was confronted with specific difficulties. Christian painting, for instance, continually made use of Christian stories and portrayed well-known incidents, and these incidents were so well known, so thoroughly coded by Church dogma, that there was nothing new illustrated or represented in these pictures. For this reason the Figures could emerge from these paintings with the sensations they carried being all which remained that might directly affect a viewer.[61] In the secular twentieth century, dominated by the photographic image with its illustrative power, however, it became increasingly difficult to escape from the tyranny of explanation and the drawing of illustrative stories from all images, a process which in turn has hampered the ability of such images to bring forth or capture sensations. In the twentieth century, then, for Bacon and Deleuze, modernist painting developed three answers to the question of how one might escape from the merely figurative, the merely illustrative: abstraction, abstract expressionism and the sensations of Cézanne or the Figures of Bacon.[62]

For Bacon, and Deleuze, the problem with abstract painting is that it is too cerebral: like illustration or the figurative, this form must pass through the brain, must be interpreted before it can be appreciated, and it therefore finds it difficult to work directly on the sensations.[63] In abstract expressionism sensation is achieved but it remains confused, thereby losing its force.[64] The middle way of Bacon and Cézanne, however, allows the production of sensation: 'the Figure is sensible form related to sensation; it acts immediately on the nervous system which is flesh'.[65] As Deleuze explains:

Sensation has one face turned toward the subject (the nervous system, vital movement, 'instinct', 'temperament', a complete vocabulary common to Naturalism and Cézanne), and one face turned toward the object ('the fact', the place, the event). Or rather it has no faces at all, it is the two things indissolubly, it is being-in-the-world, as the phenomenologists say: at the same time I *become* in the sensation and something *happens* through sensation, one by the other, one in the other.[66]

Creating the figure involves the isolation of an object. The object is extracted from its surroundings, cut off from the relations which cause it to fail to act directly on the nervous system. There are strong links here with how the image is understood to be operating in Beckett's work by Deleuze. In 'The Exhausted' Deleuze states:

It is extremely difficult to tear ... adhesions [from the language of words and voices] away from the image so as to reach the point of 'Imagination Dead

Imagine'. It is extremely difficult to make a pure and unsullied image, one that is nothing but image, by reaching the point where it emerges in all its singularity, retaining nothing of the personal or rational, and by ascending to the indefinite as if into a celestial state.[67]

The image is extracted from context because it is contexts which carry interpretations. The linking to a context, to an understanding or interpretation which has already been made, involves the process of screening which produces the representation. A pure image must be divorced from these contexts and interpretations: that is, it is necessary to create a presentation, to create a thing or an object which is presented to us, rather than attempting to represent an already interpreted object.

We see this understanding, adapted from Schopenhauer, Joyce, Proust and others, in Beckett's essay from 1931, *Proust*:

when the object is perceived as particular and unique and not merely as the member of a family, when it appears independent of any general notion and detached from the sanity of a cause, isolated and inexplicable in the light of ignorance, then and only then may it be a source of enchantment.[68]

The process of creating an image, then, is strongly tied to the idea of relation and nonrelation. It is necessary to sunder or occlude the 'relations' (or prefabricated interpretations) which adhere to an image in order to create an image capable of generating the power to properly affect an audience. The manner in which Beckett begins to develop a form capable of accommodating his aesthetic ideas is explored in the next chapter.

CHAPTER 3

Relation and nonrelation

In 'The Exhausted', Gilles Deleuze considers the image to be of primary importance to Beckett's television plays. While this idea fits neatly within Deleuze's reading, which stresses how the concept of 'exhaustion' might be seen to develop in Beckett's works, it leaves some aspects of Beckett's use of the image to one side. I will argue in this chapter that, if we pay attention to the key idea of nonrelation in Beckett's works, we can add elements to Deleuze's description of Beckett's use of the image.

Beckett's interest in developing an art of nonrelation is well known from *Three Dialogues with Georges Duthuit*[1] and has been treated by a number of critics such as J. E. Dearlove.[2] What has not been fully drawn out in these previous studies is how Beckett's aesthetic practice and his understanding of the importance and nature of relations, or connections, develops throughout his career. A close attention to the quality of these shifts sheds light on Beckett's understanding of the image.

FROM RELATION TO NONRELATION

In Beckett's abandoned first novel, *Dream of Fair to Middling Women*, which was written in 1932, the central character Belacqua describes his theory of relations for the Polar Bear.[3] He begins by referring to an image of a bridge over water, an image which reappears throughout *Dream* as it is drawn into relation with an idealised anti-hero called 'Nemo', who stands on a bridge and finally jumps from that bridge.[4] Nemo brings to mind Ulysses, among other things, as 'nobody' is the name Ulysses chooses for himself when confronting and escaping the Cyclops in Homer's *Odyssey*. He is offered as an example of a person who cannot be simply represented because he is not a simple point of relation in a system of links. He *is* a point of relation, but the linkages are multiple and symphonic rather than that of a single note following another in the manner of a melody.[5] He seems to be a prototype of Mr Endon in *Murphy*[6] and escapes irony in being idolised as an ideal outsider by the younger Beckett. The main avatar for the younger Beckett, on the other hand, Belacqua, does not escape the irony of the narrator (who is another avatar). This is most apparent when he pushes his aesthetic theories upon the Polar Bear, but this irony does not serve to undermine Belacqua's theory; rather, it is Belacqua's pomposity, not the content of his musings, which is the target of the irony. Moving, a little awkwardly, between indirect and direct speech, Belacqua's theory of relations is sketched.

The hyphen of passion between Shilly and Shally, the old bridge over the river . . . Suicides jump from the bridge, not from the bank. For me, he prattles on, he means no harm, for me the one real thing is to be found in the relation: the dumb-bell's bar, the silence between my eyes, between you and me, all the silences between you and me. I can only know the real poise at the crest of the relation rooted in the unreal postulates, God-Devil, Masoch-Sade (he might have spared us that hoary old binary), Me-You, One-minus-One. On the crown of the passional relation I live, dead to oneness, non-entity and unalone . . . the silence between my eyes, between you and me, the body between the wings.
    Ain't he advanced for his age!⁷

Dream is a book which is crammed full of aesthetic theories, and, despite the ironic interventions of the narrator, it is difficult *not* to take these seriously. That is, these theories seem to reflect an understanding of what fiction can do which, in important ways, in fact corresponds with what is attempted in *Dream*; often, indeed, it is the third-person narrator himself who elaborates the theories, as in the case of the notion of fictional characters as 'liŭ'.⁸ The image of Nemo on the bridge and Nemo jumping from the bridge⁹ is given such a particular prominence in the book that it is difficult not to read the passage quoted above as an attempt to prompt or direct our interpretations. The relation, then, at this point in Beckett's career, is stressed. After World War Two, in *Three Dialogues with Georges Duthuit*, which was written in 1949, and in a letter to Georges Duthuit of 1949, Beckett, now, conversely, stresses the importance of nonrelation, an art in the absence of relations. In this letter Beckett states:

As far as I'm concerned, Bram's painting owes nothing to these meager consola-tions. It is new because it is the first to repudiate relation in all its forms. It is not the relation with this or that order of encounter that he refuses, but the state of being quite simply in relation full stop, the state of being in front of. We have waited a long time for the artist who has enough courage, who is enough at ease among the great tornados of intuition to realise that the break with the outside implies the break with the inside, that no relations of replacement for the naïve relations exist, that what we call the outside and the inside are the very same thing. I'm not saying that he doesn't search to reestablish correspondence. What is important is that he does not manage to. His painting is, if you like, the impossibility of reestablishing correspondence. There is, if you like, refusal and refusal to accept his refusal.[10]

There are certainly important inconsistencies or paradoxes which become apparent with regard to the aesthetic musings in *Dream*. We are informed that Nemo is not a liŭ, that he is not a 'type' able to perform a specific function as in the liŭ-liŭ the narrator describes, one which corresponds to a single note which can be readily linked to others in forming a melody. He is, rather, much more complex, not a 'note at all but a regrettable simultaneity of notes'.[11] This said, however, his role in the narrative makes it difficult not to read him as a primarily symbolic character, something which is further emphasised by the choice of name, 'Nemo'. This tendency, to push us towards a symbolic reading (where the everyman 'nobody', despite the narrator's protestations to the contrary, does in fact seem to represent an idealised type) does not fully correspond with these early descriptions of the complex Nemo. This is also apparent, one might argue, in the representation of Mr Endon in *Murphy*, whose name also seems to carry a symbolic weight.

This kind of inconsistency, rather than pointing towards simple incoherence in Beckett's system, betrays a fault line within it, one which will later open in developing into the aesthetic of nonrelation. That is, the tendency to point towards a connection is drawn to the surface at the same time as that connection is refused. We see this most clearly in *Waiting for Godot*,[12] where a reading of Godot as God is both opened and openly disallowed within the text.

Further, in stressing the connection itself, the link itself, Beckett is already calling that connection into question. The bridge between is neither one shore nor the other, it is precarious, suspended, and is a place from which a definitive exit from the substantial world of one shore or the other is possible. In a way, then, the move from relation to nonrelation is not one of simple overturning. For example, the idea of 'relation' in *Dream* is already linked to an idea of 'silence', or 'the aesthetic of inaudibilities',[13] and these ideas remain consistent with the later emphasis on the nonrelation as that which both invites interpretation and calls the process of interpretation itself into question. The move from relation to nonrelation does, none the less, mark a significant shift in focus.

Some of the implications of this shift can be seen in other aspects of Beckett's writing; or rather, these other aspects can be thought of as exemplifying what is at stake in the shift from relation to nonrelation.

ALLUSION IN *DREAM OF FAIR TO MIDDLING WOMEN*

In his early works Beckett is strongly interested in the use of allusion. There is a heavy use of allusion to other writers, other intellectual contexts in *Dream, More Pricks Than Kicks*[14] and in Beckett's next novel, *Murphy*, and, indeed, elements of a compositional process which, in part at least, is based upon the incorporation of allusions or images drawn from other texts, can still be recognised in *Watt*.[15] C. J. Ackerley's extended study of allusion in *Murphy*[16] illustrates how densely packed with references to other texts this novel is. So too, the *Dream Notebook*, edited by John Pilling,[17] allows us to see how systematically Beckett sought to incorporate these kinds of allusions, following a process of composition which bears marked similarities to that of Joyce, who also kept notebooks filled with materials which were to be incorporated into his novels.

That such allusion is tied in with an aesthetic method becomes apparent in *Dream*. In expounding his 'aesthetic of inaudibilities', Belacqua begins by again highlighting the importance of the relation, the interval, the silence which comes between, and, then, by way of illustrating what he means, he offers a list of allusions to works of visual artists, theologians and poets, ending with an extended discussion of Beethoven:

I shall write a book, he mused ... where the phrase is self-consciously smart and slick, but of a smartness and slickness other than that of its neighbours on the page. The blown roses of the phrase shall catapult the reader into the tulips of the phrase that follows. The experience of my reader shall be between the phrases, in the silence, communicated by the intervals, not the terms, of the statement, between the flowers that cannot coexist ... I think now ... of a Rembrandt ... of the Selbstbildnis ... van Ryn ... the Pauline ... *cupio dissolvi*. ... Horace ... Hölderlin ... Beethofen[18]

Towards the end of the novel, in a passage reproduced in slightly altered form in the short story 'A Wet Night', which appears in *More Pricks Than Kicks*,[19] a witty exchange between the Polar Bear and a Jesuit – that is, the kind of verbal joust which itself proceeds through a scoring system based on the cleverness of allusions – ends with the Jesuit having the final word. His final word turns upon an understanding of links, of relations or connections, which are not to be simply confused with 'the drawing of accounts' or the neat tying together of things into a straightforward meaning. There is a pleasure to be had, we seem to be being told, in recognising the chords which are struck when a link is made, an allusion or pun skilfully produced. The Jesuit, having distanced himself from the mere Parish Priest, ends the exchange as follows:

'But they [the Parish Priests] are excellent men. A shade on the assiduous side. A shade too anxious to balance the accounts. Otherwise . . .' He stood up. 'Observe' he said 'I desire to get down, I pull the cord and the bus stops and lets me down.'

'Well?'

'In just such a Gehenna of links' said this remarkable man, with one foot on the pavement, 'I forged my vocation.'

With these words he was gone and the burden of his fare had fallen on the Polar Bear.[20]

At this point in his career, then, Beckett's aesthetic seems to prize the process of skilfully drawing links, something which includes the drawing of allusions. Already with *More Pricks Than Kicks*, however, a whiff of uncertainty seems to hang in the air. In this book, much like most of those that follow, the avatars for the author seem to multiply. In *Dream*, Belacqua, and the third-person narrator seem most closely identified with the author, 'Mr Beckett'. In *More Pricks Than Kicks*, Belacqua and a version of the narrator reappear, but there are other characters who also take on some of the attributes of Belacqua and 'Samuel Beckett' and are, to an extent at least, identified with these. Two such characters are Walter Draff, who, we are told, like the young Samuel Beckett is writing a book called 'Dream of Fair to Middling Women',[21] and Hairy, who appears in a number of the later pieces and comes to resemble Belacqua more and more in 'Draff' once Belacqua himself passes on in 'Yellow'. After Belacqua's death we are told, 'Hairy seemed to have taken on a new lease of life. He spoke well, with commendable assurance; he looked better, less obese cretin and spado than ever before'.[22] This is because, we are informed, Hairy is now able to make use of Belacqua, adapting his manner to remodel himself, so that 'Already Belacqua was not wholly dead, but merely mutilated'.[23]

In 'What a Misfortune'[24] Walter and Hairy go head to head in a friendly round of repartee: a kind of banter based on the witty drawing of allusions.[25] If it is a battle, though, it is a depressingly unequal one, with Hairy (prior to Belacqua's death and his own subsequent transformation into a sharper verbal duellist in the mould of Belacqua) only barely witty enough to recognise that he does not understand the greater part of what Walter is saying:

The mole is never sober. A profound mot. Hairy, having tried all he knew to say as much, hung his head, a gallant loser, consoled by the certitude that Walter would take the will for the deed. Poor Hairy, there was a great deal he understood, but he could not make this known in the absence of a battery of writing materials.

'That unspeakable invite' exclaimed Walter, 'of all things to be destitute of
enjambment!'

He was confirmed in his initial misgiving by Hairy's having clearly no idea what
he was talking about. There was nothing for it but to put it into his book.[26]

We see here, perhaps, a confrontation between avatars. The urbane
Walter, like Belacqua, is verbally sophisticated and is constantly displaying
this through these games of allusion. The uncomprehending Hairy seems
to foreshadow some of Beckett's later avatars who come to dominate after
Watt: those who do not know, who once knew but who have forgotten,
though remnants remain, haunting what they say despite their own difficulty with now making the precise connection. Molloy states: 'All I know is
what the words know'.[27] It is worth noting that the confrontation between
Walter and Hairy occurs around the process of drawing allusions, as this
allows us to map some subtle shifts in Beckett's aesthetic thinking as he
moves (intuitively or otherwise) from an aesthetic of relation to one of
nonrelation. We see this further illustrated in *Murphy*, where we see a sense
of distrust or even disgust with this kind of allusion beginning to emerge.

ALLUSION IN *MURPHY*

The importance of the allusion, and the relation on which it is built, is
stressed in *Murphy*. Building upon the aesthetic of relation early in the
novel we are told 'Murphy was one of the elect, who require everything to
remind them of something else'.[28] One of the more arresting rare words
to appear in the work is 'syzygy', which refers directly to the alignment of
bodies in astronomy or astrology,[29] and is used to describe Suk's drawing of
Murphy's horoscope (among other attempts to relate Murphy's life to a
stable meaning).[30] While allusion is still very much at the forefront, both in
the method of composition, and in the style of verbal jousting adopted by
many of the characters (if not, tellingly, Murphy himself), allusion is also
something which is now looked upon with an air of equivocation.

The main representatives of the rule of the verbal joust in *Murphy* are the
'Engels sisters': Neary, Wylie and Miss Counihan. The image of the ball
being hit back and forth as in a tennis match is used on a number of
occasions. At certain points, however, the game is seen to collapse and is
looked upon with a jaundiced eye.

'You to play, Needle.'

'And do the lady out of the last word!' cried Wylie. 'And put the lady to the
trouble of finding another! Reary, Neally!'

'No trouble,' said Miss Counihan.

Now it was anybody's turn.

'Very well,' said Neary. 'What I was really coming to, what I wanted to suggest, is this. Let our conversation now be without precedent in fact or literature, each one speaking to the best of his ability the truth to the best of his knowledge . . .'[31]

After a time the allusive, ironic, clowning of the Engels sisters becomes tiresome even to themselves. As Wylie states a little later, 'After all, there is nothing like dead silence. My one dread was lest our conversation of last night should resume us where it left us off'.[32] Indeed, such weariness was already present in *Dream*:

'The bicuspid' from the professor 'monotheistic fiction torn by the sophists, Christ and Plato, from the violated matrix of pure reason.'

Oh, who shall silence them, at last? Who shall circumcise their lips from talking, at last?[33]

Underlining this growing sense of distrust, we are given a stark contrast between Miss Counihan's tiresome cleverness built upon allusion (and the necessary drawing of learned relations beyond the immediately perceptible situation) and the naive simplicity of Celia. This simplicity is then authorised by Murphy, who stands apart from the other puppets in the novel:

'One of the innumerable small retail redeemers,' sneered Miss Counihan, 'lodging her pennyworth of pique in the post-golgothan kitty.'

But for Murphy's horror of the mental belch, Celia would have recognized this phrase, if she had heard it.[34]

Again, there is a tension here between the method Beckett uses in *Murphy*, which is full of allusion, and this drawing into question of the process of drawing allusions.

ALLUSION IN *WATT*

This fault line widens with Beckett's next novel, *Watt*, where we are still able to recognise a process of composition which makes use of the incorporation of allusions into the text. Yet this process itself is brought to the surface and called into question in the famous Addenda. The footnote to the Addenda underlines how 'fatigue and disgust'[35] at last overcame the author, who has failed to incorporate certain of the notebook materials (which mix original musings with allusions to other sources).

Of course, elements of the style have changed considerably since *Murphy*. While there is still some considerable use of allusion, this is not brought so readily to the surface. Whereas numerous characters in the previous works made use of allusion as a means of indicating intellectual superiority, in *Watt* the heavy use of references which relate ideas to other texts or contexts (allusions, in short) is made to seem ridiculous. The character Mr Spiro, the editor of 'the popular catholic monthly' 'Crux', is ridiculed, for example. He spends a good deal of time describing the prize competitions he produces for the paper, competitions which depend on the kind of recognition and regurgitation of material sighted in other texts, and at times its relation to a new context, which is essential to the drawing of allusion. He pretends to attempt to test Watt in this way, but in fact is more interested in his own response to the intellectual puzzle he sets, which he answers by alluding to numerous authorities. At a stretch one might read this whole episode as a parody of the Christian hermeneutic tradition, a tradition which has been crucial to the development of textual interpretation in the West. The drawing of relations involved in this, the mania for solving puzzles which develops the ability to make such connections and the allusion to authority as a means of developing or concluding an argument are contrasted with the indifference of Watt, who exists outside this particular logic of relation. After posing himself a series of questions related to the possible desecration of the Eucharist, Mr Spiro goes on to develop his answer:

Mr Spiro now replied to these questions, that is to say he replied to question one and he replied to question three. He did so at length, quoting from Saint Bonaventura, Peter Lombard, Alexander of Hales, Sanchez, Suarez, Henno, Soto, Diana, Concina and Dens, for he was a man of leisure.[36]

Watt, however, exists on a different plane, and it is worth paying close attention to how and what he perceives in contrast to the allusive logic of Mr Spiro:

But Watt heard nothing of this, because of other voices, singing, crying, stating, murmuring, things unintelligible, in his ear. With these, if he was not familiar, he was not unfamiliar either. So he was not alarmed, unduly.[37]

Watt hears a cacophony of unintelligible information, things, in short, he cannot draw easily into a particular relation. Importantly, however, we are told that these are neither too familiar nor too unfamiliar. If they were too familiar they would be recognised, and the process of recognition is key to the kind of understanding developed through the drawing of relations.

If they were too unfamiliar he would be thrown into complete confusion and alarmed.

The kind of relation developed in the allusion is more or less unknown to Watt. This is not to say that relation does not occur in this novel. On the contrary, a different kind of relation is developed at some length. It is so different, however, that one might ask if it should really share the same word. It is no longer *a* relation, in terms of a single bridge between shores: now it involves exhausting all the possibilities for relation which are at hand. While this might, in the end, lead to a single answer (as it does for Watt with the example of the Lynchs' dog which follows) it seems to be the exhaustion of relations which is at the core of the process. In short, Watt's drawing of relations involves the negation of relation itself through exhaustion, rather than its affirmation through the isolation of a single possibility.

What follows upon the passage cited above, then, is a different kind of drawing into relation, one which emerged in *Murphy* and is developed extensively through *Watt*, and appears again in *Molloy* with the sucking stones: the process of listing permutations which Deleuze describes in detail in 'The Exhausted'. Such a process draws out the series of possible relations between a set of elements, and in setting out to detail these series, Watt, we are told, seeks some sort of peace:

> And would he have gone into the Lynch family at such length if, in thought, he had not been obliged to pass, from the dog, to the Lynches, as to one of the terms of the relation that the dog wove nightly, the other of course being Mr. Knott's remains ... But once Watt had grasped, in its complexity, the mechanism of this arrangement, how the food came to be left, and the dog to be available, and the two united, then it interested him no more, and he enjoyed a comparative peace of mind, in this connexion. Not that for a moment Watt supposed that he had penetrated the forces at play, in this particular instance, or even perceived the forms that they upheaved, or obtained the least useful information concerning himself, or Mr. Knott, for he did not. But he had turned, little by little, a disturbance into words ...[38]

The distinction which Deleuze stresses with regard to this process of exhausting relations involves that between the exclusive disjunction and the inclusive disjunction. The realisation of the possible always proceeds through *exclusive* disjunction: you do one thing by excluding other possibilities. The exhaustion of the possible through the process of permutation, however, involves *inclusive* disjunction, and this requires renouncing all order of preference or organisation of goal, all signification.[39] This kind of relation differs markedly from that found in the allusion, then, which announces its significance by calling upon us to recognise a source.

While Deleuze claims that all Beckett's works are pervaded by exhaustive series,[40] this comment fails to take into account the subtle shifts in the strategic approach to questions of relation which Beckett develops throughout his career. This kind of permutation occurs for the first time in *Murphy* with the biscuits, and then becomes a dominant element in *Watt*. It reappears in many later works, notably *Molloy* with the sucking stones, *The Unnamable*[41] with the ceaseless testing of possibilities, but also in *The Lost Ones*,[42] *What Where*, *Quad* and *Come and Go*,[43] for example. It emerges with greatest force, however, with *Watt*, which appears at a point when Beckett begins to move definitively away from an hermeneutic aesthetic of interpretation (one which proceeds, at least in part, through allusion and the deference to authority this requires) to one which seems to be based on a combinatorial logic which includes all in exhausting all, and so ultimately excludes all. This shift corresponds with the shift from an interest in an aesthetic based on the recognition of a single relation to one understood to involve 'nonrelation'.

While this shift takes an undoubtedly complex turn with *Watt*, the broad outlines of the shift between relation and nonrelation remain clear. Increasingly Watt's words begin 'to fail him', his 'world to become unspeakable'.[44] This difficulty with drawing connections, or understanding clearly, is something which appears in many of Beckett's characters from this point on. We see it in *Mercier and Camier*: 'I don't see the connexion, said Camier/Just so, said Mercier, you never see the connexion,'[45] as well as in *Molloy*, *Malone Dies* and *The Unnamable*, and *Godot* and later in *Happy Days*,[46] when Winnie only half remembers, at best, her lessons. A failure to understand, a failure to draw connections emerges as a key aspect of many of the principal characters Beckett describes between *Watt* and *Molloy*, *Malone Dies* and *The Unnamable*, and this seems to replace an earlier tendency to work by developing allusions and drawing connections. Indeed, we have touched on the famous credo against the drawing of such connections in *Watt*, 'no symbols where none intended', in the previous chapter. We see this echoed in *Mercier and Camier*, where symbolic or allusive procedures are explicitly disavowed:

You ask me to explain, said Camier, I do so and you don't mind me.

It's my dream came over me again, said Mercier.

Yes, said Camier, instead of minding me you tell me your dreams. And you know our covenant: no communication of dreams on any account. The same holds for quotes. No dreams or quotes at any price.[47]

This is not to claim that allusions no longer occur after *Watt*. Rather, it is a good deal more complex than this. While allusions do still occur they are much less frequently brought to the surface. They are less often explicitly tied to a proper name, as in 'I who had loved the image of old Geulincx, dead young ...' from *Molloy*,[48] or 'it had the same notion at the same instant Malebranche less the rosy hue' from *How It Is*.[49] When this explicit link is made it often, more or less, comes as a surprise to the one who makes it, as we see in the comments which immediately follow the reference to Malebranche: 'the humanities I had',[50] or, in *The Unnamable*, 'No denying it, I'm confoundedly well informed'.[51] Or the one who makes it is no longer completely sure they are remembering correctly: 'It was in Latin, nimis sero, I think that's Latin' in *Molloy*,[52] or 'what is that wonderful line ... laughing wild ... something something laughing wild amid severest woe' in *Happy Days*.[53] It is clear, indeed, that the avatars after *Watt* once had learning, but that this has now been eroded, by time, by the vagaries of memory.

FAILING TO UNDERSTAND

A kind of equivocation is now stressed about the hermeneutic tradition; about scholarship in the humanities. It is recognised in *Molloy* that there are connections between things ('all things hang together, by the operation of the Holy Ghost, as the saying is'),[54] and it is recognised, as we have seen in *Watt*, and as is stressed through the description of Moran's study of the habits of bees in *Molloy*, that the pondering of the nature of connections, those links which might allow us to understand, brings a kind of peace. Yet it is also now recognised that such links are fleeting and insubstantial; that they can never fully be grasped, at least not by the kinds of people that are Beckett's people. It is worth quoting at some length from *Molloy*, where Molloy discusses his interest in the humanities, to illustrate what I mean:

I once took an interest in astronomy, I don't deny it. Then it was geology that killed a few years for me. The next pain in the balls was anthropology and the other disciplines, such as psychiatry, that are connected with it, disconnected, then connected again, according to the latest discoveries. What I liked in anthropology was its inexhaustible faculty of negation, its relentless definition of man, as though he were no better than God, in terms of what he is not. But my ideas on this subject were always horribly confused, for my knowledge of men was scant and the meaning of being beyond me. Oh I've tried everything. In the end it was magic that had the honour of my ruins, and still today, when I walk there, I find its vestiges. But mostly they are a place with neither plan nor bounds and of which I understand nothing, not even of what it is made, still less into what. And the thing in ruins, I don't know what it is, what it was, nor whether it is not less a question of ruins than the indestructible chaos of timeless things, if that is the right expression. It is in any case a place devoid of mystery, deserted by magic, because devoid of mystery. And if I do not go there gladly, I go perhaps more gladly there than anywhere else, astonished and at peace, I nearly said as in a dream, but no, no.[55]

Allusions, then, are still made, and the works remain as full of the astonishing depth of learning which Beckett had brought, with a much heavier touch, to his earlier works: the words, as Molloy says, 'know'. What has changed, now, is that the verbal 'joust' has disappeared, as has the sense of the certainty of the nature of connections. 'Getting' an allusion does, no doubt, bring something to the works, just as getting a joke allows us to see the point of the telling, whereas, when we do not get the joke, we can do little but look at one another with the forlorn air of Hairy, or pass on. Still, getting the majority of the allusions is no longer an indication of playing the game more successfully. Rather, not getting them is at times valued as, if not more, highly: failing to understand comes to be considered a considerable virtue: 'Dear incomprehension, it's thanks to you I'll be myself, in the end.'[56] This is a point whose implications have perhaps not yet been adequately recognised. We know of Beckett's struggles with producers, such as Kenneth Tynan and Laurence Olivier, who argued that the protagonists of *Play*[57] were being asked to pronounce their lines so rapidly that no one could understand them.[58] Though impossible to describe or even circumscribe, failing to comprehend, and how this might affect an audience, is perhaps as important to our descriptions of Beckett's works as our attempts to comprehend.

THE OCCLUDED ALLUSION

Allusions do occur, but they also at times are occluded or hidden. No doubt this might be thought to be the case from the very beginning, but the shifts we have traced here allow the suggestion that they are now hidden in a different way and produce different effects. Whereas in the works prior to *Watt*, tracing an allusion is clearly part of a game between writer and reader, and so finding a hidden allusion is a manner of scoring points in that game, I would suggest that a different kind of hiding of allusion occurs. This involves the use of allusions which it is not necessary to find in order to 'get'. This, I will argue, throughout this work, often proceeds through the use of images which might have been borrowed from other sources but which maintain a power that persists even when the connection to the original is not recognised.

An example of this has been mentioned above: the image which Beckett told Ruby Cohn was drawn from Casper David Friedrich's *Two Men Looking at the Moon* and staged in *Waiting for Godot*. Something is gained when we discover this connection, but we also realise that we were never seriously called upon to discover it; that the power which emerges in the discovery is not essential to the power of the image itself. Another example, which perhaps better exemplifies the shifts I am pointing to here, would be the reference to Belacqua from Dante. In *Dream* and *More Pricks than Kicks* Belacqua, of course, is referred to by name, and we are drawn back to Dante's descriptions of him.[59] That is, the image of one sitting under a great rock in the pose of absolute indifference is drawn into relation with the character of this name. I would argue that the same image, or variations upon it, re-emerges in later works, but this time without the explicit allusion to Dante. Molloy watches A and C while lying on his rock in *Molloy* for example, and in *The Lost Ones* we meet figures adopting postures much like that of Dante's Belacqua. The image still occurs, but the relation to a source is now occluded.

There is another paradox here, then, one which will be felt throughout this study: just as, while recognising their inadequacy to him and his to them, Molloy still finds peace among the ruins of connections, much of this study will pay attention to connections which have been sundered or occluded. Some kind of peace inheres in this process.

THE IMAGE AS 'SIGN'

What is at stake in this shift from allusion as an ideal to allusion as that which, where it exists, might as well be occluded is a shift from relation to nonrelation. The relation stresses the link from which the allusion draws its power. The nonrelation stresses a different kind of power, one which remains open to interpretation precisely because no ready connection is made, or such a connection remains in suspension. With regard to what has been discussed in chapter 1, we can conclude that the relation (of which the allusion is one kind) involves representation, and representation refers to that kind of description which already carries an interpretation with it. A representation works through the relation of one thing to another: in this sense it is recognised and easily understood. The presentation, on the other hand, is that which has not yet been understood, is that which remains to be interpreted and whose meaning resists being fixed.

No doubt with reference to Peirce, this kind of presentation is what Deleuze calls the 'sign' in *Proust and Signs*:

What forces us to think is the sign. The sign is the object of an encounter, but it is precisely the contingency of the encounter that guarantees the necessity of what it leads us to think. The act of thinking does not proceed from a simple natural possibility; on the contrary, it is the only true creation. ... To think is always to interpret – to explicate, to develop, to decipher, to translate a sign. Translating, deciphering, developing are the form of pure creation.[60]

As I touched upon in *Beckett and Poststructuralism*, there is a difference between Deleuze and Beckett in that, while encountering the same sets of problems, Deleuze always seeks the positive image, and Beckett the negative. Beckett might stress the failure to adequately translate, decipher, or develop a sign, but the problem encountered is more or less the same. The sign Deleuze describes is a kind of presentation, and what we fail to adequately understand in Beckett is the presentation, the object. Both, however, equally turn with dissatisfaction from the representation. For Deleuze, art does not represent, it creates. For Beckett, over time, the point of focus moves from what is represented (and this does, indeed, remain an important point of focus at least until *Malone Dies*) to what is presented to us. Asked what the late play *What Where*[61] means, Beckett is reputed to have answered, 'I don't know what it means, don't ask me what it means, it's an object.'[62] A nonrelation, then, is a sign of this kind or, to continue with the terminology we have been developing, it is a presentation.

THE ACT OF RELATING

There are, of course, other elements of Beckett's writing which link with the shifts I have been tracing from an aesthetic of relation to one of nonrelation. Briefly, one might mention the process of relating a story. The most obvious example of a shift in Beckett's aesthetic can be found in the move from the strong emphasis on the third-person narrator, which is to be found in all Beckett's prose works prior to *First Love* (first published in 1946),[63] to the first-person narrator, which is found in all the works after *First Love* until *All Strange Away* (1963–4)[64] and *Imagination Dead Imagine* (1965),[65] which return to a third person. This time, however, rather than recounting a story, that third person seems to describe a process: he is a detached observer, who, in a somewhat scientific way, describes an image or series of images. *Enough* (1965)[66] returns again to the first person, while *Ping* (1966),[67] *Lessness* (1969)[68] and *The Lost Ones* (1966, 1970)[69] return to the third person as distanced observer. The *Fizzles* (1973–5)[70] alternate between first and third, while 'Heard in Dark' 1 and 2 (as early sketches for *Company*) alternate between the third and second persons. 'As the Story

Was Told' (1973)[71] returns to a first person, but it is a first person much like that encountered in *How It Is* who recounts what he hears (relaying what is said by, one imagines, a second person) rather than recounting his own story. The final three short prose pieces – 'The Cliff', 'neither' and *Stirrings Still* (1988)[72] – at last return to a third person.

I have left to one side the 'Nohow On' trilogy of *Company, Ill Seen Ill Said* and *Worstward Ho*[73] for the moment, as I need to make some passing comments about the original shift from third to first person before returning to these late works. Firstly, it must be recognised that, as with our discussion of allusion, a lack of purity in the distinction between the first and third person narrators occurs from the beginning. That is, the third person narrators almost always enter into the stories at some point, becoming first person narrators briefly, before returning to the descriptions of what happens to the others. Yet there is a clear difference, nonetheless. The narrators of the 'Four Novellas'[74] and *Molloy* and *Malone Dies*,[75] for example, relate their stories in a manner which can be more easily connected with the presentation than the representation. That is, we are shown, to an extent (though this increases and is most apparent with *Malone Dies*) the process of telling which helps to comprise the relation, a process which includes errors in the relation and the decay of the one who relates. The process of relating, itself, is drawn to the surface or attention is drawn to it (though, of course, it is fictionalised). That is, rather than the story being highly polished, with the narrator representing a world for us which he has already himself gone some way to interpreting, the first-person narrators are presented to us as objects for interpretation who claim in large part to be themselves incapable of interpreting what they relate.

With *The Unnamable*, we find a further shift, where the narrator is no longer writing his story, but telling it, making it up and feeling that perhaps (he is not sure) his voice in fact only repeats what it has heard (a figure which is developed in numerous works after this). With 'Nohow On', particularly with *Company*, we have a fluid shifting between third, second, and first persons. The brief summaries I am offering here in no way do justice to the complexity of these shifts. They do indicate, however, how these shifts draw attention to the process of composition in such a way as to move towards the presentation of the event of relating, rather than considering relation to be a process of representation. In this way, again, the relation itself is negated at the same time as it occurs: it becomes a nonrelation. This is indicated in a passage cited below from 'The Calmative',[76] but perhaps most clearly in the well-known final lines of Moran's narrative in *Molloy*.

Something of what I mean can be illustrated in an example cited by S. E. Gontarski in his edition of Beckett's *Complete Short Prose*. Gontarski recounts how an American theatre director, Joseph Chaikin, wrote to Beckett for permission to stage *Stories and Texts for Nothing*. Beckett responded with a draft for an adaptation:

Curtain up on speechless author (A) still or moving or alternately. Silence broken by recorded voice (V) speaking opening of text. A takes over. Breaks down. V again. A again. So on. Till text completed piecemeal. Then spoken through, more or less hesitantly, by A alone.[77]

This version was rejected by Chaikin, who wanted to draw on a selection of texts rather than stage a complete text. Beckett responded: 'The method I suggest is only valid for a single text. The idea was to caricature the labour of composition . . .'[78] The process of composition, then, itself is as much imagined, or pictured within or behind the prose texts from 'Four Novellas' on, illustrating again how Beckett's aesthetic orientation has shifted from his earlier works.

In the earlier works attention is drawn to the narrator, but somewhat superficially. The opening line of *Mercier and Camier*,[79] which draws attention to the problem of how a third-person relation might be complete, echoes similar comments in *Dream*[80] and *More Pricks Than Kicks*.[81] In these texts, however, the presence of the narrator is interpreted (as in *Dream*) or his relationship with the protagonist is brought to the surface and made to seem slightly ridiculous (as is also the case in *Watt*, when the narrator meets Watt in Chapter III). There is an implied interpretation here: the impossibility and absurdity of the omniscient third-person narrative is brought to our attention. In the texts after *First Love*, however, the impossibility of the relation emerges as a given which is never adequately interpreted. An example of such a gap in interpretation can be found in the passage where Malone loses his pencil in *Malone Dies*.[82]

If there were sufficient space, other kinds of relation could be drawn into this reading: the shifts in kinds of relationship, for example. The relationships between protagonists are particularly interesting in the plays (which begin at a time when Beckett has more or less definitively shifted from an emphasis on relation to one on nonrelation). In these terms, *Godot* could be seen as a kind of throw-back. Whereas relationships have already begun to break down in the prose texts with *First Love* (which comes immediately after the story of the pseudo-couple *Mercier and Camier*), so that, increasingly isolated figures are presented to us, *Godot* brings us back to a couple, Didi and Gogo, whose relationship is relatively strong and stable (in contrast to that of Pozzo and Lucky, which continues to decay). With *Endgame*,[83] we are shown an anti-relationship: that of Hamm and Clov, and kinds of disjunction or failures to completely connect can be found in almost all the other plays and radio plays which follow. We see this in *Happy Days* with Winnie and Willie, in *Krapp's Last Tape*,[84] with Krapp's sense of disconnection with his former selves, in *Play*,[85] with the three protagonists utterly disconnected, and in *Not I*,[86] with the further disconnection of self from self ... Other examples could be drawn.

THE IMAGE, THE RELATION AND THE NONRELATION

Deleuze's reading of Beckett in 'The Exhausted' is compelling, and is made more so because he ties it to a concept, 'exhaustion', which itself is extracted from images which recur throughout Beckett's work: the image of the one who is exhausted, the one who has nothing left, an image which links with processes of extraction and taking away. It considers the issue from one side, however, and therefore still fails to notice certain aspects of it. That is, the three kinds of language Deleuze discusses in 'The Exhausted' all have in common that they interact with the question of relation and nonrelation.

'Language I', refers to the series and the permutations of series. We have already seen how this involves a drawing of relations which is, at once, a negation (or exhaustion) of relations. Yet, what Deleuze has left out in beginning at this point is how other kinds of relation were apparent, and apparently abandoned, in Beckett's early work: the kind of non-exhaustive drawing of relations (in the exclusive disjunction) which is apparent in the allusion, for example. One might argue that this occurs in works which are not yet 'mature', yet whether or not this is the case, it still occurs, and the shifts which have been noted above allow us to better focus on how the later works might be thought to function.

The 'language II' Deleuze identifies in Beckett refers to voices, and again Deleuze sheds new light upon how these function, but this language can only be thought to begin with those works which fully make use of the first person. The early narrators are only fleetingly visible prior to 'First Love': after this point, with the use of the first person, the voice of the one telling offers us the process of telling as a 'presentation'. In short, then, the nature of the voice which tells and its interaction with the story which is told can also be considered from the point of view of relation and nonrelation. There is an interplay of voices (voices which hear voices and recount what these voices tell), and this interplay involves various processes through which the point of relation loses its ground. There are points of non-connection within this interplay, then, and this aspect of the problem of the voice is equally as important in Beckett's works as that which Deleuze recognises in concentrating on the notion of exhaustion.

A similar point might be made with regard to Deleuze's 'language III', the language of the image, which we have touched upon above. Deleuze states:

language I was that of the novels, and culminates in *Watt*; language II marks out its multiple paths throughout the novels (*The Unnamable*), suffuses the works for theater, and blares forth in the radio pieces. But *language III*, born in the novel (*How It Is*), passing through the theater (*Happy Days, Act without Words, Catastrophe*) finds the secret of its assemblage in television: a prerecorded voice for an image that in each case is in the process of taking form.[87]

The image, as Deleuze convincingly displays, can be understood as being involved in processes of exhaustion. It is equally enlightening, however, to consider how processes of relation and nonrelation affect our understanding of what the image is, and what it does in Beckett's works. Yet, in order to do this, we need to recognise the emergence of the image in the earlier works (well before *How it Is*) and to consider how the image might have differed in form or function in those earlier works.

A major problem when discussing the image is how to define this term in such a way that, on the one hand, it remains sufficiently broad to encompass its many incarnations, and on the other that its particular nature can be adequately circumscribed (so that it does not become too vague to serve any purpose). In the previous chapters we began to see how the image might be understood to be a presentation rather than a representation. That is, it is something which requires interpretation, something which has not, in the manner of a representation, already been more or less completely interpreted by being drawn into a stable relation.

With Beckett it is always important to keep in mind the subtlety of these distinctions: the shift from relation to nonrelation, as we have seen, involves a subtle change. The lack of connection which ensues can be, apparently, minor. There is not a huge gulf to be traversed; rather, there are gaps, fissures, tears in the surface, but it is through these small gaps that relation turns to nonrelation. So too, what I have called a presentation will not be something which we completely fail to recognise. We will recognise aspects of it: the mouth in *Not I*, for example, is recognised as *a mouth*, but the context within which mouths are usually represented is now missing. There is a gap, in this case a gap in context, which forces us to interpret *this* mouth as 'a mouth'.[88] This is what I mean by the presentation in Beckett, and it is this aspect – the process through which something is not easily understood, the process through which something has to be actively interpreted – which is crucial to a definition of the image in Beckett.

What becomes apparent in the early works however, is how 'images' are offered which *are* brought into relation with interpretations that are more or less directed. This 'image in relation' would more commonly be called the metaphor. A metaphor is a figure which connects an image to a context or meaning. Indeed, it might be argued that all language has this effect, that all language tends to draw us towards links. This aspect of language is what Beckett seems to be drawing attention to in his letter to Axel Kaun of 1937,[89] and Deleuze recognises this in his reading of this letter.[90]

There is, however, already a tension in Beckett's use of the metaphorical image, from the very beginning. That is, some of the early metaphorical images are already straining to release themselves from the connections which are being made. This tendency, indeed, might be thought to be a common problem for the metaphor. The tendency of the image to exceed the relation into which it is drawn, the tendency of the image to fail to be domesticated and well behaved, moves towards the surface in Le Doeuff's discussions of the use philosophers make of the image. The philosopher draws upon an image to express a relation, but the image is being asked, in fact, to cover over, or leap over, a gap in an argument. The image, that is, is being asked to establish a connection where that connection remains difficult to establish. Such images, when examined, have a tendency to fail to fully carry the connections, and instead carry us in unintended directions. Such metaphors, that is, have a peculiar quality: they can be reinterpreted in a manner which diverges from the interpretation already given to us through the relation drawn to the image by the metaphor. Such a process is exploited by Derrida, among others, in developing his deconstructive readings.

In his early works Beckett seems to intend to offer us metaphors (that is, his images are always drawn into relation). As we have seen, however, he was also already very much aware of the idea of the image itself, as that which can carry affective power. I touched upon the Imagists in the previous chapter. If we look at a famous example of Imagist poetry, however, we can see how even the Imagists were drawing their images into relation, rather than drawing attention to any failure to connect. Consider Ezra Pound's 'In a Station of the Metro'

> The apparition of these faces in the crowd;
> Petals on a wet, black bough.[91]

Here we are given the image in the second line and a point of relation (which also includes an image) in the first. We tend, through habit, to turn the second image purely into a metaphor. An explicit link, it might be argued, is missing, but the framing of the two makes it difficult to dissociate one from the other. It is nonetheless clear that the lack of the explicit link does force us to consider the image of the petals fully, and the point of relation (the faces, which also offers an image) fully, and this might be developed by way of attempting to account for the power of the poem. Still, a relation occurs, and the image is read as a metaphor, or rather, each image is read as a metaphor for the other.

We see a similar use of metaphorical image (one which draws attention to the image which will be drawn into relation, but nevertheless directs us to a specific interpretation) in the first lines of *Dream of Fair to Middling Women*. The first full section or chapter of this work offers, in fact, such an image. In one way this is curious, as we are not given the normal contexts we might expect in a novel. Rather, we are given an image, which stands alone and is not incorporated into the story:

Behold Belacqua an overfed child pedalling, faster and faster, his mouth ajar and his nostrils dilated, down a frieze of hawthorn after Findlater's van, faster and faster till he cruise alongside of the hoss, the black fat wet rump of the hoss. Whip him up, vanman, flickem, flapem, collop-wallop fat Sambo. Stiffly, like a perturbation of feathers, a tail arches for a gush of mard. Ah . . .!

And what is more he is to be surprised some years later climbing the trees in the country and in the town sliding down the rope in the gymnasium.[92]

This passage can be drawn into relation with themes from the story as a whole. Belacqua rides his bicycle and is covered in shit. The connection, to this extent is clear. We clearly connect, through habit, metaphorical shit, with shit of other kinds. The event is humorous, and directs us not to take Belacqua, or his antics, or his ideas, too seriously. Colouring the humour is more than a hint of grotesque perversity. We are directed towards certain questions: 'does he like this kind of thing?' for example. Another question might be: how does this particular image of the horse's tail lifting (an image within an image, 'the perturbation of feathers') so that the shit can spew forth upon our pedalling hero, connect with the following, apparently wholesome ones of climbing trees or sliding down ropes? We begin to see

both the use of relation and the placing of the relation under pressure here. The mind – to turn new eyes upon a cliché – boggles.

The distinctions, then, are subtle, but nevertheless real. In drawing our attention to the notion of nonrelation, Beckett underlines how we habitually come to make sense in fiction or art. He underlines how we are used to being shown two things side by side and think ourselves clever in drawing a connection between them, ignoring, all the while, how the artist has led us towards this meaning. Indeed, fiction generally works through the drawing of connections; the drawing into relation of elements which are placed within the work, or referred to outside the work. The process of recognising an allusion proceeds in this manner. The author knows the relation which the reader is called upon to find: this is a kind of game, and, practised at a high level, it is a method which clearly can play an important role in the production of significant works of art. Beckett, in an interview with Israel Shenker, makes a well-known distinction between his own work and that of James Joyce which it is worth revisiting here:

With Joyce the difference is that Joyce was a superb manipulator of material – perhaps the greatest. He was making words do the absolute maximum of work. There isn't a syllable that's superfluous. The kind of work I do is one in which I'm not master of my material. The more Joyce knew the more he could. He's tending toward omniscience and omnipotence as an artist. I'm working with impotence, ignorance. I don't think impotence has been exploited in the past. There seems to be a kind of esthetic axiom that expression is an achievement – must be an achievement. My little exploration is that whole zone of being that has always been set aside by artists as something unuseable – as something by definition incompatible with art.[93]

INTENTION

In *Three Dialogues with Georges Duthuit* Beckett links nonrelation to a failure to express. Expression, here, carries the sense of representing, and to represent carries with it the idea that the work, and the artist who creates the work, develop a virtual interpretation which inheres within it. The artist who expresses, then, has something to say, and it is the role of the reader to decode this message. Others have used terms such as 'the ideal reader' to convey this idea. A different approach to taking into account this virtual interpretation would be to refer to it as an 'intention'. The intention, here, the intention to express, does not simply remain within the person of the artist, but is carried within the work;[94] it involves putting before the reader elements which are expected to be drawn into relation.

In contrast to this, Beckett's views can be taken to affirm an artform which, while not giving up the process of attempting to draw things into connection, intends to fail to do so. As Beckett says of Bram van Velde in his letter to Duthuit: 'I'm not saying that he doesn't search to re-establish correspondence. What is important is that he does not manage to.'[95] Rather, he fails to express by failing to provide the reader with materials which can be clearly drawn into relation; failing to provide clear lines of intention with which to draw connections within and without the work.

This process itself, of course, is intended, and a renovated concept of intention allows us to better grasp the apparent paradox of nonrelation. It allows us to better grasp the apparent paradox of an author who, on the one hand, provides texts which seem hostile to processes of fixing meaning and, on the other, particularly in the case of the playtexts, insists upon specific stage directions, specific 'interpretations' of these texts. Intention remains within the art of nonrelation as much as it does within the art of relation. As is well known, Beckett told Driver, 'What I am saying does not mean that there will henceforth be no form in art. It only means that there will be new form.'[96] It is less commented upon that, following this, Driver suggested to Beckett that all art was ambiguous, to which Beckett responded that this was not true, that classical art, for example does not allow 'the mystery to invade us', but that some kinds of art, his own, for example, raise questions they do not attempt to answer.[97]

This shift in intention and the possibility of its occurrence are well summed up by Morson and Emerson[98] in their reading of Mikhail Bakhtin. For Bakhtin, they argue, the problem with intentional criticism is that it does not go far enough:

Typically, intentionalists understand only one of two kinds of intention; what they overlook is the author's 'other intention' – to make his work rich in potentials. ... authors *intend* their works to mean more than their *intended* meanings. They deliberately endow their works not only with specified meanings they could paraphrase, but also with 'intentional potentials' for future meanings in unforeseen circumstances. The most important thing wrong both with the usual intentional criticism and with the most common criticisms of it is an extraordinarily impoverished understanding of intention itself.[99]

My argument is that there is a shift in the kinds of intentions which inhere to the images offered in *Dream* and those offered when Beckett comes to write *Watt*. While the images in *Dream* can and do exceed the intended relations into which they are drawn (as is often the case when images in relation – metaphors – are employed), from *Watt* on, Beckett begins to include images which are intended to no longer easily be drawn into relation.

THE BROKEN HERMENEUTIC CIRCLE

The fault lines which develop into this break, as with our discussion of allusion, can be traced from Beckett's earliest aesthetic writings. In *Dream* a clear preference is expressed for the image of the imagination or fancy, that image which can be made to appear and which then disappears.

The real presence was a pest because it did not give the imagination a break . . . the object that becomes invisible before your eyes is, so to speak, the brightest and best.[100]

The artistic image, the artistic presentation, that which Beckett develops, differs from the presentation of the real precisely because it can more readily be detached from those contexts, those links, those connections, those relations, which adhere to it. It remains a presentation, however, because it also lacks the intended interpretation which a representation includes.

As we have seen in the previous chapter there is a continuity with Beckett's aesthetic ideas concerning the image from early in his career. These ideas, however, are only fully developed into an artform capable of accommodating them over time.

A major step in this process occurs in *Watt*. We can clearly trace here a move from the kind of interpretation required of the representation (which in the language Beckett adopts in this novel is called 'symbolic'),[101] to a notion of presentation where all that is provided to us are images which do not carry intended interpretations, images that we either simply fail to understand or have to understand anew, for ourselves, at every turn:

This fragility of the outer meaning had a bad effect on Watt, for it caused him to seek for another, for some meaning of what had passed, in the image of how it had passed.

The most meagre, the least plausible, would have satisfied Watt, who had not seen a symbol, nor executed an interpretation, since the age of fourteen, or fifteen, and who had lived, miserably it is true, among face values all his adult life, face values at least for him. Some see the flesh before the bones, and some see the bones before the flesh, and some never see the bones at all, and some never see the flesh at all, never never see the flesh at all. But whatever it was Watt saw, with the first look, that was enough for Watt.[102]

There is evidently a distinction between how 'interpretation' is understood in this passage in relation to the understanding of a symbol and the process of establishing meaning by attending to the face value of what is presented to us. For Watt is not averse to attempting to establish meaning; on the contrary:

Watt could not accept them for what they perhaps were, the simple games that time plays with space, now with these toys, now with those, but was obliged, because of his peculiar character, to enquire into what they meant, oh not into what they really meant, his character was not so peculiar as all that, but into what they might be induced to mean, with the help of a little patience, a little ingenuity.[103]

Rather than simply following the trail of links offered by the work, what seems to be being developed is an art which will lead us towards seeking meaning which is not symbolic, which does not direct us to an intended interpretation, which has to be experienced, and whose uncertainties have to be encountered by the reader without assistance.

That this artform has still not completely been developed by Beckett with *Watt*, however, is illustrated by a passage which occurs later in the work. Watt enters Erskine's room and is arrested by a painting which he finds there:

A circle, obviously described by a compass, and broken at its lowest point, occupied the middle foreground of this picture ... In the eastern background appeared a point, or dot. The circumference was black. The point was blue ... And he wondered what the artist had intended to represent (Watt knew nothing about painting), a circle and its centre in search of each other, or a circle and its centre in search of a centre and a circle respectively ...[104]

Here we encounter an image which seems to implore us to read it symbolically. The break in the circle, for Watt, can only come at the lowest point, for 'It is by the nadir that we come, said Watt, and it is by the nadir that we go, whatever that means.'[105] There is a gap in the circle. The circle brings to mind, symbolically, the circle of interpretation, the hermeneutic circle.[106] The 'centre' of the circle is outside rather than in the centre, again undoing habitual logic. This image illustrates, all too well, the very idea of nonrelation in art. The relation is the drawing of connections. The broken hermeneutic circle draws us into a process of interpretation, but the process cannot be completed because a gap occurs, a failure to completely relate or connect elements, a failure to lead us to an intended meaning. I suggest this illustrates the process of nonrelation 'too well' because in doing so the image of the broken circle struggles not to take on the role of a symbol for it: it seems to represent nonrelation, because we closely connect it with the theories which have been set out for us (elements of which I have just cited above).

What we witness here, then, is the fact that while Beckett's aesthetic theories were already well developed with *Watt*, he still had not found a form which might adequately accommodate them. 'The image' has already been mentioned in dispatches on a number of occasions. It is only after World War Two, however, beginning with *First Love* that Beckett begins to find the form he has been seeking.

THE 'FOUR NOVELLAS' AND NONRELATION

The major evident change with the 'Four Novellas' is the use of the first person. As we have seen, the use of explicit allusions (which had been diminishing since *Watt*), though not renounced completely, is now greatly reduced in line with the faulty memories of the first-person narrators. We do, however, still find mentions of 'Giudecca in the hell of unknowing' (*First Love*),[107] Heraclitus ('The Expelled'),[108] d'Aubigné and the story of Joe Breen or Breem (he misremembers) ('The Calmative')[109] and the Ethics of Geulincx ('The End').[110] What we encounter here, for the first time, however, is what might be called a background image, the image of the writer writing, or, rather, the narrator narrating. This is an image which pictures the process of the creation of the story. This process of presenting the relation has a number of contradictory aspects. For example, while there is a recognition that this is all ill said, inexact and fictionalised, the sense is also conveyed that this failed relation is, nevertheless, attempting to focus on the essential aspects of a life. For example, 'The Expelled' ends as follows:

I don't know why I told this story. I could just as well have told another. Perhaps some other time I'll be able to tell another. Living souls, you will see how alike they are.[111]

And 'The End' as follows:

Back now in the stern-sheets, my legs stretched out, my back well propped against the sack stuffed with grass I used as a cushion, I swallowed my calmative. The sea, the sky, the mountains and the islands closed in and crushed me in a mighty systole, then scattered to the uttermost confines of space. The memory came faint and cold of the story I might have told, a story in the likeness of my life, I mean without the courage to end or the strength to go on.[112]

Essential to life is the understanding that, as we will see in the chapters treating Geulincx, we can ultimately understand nothing. To quote from *First Love*:

It took me a long time, my lifetime so to speak, to realize that the colour of an eye half seen, or the source of some distant sound, are closer to Giudecca in the hell of unknowing than the existence of God, or the origins of protoplasm, or the existence of self, and even less worthy than these to occupy the wise.[113]

At stake, then, is much more than some banal indication of the fictional nature of fiction. At stake is an attempt to create a form which might convey a presentation that does justice to an idea of an absence of order, an absence of system. The form is now one which includes a first-person narrator who, while once learned, now remembers ill and offers relations of events which fail to offer adequate connections and clearly expressed intentions. That is, the process of relating events is imperfect, interrupted, broken like the circle in Erskine's room. At the same time we are now, for the first time, offered a background to the story (the idea of the narrator who tells it). Among other things this figure, speaking of himself (remembering ill, recounting ill), is one who is haunted by images which persist from the past, as illustrated in *First Love*:

faint or loud, cry is cry, all that matters is that it should cease. For years I thought they would cease. Now I don't think so any more.[114]

Indeed, in 'The Calmative' the story is related by one after death. The images which persist are both of the past and in the present. They are ghostly presences which subsist, which are all the more disturbingly there in their absence:

I don't know when I died ... For I'm too frightened this evening to listen to myself rot ... So I'll tell myself a story, I'll try and tell myself another story, to try and calm myself ... Or is it possible that in this story I have come back to life, after my death? No, it's not like me to come back to life, after my death ... But there was never any city but the one ... I only know the city of my childhood, I must have seen the other, but unbelieving. All I say cancels out, I'll have said nothing ... For what I tell this evening is passing this evening, at this passing hour.[115]

In short, there are disconnections in the relation. Further, as I argue in chapter 5, we are offered a background image which gives us a picture of what it means to think; we are offered, that is, an image of thought which presents the thinking self as a series of disconnections. Rather than the stable, self-sufficient cogito of Descartes which builds a world again from belief in its own capacity to think, the cogito of Beckett's first-person narrators are suffused with ignorance, just like that cogito described by Arnold Geulincx in his *Metaphysica Vera* and his *Ethics*.

In the next chapter I will attempt to sufficiently unravel the problem of how an art of nonrelation, which now gives less importance to the drawing of allusions, still might draw upon images from philosophy to add to its capacity to unsettle and affect an audience and present that audience with problems which are real, but not solved within the texts.

CIRCUMSCRIBING THE IMAGE

We have now come some distance, and I feel it is possible to roughly outline, in very general terms, the nature of the image in Beckett. The description I will give is one which might be most readily recognised in the later plays in particular, but, when the matter is closely examined, it might be understood to hold for most occurrences of true 'images' in Beckett. While all the works make use of images of various kinds, the true Beckettian image (that which he himself terms 'the image' in 'The Image' and *How It Is*) is something which appears, or is created, and vanishes, but in vanishing leaves a strong impression, an impression which lingers or even transforms the one it affects. At times the vanishing is drawn to our attention (such as the image of the face which appears and vanishes in . . . *but the clouds* . . ., or the hand in *Nacht und Träume*, or the changing figures in *Quad*) and at times the manner in which an image persists or lingers is brought to the surface (such as the figures in their jars in *Play*, the mouth in blackness in *Not I*, the head in *That Time*, the pacing of Amy in *Footfalls*, the one who rocks in *Rockaby*, the last five in *What Where*). These are two ways of looking at the same phenomenon: the phenomenon of the image which is presented to us; the image which exceeds any relation into which it might be drawn; the image which requires us to think.[116]

The Beckettian image, then, appears, vanishes, yet lingers. It is also extracted from surrounding contexts; it is 'an autonomous mental image' like that Deleuze identifies in Bacon. It is offered to us as something which must be interpreted but which will resist easy interpretation and lacks an intended interpretation: that is, we reach out but fail to grasp it. In the theatre we become physically aware of the nature of such images, which, especially in those plays in which figures are surrounded by darkness (*Play, Come and Go, Not I, That Time, Footfalls, A Piece of Monologue, Rockaby, Ohio Impromptu, What Where*)[117] are impressed upon us as we watch and more or less burnt into our retinas, leaving afterimages which linger.

The image is apparently insubstantial, but nevertheless describes a real being, with 'real' carrying the force given to it by the Stoics: a physical reality, the reality of bodily things. The ghostly image is offered to us disconnected from the particular contexts of our socio-historical world, but these contexts – events, their meaning and the words which explain them – are incorporeal for the Stoics, whereas the ghostly image itself, as an image (something which is able to impress itself upon our senses) has a body and is therefore real. These Stoic conceptions, strange to our ears, go some way to illustrating why a peculiar work, in which figures wade through mud to torture other figures, might be called *How It Is*, and I will develop a detailed discussion of this in chapter 7.

The image is often visual, but can also be aural. Indeed, we perhaps begin to feel the haunting nature of the image in Beckett with *All That Fall, Krapp's Last Tape* and *Embers*.[118] In differing ways voices themselves become images in these works. In each case we recognise a sense of the insubstantial, as the voices, in returning (the tapes in *Krapp* or the haunting voices in *Embers*), draw attention to how they have passed away. A similar use of voice as image can be found in *Eh Joe*,[119] where the voice of the woman who pursues Joe, the voice of a once living woman, as in *Embers*, lingers, returns, fades, persists. Sounds too provide us with images: the dragging steps and the wind and the rain of *All That Fall*, the sound of the waves in *Embers*.[120]

While it is easiest to recognise these images in those works (the plays, the film, the works for television and radio) which are able to present those images to us directly, and in particular in the later works, where only one or two images might be emphasised throughout the entire piece, once we have recognised and roughly defined the nature of these images it is possible to work backwards and begin to find images in those works which are not completely dominated by them. The earlier plays, *Godot, Endgame*, and *Happy Days*, also stage images, but these emerge within works which are much more dynamic in the sense that the protagonists are engaged in many actions. If we look more closely, however, we begin to see certain points within these plays in which a particular image is held and emphasised. Estragon removing his boot, or Pozzo and Lucky falling on their faces and remaining prone, or Lucky delivering his speech, to choose a few examples among many, can be thought of as images. So too, in *Endgame*, certain images are held, momentarily, so that they might affect the audience: the opening with Hamm covered by his old stauncher, or the end where Clov stands motionless. In *Happy Days* two main images are emphasised: Winnie up to her waist in Act 1 and Winnie up to her neck in Act 2.

In the fiction, as I have touched upon above, after *First Love* and until the brief return to the third person in the late 1960s in *Ping, Imagination*

Dead Imagine, All Strange Away and *The Lost Ones*[121] (where a different image, that of the observer, is established), we are shown a background image of the narrator narrating. This, on inspection, shares much in common with the staged images we have just been discussing. The background image is apparently insubstantial (who or where the narrator is recedes and escapes our grasp should we pursue it: Moran's relation, to offer one well-known example, negates its first lines with its last). It appears as, briefly or in a more sustained way (with *The Unnamable* or *Texts for Nothing*),[122] the background comes into view. It vanishes as stories emerge and cover the background. Yet it lingers, remaining one of the elements we remember most vividly from these texts. It exceeds interpretation, and so on. In each case, we are offered an image of the cogito, the 'I think': be it a voice surrounded by darkness or a teller of a tale who tells it ill in attempting to grasp his own story, a story which presents that cogito as one suffused with ignorance.

Yet within the prose, even well before *First Love*, we can also recognise the image. Images occur, indeed, from the first lines of Beckett's fiction, as we have seen in discussing *Dream* above, although it is only after World War Two that Beckett finds a form which most effectively severs them from relations. Yet even in the earlier works, images which linger still occur, images which exceed any relations they have been drawn into. In the earlier texts these images are often drawn into relation with contexts as descriptions or metaphors. Indeed 'the image' which is made in 'The Image' and *How It Is* can be compared to a description of a young man and woman looking at a bay from a mountaintop in 'Finagal' from *More Pricks Than Kicks*, and, as we will see in the next chapter, the image of the rocking chair which is presented in *Film* and *Rockaby*[123] is first of all descibed in *Murphy*. Attention is drawn to the images, they offer themselves as meaningful, but they exceed straightforward interpretation (as for example the image of the man who approaches the station in *Watt*, but never moves any nearer and finally vanishes).[124] As we have seen, Beckett struggled to find a form which might accommodate nonrelation. In seeking this form he did not simply turn to the image alone. Many other elements contribute to his mature style. The focus of the rest of this study, however, is the way in which Beckett makes use of images drawn from philosophy and how this might shed light upon how literature and philosophy interact in his work.

CHAPTER 4

The philosophical imaginary

In the previous chapter we saw how Beckett moves increasingly away from an aesthetic of relation, an aesthetic of allusion, towards an aesthetic of nonrelation, and how his use of the image develops throughout this process. In this chapter, we will begin to consider one of the perceived problems involved in this shift with regard to the question of how Beckett's literary works interact with philosophical texts. That is, if Beckett moves away from allusion, from a direct link to philosophical arguments, how might his works be considered to still be involved with philosphical ideas? My contention is that Beckett's works continue to interact in important ways with works of philosophy. Further, I argue that, once the relations made explicit through the use of allusion are disavowed or rendered problematic, the use of the image becomes one of the principal strategies Beckett's works develop in maintaining the vibrant exchange with philosophy.

In *The Philosophical Imaginary*[1] Michèle Le Doeuff describes the importance of images to the affects produced by philosophy. While philosophy sets out to distance itself from 'myth, fable, the poetic, the domain of the image',[2] it never succeeds in developing a language which is free from images. On the contrary, 'Imagery and knowledge form, dialectically, a common system. Between these two terms there is a play of feedbacks.'[3] That is, images, and the particular qualities they bring with them, serve an invaluable function within philosophical thought. For Le Doeuff, these qualities involve an ability to offer a usefully unstable point of relation. That is, while, in the philosophical texts, the images are used within metaphors to establish a connection, or within descriptions to illustrate a point, the images used exceed these clear links: they offer unstable links or nonrelations. For this reason, the image can be used to evade a problem within a philosophical argument. Le Doeuff offers an example from Kant in displaying how he makes use of a particular image to *show* things which he claims not to *be saying* (or to show something which seems to contradict what he explicitly states). She concludes:

> Between the writing subject and his text there is a complex negating relationship, which is a sign that something important and troubling is seeking utterance – something which cannot be acknowledged, yet is keenly cherished. As far as I am concerned, taking an interest in images and enquiring into this sort of evasion are one and the same activity.[4]

The image, then, is able to paper over cracks, or to make contradictory connections possible. It can subtly hide or occlude problems.[5] Paradoxically, however, it also opens up a counter reading, of the kind Le Doeuff develops: in paying attention to the images, one is able to see the gaps. It is a matter of perspective. If there are, to use the language of Beckett's letter to Axel Kaun,[6] tears in the surface of language, the image might cover these over, or, on the other hand, the gaps might be seen in focusing on images which lie over these tears. In either case they offer an unstable connection, the kind which Beckett exploits in developing his aesthetic of nonrelation. This aesthetic, as we have seen, does not completely have done with relation; rather, it urges us to make connections while showing us how unstable these connections are. Another term for this, making use of another word which Beckett borrows from the philosophical tradition, is 'aporia': the image betrays a problem which may be insoluble within a logical system.

There are two major ideas related to the use of images in philosophy, then, which Le Doeuff wishes to draw to our attention. Firstly, that images can be used to cover over, or be seen to betray, gaps in a logical argument:

> The interpretation of imagery in philosophical texts goes together with a search for points of tension in a work. In other words, such imagery is inseparable from the difficulties, the sensitive points of an intellectual venture.[7]

There are pros and cons with such an unstable connection. While the image allows philosphers to cover over, or leap over, gaps in their logical argument, there is always the possibility that these leaps will overshoot the goal, will be understood in a sense different to that which was intended. Le Doeuff's second idea is that:

> the meaning conveyed by images works both for and against the system that deploys them. *For*, because they sustain something which the system cannot itself justify, but which is nevertheless needed for its proper working. *Against*, for the same reason – or almost: their meaning is incompatible with the system's possibilities.[8]

Le Doeuff's definition of the image, then, is consistent with the description developed in the preceding three chapters. Importantly, she recognises that the meaning of an image is not completely clear, that it is not completely pre-interpreted; rather, images 'need to be decoded before one can relate their meaning to the thought made explicit in the text'.[9] It is this element – that they require interpretation, rather than carrying an immediate, clear interpretation – which allows them to function in the manner described. The images she considers are developed as metaphors or illustrative descriptions, but, given the nature of the image, they exceed the points of relation they are called upon to establish.

There are other aspects of the image, and the kind of interaction it makes possible between philosophy and literature, which Le Doeuff helps to bring into focus. Firstly, she highlights how images are able to occlude, and this occlusive element is of key importance when attempting to describe the manner in which Beckett uses images which interact with philosophy. Images, for Le Doeuff, are able to occlude or hide problems: they therefore allow evasions to take place in a philosophical argument. This occlusion emerges from the fact that the image must be interpreted: there is a crucial potential for ambiguity apparent in an image. The image requires us to think, to attempt to understand, while not itself offering a definitive indication of what we *should* think. This is one kind of occlusion.

A second, which she also discusses in this essay, is the manner in which images might be borrowed from or adapted from pre-existing sources. For Le Doeuff images are so important to philosophy that certain images can be considered proper to philosophy: that is, certain images seem to do philosophical work:

If the images of philosophical texts are so functional, so organic in their very dysfunctionality, might we not guess that they are made to measure, that there is not just an imaginary *in* philosophy but a properly philosophical imaginary.[10]

Such a contention points toward the possibility that images (either developed by or borrowed from other sources by philosophers) are made use of by philosophers *because* they carry a philosophical character with them. They carry problems with them, in short, they picture instances of aporia which the images themselves impress upon us and ask us to interpret. She considers the use of the image of the 'island of reason' in Kant and links this to a similar image in the seventeenth-century English philosopher Francis Bacon. She goes on, however, to indicate how these images interact with other images of islands, tracing the use of the image of the island from a twelfth-century Andalusian philosophical novel by Ibn Tufayl called *Riçala* to Daniel Defoe in the seventeenth century, who comes across it in translation and develops it in *Robinson Crusoe*.[11] Le Doeuff displays how such images, even in being transferred from work to work without any attribution or direct allusion, can carry with them elements of a problem. An image might be transferred from literature or fable to philosophy, and vice versa, but because of the 'play of feedback' between 'imagery and knowledge'[12] they are able to carry common elements. For this reason it is instructive, Le Doeuff contends, to locate 'a precise source' for an image, as this will serve to unlock elements of the power of the image (by adding to, rather than reducing, the potential depth of an analysis).[13] An image, then, not only occludes (or, in negative image, betrays) a gap or an aporia: it also occludes the source from which it is drawn.

Finding that source again is a process which differs in important ways from the typical tracing of an allusion. When an allusion is traced, we recognise a connection, and the effect which results from this can be attributed both to the resonance, the harmony, which is thereby produced and to the sense of satisfaction one derives from successfully making a connection, the correct connection. When an occluding image is again associated with a source, however, the link which is made, in itself, is not of primary importance. What is of primary importance is the doubling of the problem. With regard to those images which are taken from, or have passed through, the philosophical imaginary, the problem in the Beckett text is linked to a problem (a gap, or an aporia) in a philosophical text. While we do experience recognition in linking the two, more importantly an element of consternation is doubled. That is, we are not comforted by the chord struck (which indicates a world of order) or by the recognition of an allusion. While we recognise a chord being struck, it is always ominous. Beckett's use of occlusive images points us to a properly philosophical problem which is not solved, either in the Beckett text or in the source from which it is drawn (though usually with the difference that, while the Beckett text acknowledges and draws attention to the problem of the problem, the source of the image might pretend that no problem exists).

As we have seen, in 'Peintres de l'Empêchement',[14] Beckett draws the startling conclusion that, because the essence of an object is to elude representation, no object can be represented; that all one can attempt is to describe the process of evasion. The creation of images offers one means of doing this, as the image itself evades; the image itself can be presented as an object. That the image might have a pre-history, that it might have been borrowed from a philosopher, for example, does not contradict the idea that the image must be made or created. On the contrary, Deleuze and

Guattari describe creation in these terms, as drawing materials from other sources and linking them together in new and unexpected ways. The bower bird, which collects baubles and bright things which it then arranges in its bower, is offered as an example of artistic practice.[15] Creation does not come *ex nihilo*; rather, it is implicated in a system of relays. Such a system of relays can be recognised in an example of an occlusive image drawn by Beckett from Arnold Geulincx: the image of the rocking chair.

ARNOLD GEULINCX

For a time the *Ethics* of Arnold Geulincx (1624–69) were well known. They ran to a number of editions over forty-odd years once published in full posthumously in 1671.[16] As H. J. De Vleeschauwer has shown, this success was largely due to the fact the book was seen as offering an effective means both of accommodating the still new science of Descartes to the still imperative force of theological truth, and of offering a Christian answer to the danger of the perceived atheism of Spinoza. However, early in the eighteenth century Ruardus Andala launched a series of polemics against Geulincx, arguing that only Descartes offered a truly Christian perspective within his philosophy, with Geulincx criticised for lapsing into pantheism and Spinozism.[17] After these attacks, however ill-informed, in the words of Victor Vander Haeghen, 'silence fell little by little on the name of the philosopher from Anvers, and for many years he has only ever been cited in being remembered among the pale satellites of Descartes and Spinoza'.[18] Little work of any kind has been done on Geulincx by English-language philosophers, and only in the last hundred years, with the most significant works being those of D. J. McCracken,[19] H. J. De Vleeschauwer[20] and G. Nuchelmans,[21] and recently Nadler,[22] and van Ruler.[23] Terraillon[24] and De Vleeschauwer[25] have also contributed important works on Geulincx in French. Geulincx has attracted some attention in French intellectual circles through the works of Alain de Lattre[26] and Bernard Rousset.[27] Such studies, however, remain rare, and many of these texts are not easily obtainable.[28] Until recently none of Geulincx's works had been available in English.[29] So while Geulincx's works do illuminate elements of Beckett's works, Geulincx himself remains an obscure figure.

Yet, the name Arnold Geulincx is extremely well known in the field of Beckett studies. Indeed, mention of Geulincx along with the citation of his key moral premise, 'Ubi nihil vales, ibi nihil velis' ('where one can do nothing, one should want nothing')[30] has become a critical commonplace in Beckett studies. It has been such since Sighle Kennedy[31] published a letter from Beckett (since republished in *Disjecta*) in which he states, in response to her request for a key to his work, and *Murphy* in particular:

If I were in the unenviable position of having to study my work my points of departure would be the 'Naught is more real ...' [... than Nothing: Democritus] and the 'Ubi nihil vales ...' [... ibi nihil velis: Geulincx] both already in *Murphy* and neither very rational.[32]

Further, in his biography of Beckett, James Knowlson tells us how Beckett took, 'detailed notes in Latin ... [comprising] more than fifty pages of single spaced typescript', in studying Geulincx's *Ethics* in the Trinity College Dublin library while working on *Murphy* in 1936.[33] In fact, Beckett's notes, typed in Latin, and now held at Trinity College Dublin, include notes not only on Geulincx's *Ethica* (about forty pages), but also on his *Metaphysica Vera* (about twelve pages) and his *Questiones Quodlibeticae* (one page).[34] These notes, indeed, are direct transcriptions of passages selected from Geulincx's texts. Given the challenge to critics that Beckett poses, both in this letter to Kennedy and in the existence of his notes, it is surprising that so little work which carefully relates elements of Geulincx's system to problems encountered in Beckett's works has thus far been undertaken. Chris Ackerley develops some useful readings of particular allusions to Geulincx in *Murphy* in his *Annotated Murphy*.[35] Apart from this, the major attempt to engage in detail with some aspect of Geulincx is Rupert Wood's article 'Murphy, Beckett, Geulincx, God',[36] and I will discuss this in some detail below. A few others have made interesting comments in passing about Geulincx but none of these have examined his system in any depth or dedicated more than a few pages to him.[37]

Such an absence in the field, however, is less surprising when one considers the difficulty of accessing Geulincx's works. In a letter to Thomas MacGreevy of 1936[38] Beckett wonders whether his interest in Geulincx might in part stem from the philosopher's very obscurity, but then dismisses this idea, as he feels there is a genuine chord struck between his own ideas and those of Geulincx.

I have been reading Geulincx in T. C. D. [Trinity College Dublin], without knowing why exactly. Perhaps because the text is so hard to come by. But that is a rationalisation and my instinct is right and the work worth doing, because of its saturation in the conviction that the sub specie aeternitatis [from the perspective of eternity] vision is the only excuse for remaining alive. He does not put out his eyes on that account, as the Israelites did and Rimbaud began to, or like the terrified Berkeley repudiate them; one feels them very patiently turned outward, and ... inward.[39]

Geulincx, of course, did not set out to be obscure. At the time he wrote Latin was a 'universal' language which offered a greater, rather than a more restricted, potential audience. He also translated his own work into the Dutch vernacular.[40] Unlike Spinoza, who did not publish his *Ethics* in his own lifetime for fear of reprisals from the religious, political and intellectual establishments,[41] Geulincx published the greater part of his *Ethics* and continued to teach his controversial doctrine despite apparently strong opposition. It was quite likely to have been such opposition, manifested through powerful academic enemies, which led, directly or indirectly, to Geulincx being stripped of his professorial position at the University of Louvain in Catholic Flanders in 1658. The university process which led to this expulsion was held in camera, and the reasons for his expulsion remain unknown, but are likely to have been linked to his adherence to Cartesian philosophy at a time when this was considered impious by the Christian Aristotelians who dominated the academy. He removed to Holland, where he began to teach in a lowly position and in virtual poverty at the University of Leiden. Told that he could teach only Aristotle, and under the cover of doing so, he in fact continued to teach his own version of Cartesianism.[42] Some of his distress at misunderstanding and persecution and the determination nevertheless to continue teaching what he knew to be true can be seen in an unusually emotive passage from his *Metaphysica Vera*:

The vulgar ... believe that to suppose something false is to propose falsehood, an opinion that has imperilled many in our time who for the sake of argument have supposed (among other falsities) that God does not exist. This is an example of how the vulgar defame those who dare to make abstractions: however virtuous and admirable such a man may be, let him be put on the rack. But the philosophical view of abstraction is that therewith the mind and spirit are abstracted from sensations and passions; and that thus abstracted a good man may be happy, though he suffer greatly.[43]

He seems not to have shirked such conflict; indeed, accepting the trials of fortune with indifference, as things outside one's power, is a principle of his *Ethics*. His motto was 'serio et candide' ('with seriousness and candour'), a notion of openness and expressing oneself without reservation, despite the catastrophic potentials of this when confronting powerful opponents. One can contrast this with the more pragmatic practices of Spinoza, whose motto 'caute' ('be cautious'), which was something he practised in avoiding the sorts of conflicts which overtook Geulincx, was engraved on the underside of his signet ring,[44] and Descartes, whose motto was 'bene vixit, bene qui latuit' ('he lives well who is well hidden'), which was also something he practised.[45] Interestingly, Beckett provided the unnamable with a Latin motto in similar form:[46] '*De nobis ipsis silemus*'[47] ('we say nothing about ourselves').

WOOD, BECKETT, GEULINCX

While Rupert Wood's article of 1993, 'Murphy, Beckett; Geulincx, God', is a good attempt both to use philosophy to consider Beckett's works and to shed light on how philosophy and fiction might come into contact within those works, its scope is necessarily limited, and it is imprecise with regard to one or two important questions. Wood focuses primarily on the relation between mind and body in *Murphy* and Geulincx, arguing that this relationship in turn affects the relations between narrative voice and the voice of the character Murphy. Yet what interests me here are conclusions Wood draws concerning the general question of the relation of Beckett's writings to philosophy.

Early in his essay, Wood quotes Beckett (in conversation with Gabriel d'Aubarède in 1961):

'I wouldn't have had any reason to write my novels if I could have expressed their subject in philosophic terms.'

'What was your reason then?'

'I haven't the slightest idea. I'm no intellectual. All I am is feeling. *Molloy* and the others came to me the day I became aware of my own folly. Only then did I begin to write the things I feel.'[48]

While these statements are important in helping us to understand how philosophy might relate to Beckett's works, Wood's conclusions as to why are questionable. Wood contends that *Murphy* might be seen as a testing ground for 'stylistic devices, for various philosophical ideas, most of which do not reappear in later works',[49] and these trials, he concludes, lead to the 'abandonment of philosophy'[50] in Beckett's subsequent works. He links this conclusion to his contention that Geulincx's philosophy and philosophy in general suffer from the folly of attempting to describe all reality (be it 'external' or 'internal' to any individual) from a transcendent position, a position which, he claims, is self-contradictory, as human existence does not allow us access to such a God-like perspective:

The perspective of the philosophizing voice [in *Murphy*] replicates the perspective of God in Geulincx's system, for He alone is able to see and to know the connection between body and mind. In each case ... the microcosm or mind, is enclosed, hermetically sealed from direct contact with the first [the macrocosm or world] ... The ironic distance between narrator and Murphy is there to guard against the presumed folly of Murphy, yet what the novel begins to show, whether wittingly or not, is the folly of the distanced perspective, which is the folly of philosophy itself.[51]

While there is something in the connections drawn here, Wood's claims do not do justice to the subtlety of Geulincx's philosophical system. Rather than simply conflating the position of the philosopher with that of God, Geulincx goes to great lengths to establish the nature of human ignorance (including that of philosophers). That ignorance is not absolute, however: one understands, for example, that one is *ultimately* ignorant – even while there are various kinds of knowledge to which one does have access – but above all one knows with absolute certainty that God exists and that He knows all. The philosopher, then, does not pretend that he understands how the big world acts on the little world; rather, he explicitly states that this relation is ineffable, known only to God, and all that he knows about it is that it is controlled by God's agency.

The key point on which Wood might be challenged in his reading of Geulincx concerns his understanding of the relation between the mind and the world. At first Wood offers subtle readings of both Geulincx's idea of the workings of the mind and the image of Murphy's mind offered by Beckett: he accurately describes how Geulincx distinguishes between those things presented to the mind through the senses (with the body acting as the ineffable instrument through which we are made aware of these images) and those things which emerge from the mind itself (reason and desire). He states, 'the picture [Geulincx] presents is *not one of a hermetically closed sphere* [my italics], but one of a discrete mind deposited in the middle of a stage'.[52] He then links this to Murphy's mind, where the zone of the actual (those images presented to the mind via the body) gradually descends into another zone termed the virtual (those images and ideas which belong to the mind alone). Within a few pages, however, Wood has radically simplified, indeed, contradicted this description, stating:

The picture that Geulincx, in his philosopher guise, presents is one which the mind, as he describes it, cannot have. The mind cannot at the same time *be closed* [my italics] and know of its enclosedness from, as it were, the outside.[53]

Wood seems to have forgotten that the mind is, for Geulincx, ineffably presented with images and sensations by God through the brute instrument which is the body, and that it, therefore, opens out to the world and can be affected by it although it cannot directly affect that world. That is, as Wood himself contends on page 40, the mind described by Geulincx is *not* hermetically closed. The contradiction, or folly, he points to in Geulincx's reasoning, then, evaporates, and with it certain of Wood's conclusions become untenable. Chief among these is the notion that Beckett 'abandons' philosophy in his later works because of his alleged recognition of this philosophical 'folly'.

My contention, then, is that rather than discarding philosophy in general, and his interest in Geulincx in particular, Beckett begins to use philosophy differently. That is, he has done with certain ways of using philosophy and retains and develops other ways.

'ALL I AM IS FEELING'

Wood, and many others, have drawn attention to Beckett's interest in 'the shape of ideas' and this interest in the structure and shape of philosophical systems and arguments, first articulated in 'Dante ... Bruno. Vico.. Joyce',[54] is one *modus operandi* he retains in subsequent works. Wood also points to examples of, though does not precisely identify, the other key way in which Beckett uses philosophy after *Murphy*: that is, through the use of images drawn from philosophers. As with the origins of borrowed structure or shape, however, these images are only sometimes directly identified as being drawn from philosophers (and Wood's discussion of Beckett's reticence in this area is also worthy of attention).

What Wood does not see, however, is that Beckett specifically turns to the use of 'shape' or structure and images drawn from philosophy because these are already able to produce feelings and sensations. That is, while, as we have seen, one of the qualities of the image (that quality, which, following Le Doeuff, seems of most interest to philosophy) is its ability to occlude a problem, the image has other qualities which make it attractive to artists. Chief among these is the ability to produce an affect; to produce feelings and sensations. It is worth looking again at one element of the already cited comments Beckett made to d'Aubarède: 'All I am is feeling. *Molloy* and the others came to me the day I became aware of my own folly. Only then did I begin to write the things I feel.' To interpret this to mean that Beckett abandons philosophy or the use of philosophy after *Watt* is too simplistic and obscures the achievement of a powerful way of thinking through literature developed in the later works. Rather, Beckett's comments might be understood as involving self-criticism of the works before *Molloy*, which might be considered inferior by the Beckett of 1961 because they too overtly make use of materials which are not, properly speaking, involved with sensations or feelings, and which therefore damage the fabric of the works. In *What is Philosophy?*, discussing points of overlap between art and philosophy and science, Deleuze and Guattari suggest that if one attempts to insert one form of thought (say, a concept which necessarily utilises philosophical methods) into another form (say, a work of art), then the 'interfering discipline must proceed with its own methods',[55] so that, for example, the artist stops being an artist while using concepts and becomes, momentarily, a philosopher, thereby, quite possibly, botching things.

Beckett's novel *Murphy* might at times be said to relate to problems philosophically rather than in terms of sensations, and this would explain the comments Beckett makes in self-criticism of his early works. Elsewhere I express this in the pairing 'concepts of sensations' (where philosophers create concepts which are concerned with sensations) and 'sensations of concepts' (where artists create sensations which express how ideas *feel* or are experienced). Should a writer start to use a concept as a concept, however, there is a danger that the work of art will lose its shape; that is, that it will stop giving us sensations in starting to give us concepts.[56]

Numerous theorists have explained that polemic is dangerous to the artist because once you become too polemical you run the risk of ceasing to write fiction and starting to write dogma. The Bakhtin school shows how the novel is unique in that it can present many sides of a problem without choosing between these sides:

> The artist has nothing to do with prepared or confirmed theses. These inevitably show up as alien bodies in the work, as tendentious prosisms. Their proper place is in scientific systems, ethical systems, political programs, and the like. Such ready and dogmatic theses have at best only a secondary role in the literary work; they never form the nucleus of its content.[57]

That is, elements of the sensation re-experienced by a reader rest in the choice which, in order to be successfully achieved, must be taken by each reader and not predetermined by the text.

DOGMATIC USES OF PHILOSOPHY IN *MURPHY*

Examples of an overly categorical use of philosophical material can be seen in *Murphy*, about the middle of the novel, where the tone changes from a playful irony (in which, while ideas and concepts are brought into play, they are only there, in an image used more than once in *Murphy*, to be struck back and forth as in a tennis match) to a cloying seriousness, in which one kind of experience is put forward not only as true, but as *the* truth of the elect.[58] Murphy, for example, has been shown the true way, but others (the mere puppets) such as Ticklepenny could never possibly understand this way, which Murphy sees in the aspect of the inmates of the asylum in which he works (and in the aspect of Mr Endon in particular). We witness this polemical philosophical seriousness when Ticklepenny asks Murphy to explain what kind of person he thinks he is, what kind of being he thinks he has:

'Then what?' said Ticklepenny. 'If it is not a rude question.'

Murphy amused himself bitterly and briefly with the question of the answer he would have made to a person of his own steak and kidney, genuinely anxious to understand and desirable of being understood by, a Mr Endon at his own degree of incipience for example. But before the imperfect phrase had time to come the question crumbled away in its own absurdity, the absurdity of saddling such a person with the rationalist prurit, the sceptic rut that places the objects of its curiosity on the level of Les Girls. It was not under that the rare birds of Murphy's feather desired to stand, but by, by themselves with the best of their attention and by the others of their species with any that might be left over. It was not in order to obtain an obscene view of the surface that in days gone by the Great Auk dived under the ice, the Great Auk now no longer seen above it.[59]

If this passage does not *work*, it is not so much for the ideas (with which one certainly might take issue) but because the issue moves so palpably to the surface as that with which one can only agree or take issue. In a letter to Thomas MacGreevy of 17 July 1936, quoted in *Disjecta*, Beckett states: 'There seemed to me always the risk of taking him too seriously and separating him too sharply from the others. As it is I do not think the mistake (Aliosha mistake) has been altogether avoided.'[60]

That is, one no longer *feels* what is happening here; one finds oneself drawn into an intellectual confrontation, one, moreover, which involves a perhaps overly earnest description of a certain kind of self – Murphy – whom the narrator has told us is the only character in the book who is not a puppet. The novel is not generally unsuccessful in its use of philosophy, but this is precisely because, for the most part, this use is so markedly provisional.[61] It places itself in peril when competing philosophies are trumped by *the one true system which is Murphy's* as here its tone becomes too evangelical.

The novel struggles to recover from the moments of earnestness expressed at this stage by sending the comedy back into overdrive with the full-volume interplay between Neary, Miss Counihan and Wylie, a grouping which Miss Counihan dubs 'The Engels sisters'. The pun on the Marx Brothers is strained in a way which indicates a kind of desperation to please, to sweeten the bitter medicine of philosophical polemic we have just been forced to swallow. This in turn throws the balance of sensations out of kilter, as Celia's character labours to achieve the kind of pathos she effortlessly carried with her in the first half of the book. Her suffering, which we felt acutely before the polemics, is simply drowned out by the clowning of the Engels sisters and only finds its feet again when she is reunited with Mr Kelly in the beautiful final scene in which the latter loses his kite.

My contention, then, is that when Beckett says he is turning from philosophy he is in fact turning from this kind of polemic, and that the works from *Molloy* on are concerned with sensations alone. This is not to say, however, that they no longer interact with philosophy: on the contrary.

PHILOSOPHICAL IMAGES FROM GEULINCX

One way forward, which Beckett found, involves the use of images drawn from philosophy, since images can carry elements of conceptual power with them but still function largely through feeling. So as to better illustrate what is at stake here I will turn to a reading of Beckett's use of images drawn from Geulincx.

As we will begin to see in the next chapter, certain points of emphasis and interest led Geulincx into developing a cogito, which, despite initial appearances, is quite different from the well-known Cartesian cogito on which it is based. As I will attempt to establish there, Beckett draws more heavily on the image of Geulincx's cogito than on the image of Descartes's cogito. Further, the Geulingian image and the presuppositions it brings with it, occluded all this time by a failure to properly distinguish it from the cogito of Descartes, haunt Beckett's text, adding complexity to our understanding.

Yet, this is not the only image which Beckett draws from Geulincx. The mention of Geulincx from *Molloy* is well known, but that Beckett tied it to another image is often not remarked upon. Trying to describe freedom, Molloy offers an example:

I . . . loved the image of old Geulincx, dead young, who left me free, on the black boat of Ulysses, to crawl toward the East, along the deck. That is a great measure of freedom, for him who has not the pioneering spirit.[62]

As I have previously brought to light,[63] a letter exists in which Beckett explains these allusions to the first German translator of *Molloy*, Dr Franzen. It is worth citing Beckett's explanations again here:

This passage is suggested (a) by a passage in the *Ethics* of Geulincx where he compares human freedom to that of a man, on board a boat carrying him irresistibly westward, free to move eastward within the limits of the boat itself, as far as the stern; and (b) by Ulysses' relation in Dante (Inf. 26) of his second voyage (a medieval tradition) to and beyond the Pillars of Hercules, his shipwreck and death ... I imagine a member of the crew who does not share the adventurous spirit of Ulysses and is at least at liberty to crawl homewards ... along the brief deck.[64]

The image of Geulincx, which brings notions of restricted freedom with it, is mixed here with an image from Dante, which brings with it notions of preordained doom. The Geulingian image is thereby slightly modified: one is not only free in the most marginal of senses, but one is not even free to escape certain doom, one is not even free to defend oneself from inevitable destruction. At the same time, this is mixed with Molloy's chipper attitude to such a fine mess. The ship image recurs on three occasions in *The Unnamable* with the voice imagining itself as a slave on board the ship heading beyond the Pillars of Hercules, who has slipped out of the galley at night unnoticed and, crawling between the thwarts, wonders perhaps whether he might throw himself from the boat to find freedom.[65] Suicide is considered, then, as a means of thwarting the horror of predetermined existence. This image clearly resonates not only with Molloy's example, but with Geulincx's image, and the Geulingian image in turn depends upon the notion of the will, which, although inhabiting a world which is utterly interfused with predestination, is alone free to go against the desires of God. Yet, as we will see below, even (or rather, especially) this gesture and the apparent 'freedom' it brings with it is put under close scrutiny by Geulincx, and then by Beckett through an image he chooses to draw from Geulincx.

There are other images from Geulincx which find resonance in Beckett including the famous image of the two clocks which Geulincx uses to explain the relation of the mind and the body (which Leibniz later developed, without reference to Geulincx, to describe pre-established harmony).[66] This appears in *Molloy* and in *Murphy*. In *Molloy* it appears as a gong, which Molloy hears at the end of his narrative and which calls Moran to his dinner. Taking a lead from the Geulingian image one might argue that this, otherwise curious, correspondence indicates how Molloy and Moran, the former dominated by his bodily responses, the latter by his rational mind, are 'out of sync'.

THE CRADLE AND THE ROCKING-CHAIR

However, the image which seems to recur most in Beckett's works and which might be traced to Geulincx is the rocking-chair. The image of the cradle is used by Geulincx to explain the relation of our will to the will of God, and I will argue that Beckett develops this in *Murphy*, *Film*,[67] and *Rockaby*[68] via the image of the rocking-chair.

Geulincx, as is well known, sets out a kind of occasionalism, one which denies that human beings have any real power over their actions. As I discuss further in the next chapter, we seem to act and think we act, but this is an illusion brought about by our ignorance. It is worth summarising some of this here in order to orient ourselves better for the arguments which follow.

If we look into the matter carefully, Geulincx argues, we will recognise that we do not understand how even the simplest movement of our own body is accomplished. Furthermore, even if we do have some kind of knowledge of certain aspects of this – a scientific knowledge of the nature of the circulation of blood, for example – this knowledge is not what causes our blood to circulate. In fact, Geulincx argues, we have a completely inadequate understanding of how our bodies function. He then ties this realisation to a proposition which he uses to buttress his philosophical system again and again: if you do not know how to do something, if you do not have full control over it, you cannot in fact be said to do that thing. I do not know how my body works, so I cannot be said to work it. From here, Geulincx goes on to argue that it is God who possesses this knowledge and therefore it is God who really controls my actions. I am merely a spectator of the machine which is my body. Yet, if I do not have any physical freedom, I do, for Geulincx, have complete freedom of will. I can desire to do whatever I please. Such desires, however, will often only reflect my ignorance and my true powerlessness. I might desire to fly across the room, for example, but I simply cannot do this, and the desire to do what I cannot do is an example of sin, for Geulincx, because it exemplifies my inability to accept the will of God.

So on the one hand we can want what we like, on the other, we are completely powerless to bring things to fruition. Things are only realised with a great deal of assistance from forces much more powerful than us. He gives the example of a paralysed person to illustrate this idea. The paralysed man wants to lift his leg but simply cannot. There is clearly no necessary link between our will and the actions of our bodies. Through vanity and self-deceit, we pretend we in fact do things which have been brought about by a higher power.

One of the places in which this problematic relationship between free will and physical powerlessness is brought to the surface is in Geulincx's discussion of suicide. Geulincx argues that suicide is, effectively, impossible, because ultimately we do not control our own bodies, and he gives examples of those who try to kill themselves, and fail, to back this up. He further argues, however, that it often occurs that something we want to happen does in fact take place. That it does successfully take place comes about through the will of God. We are in sin, then, not because a given sinful action takes place, but because we wanted it to take place. It is only our will that is free in Geulincx's system, but so too, it is only our will that is judged.

In illustrating this in relation to suicide, however, Geulincx chooses a curious image. He suggests that what we want to happen often does happen. We think we bring it about, but in fact something else brings it about. He likens this to a newborn baby (the epitome of powerlessness). The baby cries because it wants the cradle in which it lies to be rocked. And the cradle is rocked, but not by the baby; rather, it is rocked by the hand of the mother or the nurse, who in turn rocks the cradle because she thinks the baby wants the cradle to be rocked. To the baby it might seem that there is a direct relation between the desire and the action, but the action is in fact brought about by another. Geulincx likens this to our situation in relation to God. We want something and God might bring it about, not because we want it but because God wants it. Geulincx states:

And even though under the influence of silly and stupid arguments I might be in the habit of believing that I can die when I want, it is nevertheless not the case, as my Inspection of Myself has unequivocally taught me. First of all, I am not going to depart from my body merely by wanting to depart from it: I am most intimately aware that I cannot. When I have decided that I want to depart from my body, I will have to raise my own hands against my body, to defile, injure and oppress it. But I cannot yield my body to whips and scourges without motion; and I cannot cause motion in my body (honest Inspection of Myself makes that transparently obvious to me). I can only will it, and when I will it, God usually imparts the motion that I will; not because I will it, but because He wills that the motion that I will should be imparted. For example, if a baby wants the cradle in which he has been laid to be rocked, it is usually rocked; though not because *he* wants it, but because his mother or nursemaid, who is sitting by the cradle and who can actually rock it, also wants to do what he wants. Therefore, if I should contemplate something more serious with regard to myself, such as deciding to stab myself in the heart with a dagger or hang myself, I shall not be able to create the motion required to bring this about. Perhaps God will create it, and thereby despatch me; though not because I have decided to depart, but because He has decided what I have decided. But it is impious of me on my own judgement and counsel to depart without God's authorisation, impious of me to depart without being summoned, insofar as it is my business, which is to say that I wished to depart before knowing that I had been summoned.[69]

What is curious about this image is the context in which it is chosen. It is an image of comfort, mercy, empathy, and love ... the mother and child forcefully bring these associations with them. Yet it is used to explain suicide. God is like the mother, and the person who wishes to die is like the child. It is also important to note that this is one of the most striking images used by Geulincx to illustrate the notion of our true powerlessness. Rather than it being a comforting image, however, one which would point us towards the stoicism of 'Ubi nihil vales, ibi nihil velis' it is an image of desire, the desire to be at ease, to be calmed, to be soothed, to be at peace. Yet because it is an image of a desire, which we know can never properly be fulfilled, it is harrowing rather than comforting. Strangely, then, rather than reconciling us to our impotence, it brings to our attention how awful such an impotence is. The cradle is a striking image: at once it brings with it a sense of comfort and being comforted and a sense of our utter power-lessness to realise our desires (the most cherished of them along with the rest).[70]

Beckett read this passage, and it appears in his forty pages of notes to the *Ethics*.[71] Geulincx mentions the mother or nurse rocking the cradle on three occasions throughout the entire *Ethics*, and Beckett copies elements of these passages on each occasion.[72] The Latin word 'cunae' means cradle, but the cradle and the rocking-chair are strongly associated in Beckett. This strong association is most apparent in *Rockaby*. This word, which we associate with the rocking-chair in the play, clearly also refers to the cradle song or lullaby and to one such lullaby in particular.[73] Furthermore 'w', the woman who rocks, seems, in many ways, like an infant. The play text tells us that the rock is 'Controlled mechanically without assistance from w'.[74] The chair also possesses 'Rounded inward curving arms to suggest an embrace'.[75] She listens to a voice – which might be her own, indeed, but which soothes her like a lullaby recited by a parent – and, other than echoing the final words that 'v' speaks before falling silent, she herself only speaks in demanding – much like a crying baby – that the soothing words and the rocking which accompanies them continue: 'More.' Beckett still further underlines this association of rocking-chair and cradle in the French version, where the French word *berceuse* is associated with the lullaby, the cradle song, the nurse who rocks the baby and the rocking-chair. Indeed, the word is etymologically derived from *bercer*, the French word for cradle.[76] The woman who rocks also wants to stop. She wants to end, and this is made clear by the repetition of this desire, the very desire we have seen so strangely expressed in Geulincx's image:

so in the end
close of a long day
went down
let down the blind and down
right down
into the old rocker
and rocked
rocked
saying to herself
no
done with that
the rocker
those arms at last
saying to the rocker
rock her off
stop her eyes
fuck life
stop her eyes
rock her off
rock her off
[*Together: echo of 'rock her off', coming to rest of rock, slow fade out.*][77]

If we look at this passage closely we can see that, at last, the woman in the story stops addressing herself and instead speaks to 'the rocker', telling, or asking that which rocks, to 'rock her off'. Implicit here is an understanding that power over her own life – the ability to end it – does not rest with the woman herself but with something outside her, so that it is the rocker (the chair, or the unseen power which causes it to move) that is implored in the end, the rocker that is asked to intercede on her behalf. There is a strong resonance, then, between this image of the rocking-chair and Geulincx's cradle.

It is important to note the consistency with which Beckett uses this image of the rocking-chair. It first appears in *Murphy*, of course – soon after Beckett immersed himself in Geulincx at the Trinity College Library – in a novel in which Geulincx is mentioned explicitly. As stated above, this image is included in notes Beckett took to his reading of Geulincx which are currently held in Trinity College Dublin.[78] As is also well known, this is the novel Beckett was referring to when he suggested to Sighle Kennedy that she look to Geulincx as a point of reference in interpreting it. We will remember that Murphy too, if not wanting to end, wishes to achieve some sort of oblivion when he retires to his chair, and that he is in his rocking-chair when his flat catches fire and he dies. The rocking-chair appears on the first page of the novel, where Murphy is introduced in his favoured position: naked and tied to the chair by seven scarves. That is, Murphy is both as naked as a babe and as physically powerless as a babe as 'Only the most local movements were possible'[79] on account of the scarves. The chair is praised because it gives Murphy ease, appeasing his body and thereby setting his mind free.[80] The chair, then, as with Geulincx's cradle, is linked with ease, with comfort, as well as with physical impotence. It is further seen as a release from despair: Celia looks to the chair for comfort after Murphy has left her.[81] So too, as is apparent with Murphy's demise (he burns to death while helplessly bound to his chair), the chair is linked with death.

Similarly, after having covered over all of the eyes in the room that were watching him, O, the protagonist of *Film*, sits in the rocking-chair. Indeed, the process of blocking out these eyes might be understood as involving the occlusion of certain images. To quote from the screenplay:

The room sequence falls into three parts.
1. Preparation of room (occlusion of window and mirror, ejection of dog and cat, destruction of God's image, occlusion of parrot and goldfish).
2. Period in rocking-chair. Inspection and destruction of photographs.
3. Final investment of O by E and dénouement.[82]

It is not just the rocking-chair that makes one think of Geulincx here. The entire process brings to mind his 'autology' which Beckett first mentioned in *Murphy*. As will be discussed more fully in the next chapter, 'autology' (a term Geulincx understood as a kind of science of the self) involves a shutting-out of all extraneous perception followed by two process: the *inspectio sui* and *despectio sui*. We see here the shutting-out in the preparation of the room. This is followed by an inspection of and then a disregard for the self which is displayed in the photographs. The photographs show O at various ages: photo 1, an infant of 6 months; photo 2, a child of 4 years; photo 3, 15 years; photo 4, 20 years (graduation); photo 5, 21 (with fiancé); photo 6, 25 (enlisted in the army and holding his own baby daughter); photo 7, 30, patch over eye as now. This moves from birth towards his present state, passing by certain cardinal points in his life story. O then reverses the process in destroying the photographs; beginning with 7, he rips each in four in turn, ending with 1.[83] He moves back, then, from the present toward the cradle, forming a kind of circle. That is, as he seems to near death the rocking-chair comes to resemble the cradle once more. O and E confront one another and O faints away and may even die. The

rocking-chair, then, carries with it traces of finality, of peace, or at least the coming of an end that has been long sought. After O meets E's gaze and starts in horror, the screenplay ends as follows:

O closes his eyes and falls back in chair, starting off rock. He covers his face with his hands. Image of O rocking, his head in his hands but not yet bowed. Cut back to E. As before. Cut back to O. He sits, bowed forward, his head in his hands, gently rocking. Hold it as the rocking dies down.[84]

We witness here, then, several examples of the kinds of occlusiveness of the image we have discussed above. The original image, from Geulincx, of the 'nurse or mother' hides an aporia: one which has already been mentioned in a footnote to De Vleeschauwer[85] above. That is, Geulincx, while he offers an image which is meant to help us understand the futility of suicide, in fact seems to protest too much: the idea of death invades the image of the powerless child at birth. Further, there is a problem within the analogy which Geulincx draws. He offers us an image, the mother or nurse rocking the cradle, and draws this into relation with our own will (which in turn is discussed with the problem of suicide in mind); yet the relation he draws is somewhat strained. Are we to believe that God's feelings for us when we plead to be allowed to leave this earth are like those of the mother for the child? If they are different, how are the different? Geulincx was aware of this problem, and so too was Beckett, who copies the passage in which Geulincx specifically tries to address it:

the analogy of the baby and his mother on the one hand, and of God and me on the other hand, is a lame one . . . (God makes motion, the mother does not make it; the baby moves his mother to move, I do not move God). On the contrary, the whole force and energy of the analogy turns on this, that just as the motion or rocking of the cradle is made with the baby willing it, though the motion is not made by the baby, so equally, motion is often made with me willing it, though I never make it.[86]

So, having made the image, Geulincx wishes to circumscribe how we read it, to, in short, forcefully attach an interpretation to it, one which would (like all representations drawn from images) substract from the image itself. Beckett, in making his note, draws attention to this gesture, which, despite Geulincx's best efforts, fails to completely control or discipline the image in question. The image is occlusive in that it hides a problem in the philosopher's system. It hides it insufficiently, however, and in this way it also betrays that problem.

Beckett, for his part, returns affective force to the image. This is an image of isolation now: the mother is removed, those who rock are removing themselves from the world (Murphy, Celia, 'O' in *Film*, 'w' in *Rockaby*). The image is extracted from a context: this is most clear in *Rockaby*, where the woman and the chair are surrounded by darkness, but is there in *Film*, in the sense that 'O' has sought to free himself from all extraneous perception (all the other eyes in the room) before sitting in the chair. It is also there, at least thematically, in the sense of extraction from the world which is described in relation to the use made of the chair by both Murphy and Celia in *Murphy*. Other contextual elements remain, however, and, tellingly, these are connected with death in all three works: the death of Murphy in the chair (not to mention the death of desire both he and Celia experience within the chair), the apparent death of 'O' in *Film*, and the imminent death of 'w' in *Rockaby*. They are also all connected with some form of comfort (all are comforted by the chair). This comfort, in each case, however, is incomplete: once the chair stops the only hope for comfort is that it starts again ('w': 'more'), or that everything ends. The most telling connection Beckett adds, however, concerns the manner in which he shifts the image of the cradle (related to birth) to that of the rocking-chair being used near death. As I have argued above, the connection of the two is already strong, so that, at least in one of Beckett's languages, the two are conflated in the word *berceuse*, and in the other he underlines the connection through the choice of the word 'Rockaby'. In short, the Beckettian image is one of being rocked into death. When one closely inspects the image from Geulincx, however, it is apparent that this image was already there in occluded form: in the image of the suicide, rocked to death by the maternal hand of God.

CHAPTER 5

Cogito nescio

I, of whom I know nothing[1]

In *Difference and Repetition*, *Proust and Signs* and (with Félix Guattari) *A Thousand Plateaus* and *What is Philosophy?*, Deleuze develops the concept of 'the image of thought'. This idea seeks to express how the notion of what it is to think is envisaged or pictured at a given time or place. Such ways of thinking form the basis of implicit presuppositions which underlie ideas and conceptual systems. An 'image of thought', then, is a kind of canvas of underlying assumptions upon which the works of a given period are sketched. Deleuze sums up the idea in *Negotiations*:

By the image of thought I don't mean its method but something deeper that's always taken for granted, a system of coordinates, dynamics, orientations: what it means to think, and to 'orient oneself in thought' . . . The image of thought is what philosophy as it were presupposes; it precedes philosophy, not a nonphilosophical understanding this time but a prephilosophical understanding.[2]

In *Difference and Repetition* Deleuze describes a 'dogmatic' image of thought which has been dominant throughout the history of philosophy,[3] but in *A Thousand Plateaus*, *What is Philosophy?* and *Negotiations* he emphasises how the image is subject to change over time. He asks, 'Do we, for instance, have the same image of thought that Plato, or even Descartes or Kant, had?'[4] In *What is Philosophy?* Deleuze and Guattari discuss such shifts in some detail in their descriptions of 'the plane of immanence'. The plane of immanence comprises the combination of an image of thought and a 'substance of being' which is presupposed by each philosopher in developing their system and creating their concepts. For Descartes the image of thought (the way in which he pictured thought as being possible) involved, 'a subjective understanding implicitly presupposed by the "I think" as first concept', whereas for Plato 'it is the virtual image of an already-thought that doubles every actual concept'.[5]

Although Deleuze and Guattari do not attempt to fully draw out the implications of this,[6] it is clearly possible for thinkers, in throwing down their own plane of immanence, to implicitly or explicitly challenge and attempt to overturn the image of thought used by earlier philosophers, and these new presuppositions are often signalled in themes or concepts which are developed in the competing system. The Ancient Stoics, for example, develop a kind of spiritual materialism which is not compatible with Plato's idealism. The condition of possibility for thinking for the Stoics is not 'recollection' but the 'comprehensive image': an image directly impressed on our senses whose truth is immediately apparent and to whose truth we immediately assent.[7] As Bréhier explains: 'It is not, therefore, reason which, in one way or another, renders the representation comprehensive; this characteristic is immanent to the image; the image possesses it before any activity of reason.'[8] While Platonism seeks immutable truth in the Ideas, which are only understood through recollections explained through the myth of another realm above the world in which we exist, the Stoics sought to establish a similarly immutable truth in the very appearances of this world.[9] Clearly, then, the Stoic image of thought seeks to challenge and overturn the Platonic image. Such shifts are instructive as they allow us to grasp important implications of each system. Recognising this point is of use to the present study as it offers one way in which we might begin to question which kinds of philosophy seem to interest Beckett and how these kinds of thinking (and the presuppositions they bring with them) might help us to understand his use of them in his works.

The concept of the image of thought is important to this study for two reasons. Firstly, although he refers to and uses numerous philosophical sources which are spread across the long history of Western philosophy, Beckett can be shown to be drawn to certain kinds of philosophy, and the manner in which the philosophers he chooses might be thought to intersect, the things they have in common, might be better understood by questioning the images of thought they carry with them. Some of the outlines of this problem will be lightly sketched in this and the next two chapters. Secondly, and perhaps more importantly, Deleuze's concept, developed in relation to philosophy, can be usefully adapted to an understanding of literary practice, and this might not only allow us to see how Beckett draws upon philosophy as a source of ideas, but also how images he develops might in turn be adapted to, and made use of by, philosophers in a system of relays. That is, I will argue here that Beckett borrows and develops an image of thought (a way of imagining what it means to think) from Arnold Geulincx, and that, in turn, this image is taken from

Samuel Beckett and adopted (again, being enhanced and developed) by a number of post-World War Two philosophers.

While for the most part developing the concept in relation to philosophy, Deleuze does use 'the image of thought' in relation to literature on one occasion. In *Proust and Signs* he describes how 'Proust sets up an image of thought in opposition to that of philosophy'.[10] On the one hand, the 'dogmatic' image of thought developed by philosophy sees thought as being possible because of the goodwill of thinkers who agree on the meaning of words and things[11] and who openly share the truth in a spirit of friendship (as each philosopher is a 'friend' or lover – 'philo' – of wisdom – 'sophia'). Proust, on the other hand, offers an image in which no goodwill is necessary, one which, in effect, understands the truth not as revealed but as 'betrayed', not as openly shared or communicated, but interpreted through the reading of signs which are presented to us involuntarily.[12] The jealous lover finds the truth by discovering a lie on the face of the loved one (who is betrayed by an involuntary expression), just as the sensitive person feels the truth through the violence of an impression.[13]

Proust, then, challenges philosophy and its pretension to offering the only proper means of discovering the true. The truth is not uncovered through goodwill; rather, in a manner similar to the 'comprehensive image' of the Ancient Stoics, it is created through sensations, or the direct impressions which we ourselves experience through our own senses and know to be true (with a truth which has to be sought via interpretation, via the reading of the signs these images offer to our senses). In *A la recherche du temps perdu*, Proust states that Victor Hugo might be seen to write philosophy in his early poems rather than true poetry as he 'still thinks, instead of being content, like nature, to lead to thought'.[14] Deleuze clarifies this distinction between poetry and philosophy by quoting Proust at some length. The distinction, which reminds us of the understanding developed by William James (cited by Paul Redding and touched upon in chapter 1) of how the presentation underwrites the validity of the representation,[15] is outlined by Proust as follows:

The ideas formed by pure intelligence have only a logical truth, a possible truth, their choice is arbitrary. The book whose characters are figured, *not traced by us*, is our only book. Not that the ideas we form cannot be logically exact, but we do not know whether they are true. Only the impression, however paltry their substance seems, however unlikely their traces, is a criterion of truths and on this account alone merits being apprehended by the mind.[16]

The essential, for the poet, is not thought, but what 'leads to thought', what forces us to think.[17] Deleuze suggests that Proust is a Platonist in the sense that he develops an idea first outlined by Plato. This contends that there are different kinds of things which confront us: one kind is simply and easily recognised, while another is not easily recognised. This second object puzzles us and causes us to think.[18] Proust, for Deleuze, seeks to describe processes of cognition, and certain kinds of memory in particular, as partaking of the second kind of object. This thinking opposes the 'Logos' of philosophy with the 'hieroglyph' (an image-sign), and Deleuze concludes that 'to think is therefore to interpret, is therefore to translate'.[19] Art partakes of this second kind of thinking because it requires that we interpret, that we translate what it presents into meaning for ourselves. We can begin to see how this connects with the discussion of the presentation as opposed to the representation described above: the former needs to be interpreted; the latter already carries an intended interpretation.

With Proust and Deleuze, one might contend that literature is a kind of thinking and has always functioned as such, even when it has not been understood as being such. Understanding it as a kind of thinking (as something which can affect readers and in some way encourage them to think) presupposes an image of thought. Literature differs from philosophy in that, while the latter might be understood to offer a kind of thinking, the former might be understood to develop or encourage thinking in its audience. This thinking is one kind among others (in *What is Philosophy?*, Deleuze and Guattari compare philosophy, science and art); the process of thinking, however, is different in art. Art, rather than describing or developing a line of thought, indicates problems about which we are required to think. It leaves gaps and does not instruct us as to how we might bridge them.

Yet literature itself has also long been interested in describing or creating images of what it means to think. This tendency is particularly pronounced in the modernist novels of Joyce, Woolf and Faulkner, for example, where the 'stream of consciousness' can itself be understood as an attempt to picture or present thought processes. We have seen in chapter 3 how Beckett moves from an art of relation to one of nonrelation. In the following section, by offering the first critical reading of Beckett's notes to his reading of Arnold Geulincx, I focus upon how Beckett develops an understanding of thought which stresses how our thinking is intimately interinvolved with ignorance. That is, I will argue that, following Geulincx, he identifies the cogito (the 'I think') with a nescio (an 'I do not know').

IMAGES FROM GEULINCX AND BECKETT'S NOTES TO THE *ETHICS*

The *Ethics* of Arnold Geulincx, as it was finally published in full after Geulincx's death in 1671, comprises six Treatises. Of these, only the first could be understood to be complete. This, along with the extensive notes which accompany it, was published separately by Geulincx in his lifetime and translated by Geulincx from Latin into the Flemish vernacular he spoke. Of the 350 or so annotations in the *Ethics*, all but the last eight relate to Treatise I, *On virtue: And its prime attributes, which are commonly called cardinal virtues.* The other five Treatises are: Treatise II, *On the Virtues Commonly Called Particular*; Treatise III, *On the End and the Good*; Treatise IV; *On the Passions*; Treatise V, *On the Reward of Virtue*; and Treatise VI, *On Prudence.* These were reconstructed by students of Geulincx for publication.

Beckett's notes to the *Metaphysica Vera, Questiones Quodlibeticae* and the *Ethica*, which are held at the archives of Trinity College Dublin, comprise literal transcriptions from Geulincx (except in one or two minor cases).[20] With regard to the *Ethics*, these notes all relate to Treatise I and the Annotations to Treatise I. Beckett's method is to indicate the section (from the main text of Treatise I) by using a capital letter to correspond to the paragraph in Geulincx (which in the Land edition Beckett consulted at Trinity College are marked by numbers). Beckett also generally indicates when a passage is taken from the Annotations by including a small 'a' in brackets after a passage has been cited. He does not keep the passages from the Annotations separate in his notes; rather, he includes them amongst the passages he cites from the main text. The majority of the text he cites, indeed, is drawn from the Annotations (which are significantly longer than main body of Treatise I). It is clear from this that Beckett, as one might expect, read the main text and moved to the annotations at the back of Land's edition as they were indicated in the main text.

Beckett's notes themselves comprise two typed fair copies and the remains of a (probably original) handwritten copy. The two typed copies in large part overlap, though there is significant material in the second copy which does not occur in the first. The handwritten copy available at Trinity begins from where the second copy ends (at Treatise I, Chapter 2, Section 2, Number 10, paragraph 1). This is difficult to decipher, but (given the indication of paragraphs through capital letters mentioned above), extends from Treatise I, Chapter 2, Section 2, Number 10, paragraph 2, to Treatise I, Chapter 2, Section 2, Number 11, paragraph 1 (that is, it covers an additional four paragraphs). This takes Beckett's notes very near to the end of Treatise I at Chapter 2, Section 2, Number 12, paragraph 2 (that is, the Treatise ends five additional paragraphs from where Beckett's handwritten notes leave off).

In discussing the cardinal virtues in Treatise I, Geulincx indicates that his cardinal virtues differ from the common cardinal virtues. The common cardinal virtues are: prudence, justice, fortitude and temperance, while Geulincx's cardinal virtues are diligence, justice, obedience and humility.[21] Section I of Treatise I treats the first three of these. Section II, which comprises the rest of the Treatise, treats the final virtue, humility. Beckett's notes pay particular attention to Section II, which begins by defining humility, and then indicates, firstly, how humility might be achieved, and secondly, lists the obligations which flow on from this understanding of humility.

The three other virtues, for Geulincx, are all connected to humility: Diligence involves carefully listening to reason, and ethical action itself is defined as acting only on the instructions given to one by reason (which is the image of God's will); justice involves doing neither more nor less than reason dictates (banishing both excesses and defects from one's actions); obedience involves doing what reason instructs and only what reason instructs. One must act with humility in all these cases. For Geulincx, then, humility can be readily achieved by listening with diligence to reason and obeying its commands with justice. One does this in the first instance through a close inspection of the self. When one closely inspects the self (*Inspectio Sui*, Section II, Number 2), he argues, one recognises that one is ultimately ignorant. This recognition leads to the disregard of one's self (*Despectio Sui*, Section 2, Number 3).

Having recognised one's own impotence and ignorance (as I both do not know and cannot act), and equally recognised the omnipotence and omniscience of the One who does know and can act (God), a number of obligations follow. The first obligation (Section 2, Number 4), is to leave this life, willingly and immediately, when God calls you from it. The second obligation (Section 2, Number 5) is to not attempt to leave this life, or want to attempt to leave this life, until such time as God summons you from it. The third obligation (Section 2, Number 6) is to refresh your body so that it might continue to thrive. The fourth obligation (Section 2, Number 7) is to acquire some skill with which to make a living; to stick to it where it suits you, to change if it is apparent it does not suit you, but not to change in a casual manner. The fifth obligation (Section 2, Number 8) is to do many things, suffer many things, in accordance with the lot one is given in life. The sixth obligation (Section 2, Number 9) is to frequently relax the mind so that you do not become jaded. The seventh obligation (Section 2, Number 10) is to look upon your own birth as good, to never detest it, or those who have brought it about. Section 2, Number 11 describes the 'Adminicule' of humility, and Section 2, Number 12, the final number in this Treatise, sets out the fruits of humility.

Beckett's notes cover most of this, but he gives particular attention to Section 2, Number 2, 'The Inspection of Oneself', and to the second obligation, Section 2, Number 5, (not to attempt to leave this life until one is called by God). We have already seen how Beckett makes use of an image which is related to the second obligation (the image of the cradle). What I would like to focus on now is how other images or described states in Geulincx can be seen to be used by Beckett to create images in his works. Further, I want to indicate how these images resonate; indeed, how they form one single situation which emerges in many of Beckett's works: the situation of one confronted by ignorance, suffering that ignorance. This situation is at times borne with apparent patience, as is the case with Molloy and Malone; but at times it is encountered with utter fear and torment, as is the case with Moran, the Unnamable, the figures in the jars in *Play*, or by the mouth in *Not I*. While these situations might all be thought to be related when one takes into account Beckett's notes to his reading of Geulincx, they clearly do not engender a single image. Rather, images are drawn from this situation: either emerging from it, or being created in response to it.

I would suggest, however, that the situation itself comprises an image of thought, with thought imagined as involving or being 'grounded' upon the extremely unstable foundation of ignorance. Whereas the ancient imperative was 'Know Thyself', this image of thought (at least as it is adapted from Geulincx by Beckett) affirms that the self, which nevertheless remains the ground for all subsequent knowledge, cannot be known: as we have seen, the motto of the Unnamable, via Bacon and Kant, is 'de nobis ipsis silemus' (we can say nothing about ourselves). In this Beckett is not in complete agreement with Geulincx, who, as will be discussed in detail below, grounds knowledge again in God. Beckett, for his part, does not make such a use of God, and so one is left with a groundlessness and a self which disperses when one attempts to fix its identity.

THE INEFFABLE AND NONRELATION

Beckett's *The Unnamable* has long been associated with the cogito of Descartes, with it being suggested that, in effect, this work pictures the state Descartes describes where all knowledge is stripped away. I will argue here that this is imprecise; that the image of the cogito apparent in Geulincx (which no doubt owes something to Descartes, whose philosophy he follows and develops) much more closely resembles the state described in *The Unnamable*.

In chapter 3 I sought internal evidence from Beckett's works to develop a description of how the idea of nonrelation can be seen to develop throughout those works. In turning to Geulincx, however, and his understanding of human ignorance, we begin to see how the concept of 'the ineffable' Geulincx describes is in strong sympathy with Beckett's notions of nonrelation. Under 'Reason' (Treatise I, Chapter 1, Number 2, paragraph 2) Geulincx explains how obeying reason is not identical with obeying God, as we will obey God whether we like it or not, and in some cases, attempting to understand God's will is vain. Footnote 8 to this paragraph is in part cited by Beckett, and the passages he cites resonate with the descriptions he develops of nonrelation in art:

the *power* of God has to be reconciled with His *goodness*. The *power*, by which He does all things, that is, all genuine things, in such a way that nothing untoward occurs, still less anything against His will; and the *goodness*, by which he does not desire sin, but rightly condemns it in us, and punishes it ... with our finite intellect we can have no hope of effecting such a reconciliation. This craving of human ingenuity to reconcile things that exceed its understanding involves no small measure of impiety ... once we have rid ourselves of this craving for reconciliations, it should be enough for us to distinguish each term of the reconciliation clearly and distinctly ... understanding quite clearly that nothing happens unless God directly wills it to happen (which is one term), and that, on the other hand, He blames us for our sins, and punishes them severely (which is the other term).[22]

The relevance of the Geulingian definition of the ineffable is made still more apparent in a passage which Beckett cites from footnote 29 to 'The Inspection of the Self':

Something is said to be *ineffable* not because we cannot think or speak of it (for this would be *nothing*, *nothing* and *unthinkable* being the same ...) but because we cannot think about or encompass with our reason how it is done. And in this sense God is ineffable not only in Himself but in all His works. For example, I, as a man, am his work; I know of that work, in fact I know nothing so well as that I am that work; but the manner in which He made me a man and joined me to my body . . . I do not understand; I understand only that I can never understand it . . . The same is true of the rest of God's works, for when they are thoroughly investigated, in the end an ineffable something is always missing. Therefore . . . it is quite inept to deny a reality because you cannot grasp how it works; and here the Sceptics . . . are very imperceptive . . . Impious one and all, they would deprive men of the first and greatest attribute of divinity, namely, ineffability[23]

The ineffable, then, is a kind of nonrelation: while things may be connected, while there is a genuine manner in which they might be reconciled, we are not always able to understand that connection. The kinds of gaps discussed above point towards this kind of ineffability. They further indicate how all of this occurs because of the state of ignorance we find ourselves in.

THE IMAGE OF THE VOICE

For Geulincx there are two kinds of ignorance: vincible ignorance, which can be overcome by diligently listening to the voice of reason which we find within ourselves, and invincible ignorance, which cannot be overcome because it concerns what is ineffable or unknowable by us.[24] We see both kinds reflected in Beckett, and both of these are related to the image of a voice which instructs but, in Beckett, if not Geulincx, without complete clarity: 'it is solely a question of voices, no other image is appropriate'.[25] Beckett's notes cite passages from Geulincx which indicate the importance of listening to reason. As we have seen, the Cardinal Virtue 'Diligence' is defined as 'listening to Reason';[26] yet it is possible not to hear the voice of reason clearly. For Geulincx, this is because the voice has been obscured by passion or desire; 'anyone who led on by passion seeks Reason never finds it, for he is always being led away from Reason by passion'.[27] This brings to mind the end of Moran's relation in *Molloy*:

I have spoken of a voice telling me things. I was getting to know it better now, to understand what it wanted. It did not use the words that Moran had been taught when he was little and that he in his turn had taught to his little one. So that at first I did not know what it wanted. But in the end I understood this language. I understood it, I understand it, all wrong perhaps. That is not what matters. It told me to write this report. Does this mean I am freer now than I was? I do not know.[28]

This passage is full of resonances from Geulincx: it is not just the voice but also the response to it which brings to mind Geulincx. For Geulincx, listening intently to reason and obeying it completely is, in fact, the definition of freedom. Beckett quotes the following passage in his notes: 'The Fruit of Obedience is Freedom. He who serves Reason is a slave to no-one, but rather is on that account completely free'.[29] The voice, as reason, which may nevertheless not be understood (should my passions or bad habits drown the voice out) is something which is pictured elsewhere when Geulincx explains the seventh obligation (not to wish one had never been born). Here a situation which seems to strongly resemble that experienced by the Unnamable is described (and though obscured by Beckett's difficult handwriting, a crucial line from this passage – underlining that my desires drown out the voice of reason – is cited in Beckett's notes):

I shall assiduously scratch and pick at that scab which the gross injustice of the world has raised on me. My Master does not mutter to me, He does not whisper into my ear either that I must hesitate, or doubt whether He commands anything, and if so, what. What He wants me to do, He intones in a lordly manner. I would hear it well enough, but for the impatient clatter and drumming of my desires. He is not ignorant of my tongue, He does not speak to me through an intermediary, or, being absent, by courier. If he should decide to advise me of my duties through others, He gives them a signal (Reason) that is beyond doubt, so that even in this case it is He rather than they who speaks to me, which He does not regard as beneath His dignity. An idle and foolish servant, who fails in his duty, and goes to do what, at night, he dreamt his master commanded; or in broad daylight goes dancing and capering in public because some trickster has told him his master wants it: what if his master should return, and if his master had expressly commanded him not to obey the orders of anyone but himself? Then he really is a worthless servant, and deserving of the pillory.[30]

The voice of reason, then, is one we do not struggle to hear, and an image of this clarity is offered by Geulincx but, paradoxically again, he offers this image in negative form, indicating the kind of struggle *that does not take place* unless I have drowned this clear voice out with my desires. Beckett, in turn adapts this negative image and develops it. In *The Unnamable* the failure to hear or attend to this voice properly is also recognised, in line with Geulincx, as some kind of damnation.

For it is difficult to speak, even any old rubbish, and at the same time focus one's attention on another point, where one's true interest lies, as fitfully defined by a feeble murmur seeming to apologize for not being dead. And what it seemed to me I heard then, concerning what I should do, and say, it seemed to me I only barely heard it, because of the noise I was engaged in making elsewhere, in obedience to the unintelligible terms of an incomprehensible damnation.[31]

Elsewhere we find other situations of struggle described in Geulincx. On one occasion the contrasting situations of Molloy and Moran seem to be being described (in passages which, again, are directly quoted by Beckett in his notes). In paragraph 3 of the second obligation (which is not to seek to leave this life when not summoned by God; that is, not to attempt suicide) Geulincx describes two possible situations of life: two contrasting situations. He does this, interestingly, after having switched from standard text to italics. The italics seem to mark a shift into a fictional discourse, one in which the philosopher imagines himself confronted by given situations. Firstly there is the situation where I have become unfortunate, a situation which seems to resemble how Molloy might appear to the others he encounters:

let my body be consumed by starvation, scab, and consumption; let fear, pain, tedium, and consciousness of evildoing oppress my spirit; let lethargy, bewilderment, listlessness, and stupidity possess my mind.[32]

In these circumstances I shall not want to either bring death on or delay it; rather, I will simply carry the burden and wait upon the will of God. So, indeed, it might be argued, does Molloy carry himself, with a kind of indifference to his plight, as expressed in the last line of Molloy's relation: 'Molloy could stay, where he happened to be.' Next there is a quite different, even opposite, situation, where I am apparently fortunate. This situation seems to closely resemble Moran's view of himself at the beginning of his relation in *Molloy*:

though my body may be robust, shapely, vigorous, and perfect in every part; my demeanour lofty, secure, and genial, reinforced by the consciousness of acting rightly; my mind acute, shrewd, always nourished and well-stocked with ideas to be investigated and considered.[33]

This situation, we are told, will not 'furnish me with a pretext for remaining here'.[34] We will remember how having to leave, and the pain and suffering which is attendant on this, is one of the things which most causes Moran distress.

Does this mean I shall one day be banished from my house, from my garden, lose my trees, my lawns, my birds of which the least is known to me and the way all its own it has of singing, of flying, of coming up to me or fleeing at my coming, lose and be banished from the absurd comforts of my home where all is snug and neat and all those things at hand without which I could not bear being a man, where my enemies cannot reach me, which it was my life's work to build, to adorn, to perfect, to keep? I am too old to lose all this, and begin again, I am too old! Quiet Moran, quiet. No emotion, please.[35]

In both cases then, the images of the suffering and the fortunate man seem to be sketched in Geulincx and extensively developed in Beckett. Again, in both cases the situation which seems to be described is that of one confronted by ignorance, suffering that ignorance.

NESCIO

If the importance of Geulincx to *Murphy* is recognised by Beckett critics (if yet to be fully explored), *The Unnamable* has been seen almost universally as using Descartes's cogito as a point of departure. The reading is sustainable up to a point when the well-worn narrative of radical doubt leading to *cogito ergo sum* is recited again. Once we become aware of Geulincx, however, and his reading of Descartes's cogito, it begins to become apparent that this connection might be a less precise formulation than has been thought. Beckett was no doubt also playing with Descartes's system, yet the Geulingian system, although developed from Descartes, offers a significantly altered focus which is much closer to the image of thought offered in *The Unnamable* and illuminates the play of light and dark, knowledge and ignorance, in Beckett's art.

DESCARTES AND GEULINCX

In order to outline these distinctions, and how they relate to Beckett's works, properly, it is necessary to compare elements of the systems of René Descartes and Arnold Geulincx. As is well known, in Descartes doubt leads to the certainty that one thinks and is. From here, in the *Principles of Philosophy*, he further attacks doubt by underlining our ability to give or withhold assent.[36] I can refuse to believe anything and therefore not be fooled by deceit; paradoxically, then, using passive being and pure negative will as starting points, I am able to build the world again. God becomes crucial to the system as it is affirmed that the recognition of God's existence is as, if not more, certain than my own being.[37] Added to this we become certain that God, as a supremely perfect being, is perfectly positive and so cannot deceive. Therefore clear and distinct ideas which must be revealed to our minds by God offer us a means of establishing knowledge.[38] This knowledge is finite and is only certain when it emerges from our thoughts as we cannot truly know what is external to us, and so our sensations or perceptions of the external remain unreliable. There is an interest in ignorance in Descartes, then, but the emphasis of the *Principles*[39] and *Meditations*[40] and the *Discourse on Method*[41] is the manner in which knowledge is built up, the manner in which it is possible.

While numerous similarities exist between Geulincx and Descartes, to the extent that Geulincx is rightly considered a Cartesian philosopher, there are also original aspects to Geulincx's work which are key to the question at hand.[42] In his recent book on Geulincx Bernard Rousset argues that Geulincx is of interest to historians of philosophy in that he provides an important negative influence on Spinoza.[43] Rousset readily admits that the evidence these two knew each others' work is only circumstantial, but it is strongly circumstantial as they lived in the same small university town of Leiden, shared at least one close contact, Lodewijk Meyer, a friend to Spinoza and student to Geulincx, and both produced major works more or less at the same time and place entitled *Ethica*. He also draws upon textual evidence to suggest that Spinoza's terminology might be seen to change between the first and second stages of composition of the *Ethics* (which scholars consider to have been separated in their composition by a gap of some years), and that comparison with terminology in Geulincx suggests Spinoza might have been directly confronting Geulincx on certain points. He argues that Geulincx represents, in effect, a kind of anti-Spinoza: beginning with quite similar understandings of physics, derived largely from Descartes, they reached widely diverging positions, because Geulincx embraced the transcendence of God, the immortality of the soul and the primacy of mind over brute extension, while Spinoza embraced immanence, the dissolution of our mortal mind with our mortal body and the parallelism of thinking and extension. The other main element which distinguished the two, and that which, for Rousset, is the most telling, is that Geulincx bases his entire ethical system on human ignorance and powerlessness while Spinoza offers the potential, at least, of becoming eternal through knowledge of a certain kind and recognises the power of all beings (through his understanding of conatus) as a key component of his system. In short, Geulincx is a philosopher of negation and ignorance (representing, for Rousset, the most extreme example of this position in the history of philosophy) while Spinoza is the extreme example of a philosophy of affirmation.[44]

Rousset underlines the importance of ignorance to Geulincx; he indicates the prevalence of the word *nescio* (to not know) throughout Geulincx,[45] as a key word, just as Beckett stated 'perhaps' was the keyword to his own plays.[46] It is interesting to compare, then, the use of God as foundation in Geulincx and Descartes. God provides the firm Christian foundations on which (finite) knowledge is built for Descartes, and this role, as guarantor of human knowledge is one of the key functions He performs. Gaukroger has argued that Descartes' metaphysics are, primarily, a way of presenting his physics, and so, in effect, his metaphysics are haunted by this new science.[47] Geulincx's metaphysics, however, and his ethics are haunted not by his physics (which bears a marked resemblance to that of Spinoza on some points as well as the Cartesian system on which it is based) but by the concerns of theology (which is the title of Book 3 of Geulincx's *Metaphysics*).[48] If Descartes uses his metaphysics as a means of allowing the reception of his physics by rendering them compatible with Christian tenets, Geulincx uses his metaphysics to reaffirm the ongoing importance of the Christian God, not only in the face of the true philosophy and the true science based on Descartes, but through and in that true philosophy and science as the prime mover of all.

In practice, this difference translates into God providing different kinds of certainty to the Geulingian as opposed to the Cartesian system. Whereas God underwrites the clear and distinct ideas of Descartes,[49] for Geulincx God provides the overriding human certainty: that we do not have adequate knowledge of things. Not only do we not know anything, for Geulincx, we are certain that we do not know anything.[50]

It is important to recognise the nature of this ignorance, however. Geulincx's categorisations of knowledge closely resemble those of Spinoza. Spinoza offers three kinds of knowledge, which are, loosely speaking, imagination (sensory experience and all that is involved in consciousness); science (or reasoned understanding); and the third kind, adequate knowledge (sometimes described as 'intuition').[51] Geulincx, for his part, offers four kinds, which map on to Spinoza's categories. The first two kinds might be seen to relate to Spinoza's first kind and involve i) sensory perception, and ii) consciousness; the third kind relates to Spinoza's second kind and might be called iii) learning (this is clear knowledge built through reasoning based on eternal truths, but it does not penetrate the thing, it remains external to it), and the fourth kind is what he calls iv) wisdom (which involves an understanding of the thing through the idea: the thing in itself). It is this final kind of true or adequate understanding, which we lack in relation to anything but God, which leads Geulincx to affirm our ignorance (a position which leads to his occasionalism) as true action involves adequate (complete) understanding of the act, and as we lack such adequate understanding, our actions could not ultimately be said to be our own. They must, rather, be the actions of something or someone who does understand and can therefore act, and this someone, who has created and is creating the universe and the interinvolved destinies of everything in it, is God for Geulincx.[52]

The distinction between the third and fourth kind of knowledge in Geulincx is of key importance. As he affirms, 'It is very true (and passes with the vulgar for a proverb) that there are many learned men with little wisdom.'[53] One can understand, for example, that God (or Nature, to use Spinoza's terms) is the prime mover of all, and one can develop science in the manner of Descartes, but knowing, say, the framework and functioning of elements of the nervous system to a given body does not mean one knows how or why such a body, which is brute matter, affects others, is affected or *is* (the thing in itself); one does not know, that is, the true mode or meaning of its being.

When I want to speak, my tongue flaps about in my mouth; when I want to swim, my arms splash about; when I want to walk, my feet are flung forward. But I do not make that motion. I do not know how such a thing is brought about, and it would be impudent of me to say that I do what I do not know how to do. I do not know how, and through which nerves and other channels, motion is directed from my brain into my limbs; nor do I know how motion reaches the brain, or even whether it reaches the brain at all. With the aid of Physics and Anatomy I may be able to trace this motion for some distance, but I still feel sure that in moving my organs I am not directed by that knowledge; and that on occasion I have moved them just as promptly, or perhaps even more promptly, when nothing could have been further from my mind.[54]

Both our limited understanding and our absence of knowledge are confirmed by the true knowledge that firstly, we do not adequately know how or why anything is, and secondly, that God does. In *The Unnamable*, of course, there is neither the third or fourth kind of Geulingian knowledge: even ignorance is in doubt.

Still, this assertion of human ignorance is not only key to the understanding of Geulincx's ethics but strikes a profound chord with Beckett, who stated: 'I think anyone nowadays who pays the slightest attention to his own experience finds it the experience of a non-knower, a non-can-er (somebody who cannot).'[55] We have seen how Beckett pointed to the formulation *Ubi nihil vales, ibi nihil velis* as being of interest to him, and it is this formulation around which Geulincx builds his ethics. Only God has adequate knowledge.[56] It is one of Geulincx's key statements of human ignorance in his ethics and finds a corollary in his metaphysics in the key formulation *Quod nescis quomodo fiat, id non facis* ('What you do not know how to do is not your action').[57] Geulincx returns to these two key tenets to secure his system repeatedly. It is important to notice not only the emphasis on human ignorance they affirm but the concomitant powerlessness this ignorance brings, especially when we begin to consider *The Unnamable*;

the Unnamable tells us (and shows us) he is 'all-impotent' and, developing Geulincx's favourite word *nescio* ('I do not know') 'all-nescient'.[58] Mixing Geulincx with Democritus, he says: 'Nothing then but me, of which I know nothing'.[59] In his notes to Geulincx Beckett cites the following passage:

I say, therefore, that if you are willing to describe yourself as the doer of anything that you do not know how to do, there is no reason why you should not believe that you have done or do anything that happens or has been done. If you do not know how motion is made in the organs of your body while being nevertheless quite sure that you made it, you could say with equal justification that you are the author of Homer's *Iliad*, or that you built the walls of Nineveh, or the Pyramids; you could say with equal justification that you make the Sun rise and set for us all, and the succession of days and nights, and of winter and summer. Why are these not your actions, why are you conscious that they are not your actions, if not because you do not know how to do them? This is the first thing we usually say when we want to convince others most forcefully that we have not done something: *I do not understand how it is done, I do not know how to do it.*[60]

This all-permeating ignorance extends not just to human beings, who as minds are also modes of the universal mind of God for Geulincx, but also to all things beneath God, all modes of His supreme being. Only God knows how and so it is God alone who truly acts, which leads directly to Geulincx's particular form of occasionalism.[61] I do not know how my body *is*, so how could I be said to control it? God must control it. I feel no internal power over my own ability to exist or not to exist, therefore it must be only within the power of God. I may be called a 'father' but I have no true understanding of the processes through which the lives of 'my' sons was brought into being and so it is God, not I, who must be considered their true father. Further, I am trapped within myself, nothing can extend from me to affect others, neither my works nor my actions, without those others being affected or affectable through God's will and his use of the instruments that are bodies.[62]

These points of emphasis and interest lead Geulincx into developing a cogito, which, despite initial appearances, is quite different to the well-known Cartesian cogito on which it is based. Whereas the conceptual persona in Descartes empties his mind in order to get rid of the baggage of false opinions about the workings of things he has carried since childhood, so as to open the way for clear and distinct ideas,[63] Geulincx's conceptual persona empties his mind not to this end but in order to focus more fully on the self. Descartes's well known formulation is 'I think therefore I am'; that of Geulincx, however, is much closer to the formulation we find in Beckett: 'I, of whom I know nothing'.[64] In his *Metaphysics* this intense focus on the self and what the self knows or properly does not know is called autology, and Rousset considers this to be the most original component of Geulincx's thought.[65] In the *Ethics* this focus leads to what he calls the *Inspectio Sui*, or inspection or examination of the self, which leads immediately to a *Despectio Sui*, or disregard for the self or its worth. The individual cogito is isolated by doubt so as to understand its worthlessness in the face of God, and this understanding should lead to the prime virtue of humility. All this, following the tenet Geulincx adapted from the Stoics,[66] *Ubi nihil vales . . .*, provides the basis for an ethical system requiring the acceptance of the ineffable will of God. We see this referred to, along with the recognition of ignorance, in *The Unnamable*:

I must know something else, they must have taught me something, it's about him who knows nothing, wants nothing, can do nothing, if it's possible you can do nothing when you want nothing, who cannot hear, cannot speak, who is I, who cannot be I, of whom I can't speak, of whom I must speak.[67]

Descartes leads us from obscurity to clarity (knowledge), whereas Geulincx leads us into obscurity (and offers no real hope of our departing from there) so that we might recognise our own ignorance and in turn recognise the omniscience and omnipotence of God. Paradoxically, then, for Geulincx, God is revealed not through the light of truth, but through the obscurity of our ignorance. Beckett's notes from Geulincx include the following quotation

my body is a part of the world, an inhabitant of the fourth region, and claims a place among the species who walk over it, *I*, as one who can depart from his senses, and who in himself can neither be seen, heard, nor touched, am by no means a part of the world. These senses all have their seat in my body, and nothing can pass from them into me. I elude every appearance: I am without colour, shape, or size, I have neither length nor breadth, for all these qualities belong to my body. I am defined by knowledge and will alone.[68]

WILL AND FREEDOM

We have already seen how this 'knowledge', like that of the Unnamable, is everywhere limited by ignorance in Geulincx. Yet, as with Descartes, human will provides a special case for Geulincx. For Descartes the human will is the only part of human being or any kind of being under God which can properly be called infinite.[69] For Descartes most other kinds of 'infinity', such as that supposed to pertain to the physical universe, should instead be termed 'indefinite': the physical universe does not encompass everything for Descartes (the mind of God being prior to it).[70] The human will, however, is properly infinite because it is able to encompass all things, including those things which are beyond its power. Human will also provides an exception for Geulincx. Our will, in effect, is the only aspect of our being which might be considered free of the power of God. It is the only aspect of our being which might be considered active, and for this reason it takes on added importance. I might ultimately kill someone through actions which are brought about by God (as I am unable in fact to act physically) but what makes me a murderer is that I have wished to kill; that it has come about in accordance with my own will. God, Geulincx tells us, as we have seen in the previous chapter, often has it that that which we desire is brought about.[71] In fact he does this most of the time wherever this will is in accordance with his laws of nature, and it is this correspondence between our will and the actions brought about which lead us to falsely assume we have power over our actions. Such false assumptions lead, in effect, to the sin of pride, the worst of sins for Geulincx, through which we imagine ourselves to be gods in control of our own destinies.[72] The will, then, and how we use it, is directly related to our own salvation or damnation.

IMAGES IN ARNOLD GEULINCX AND SAMUEL BECKETT

To accept and recognise the power of God is to turn toward Him, to reject that power is to turn away from Him. In the *Metaphysics* Geulincx describes the kind of existence we might experience after death, and this involves the soul, released from the body and having shed the memories and sensations for which that body was (through God's intercession) the instrument, either turning toward God and realising the joy of that understanding, or turning from God and recognising the hell of utter confusion.[73] An image which offers a striking expression of this ignorance occurs in Geulincx's *Metaphysica Vera*, when he is explaining what hell would be like. Hell is a place where the guidance of God is removed from us and we become completely unknowing, completely at the mercy of our ignorance.

If death should befall me ... All I can do is await His decision concerning me ... He can leave me without a body at all, and absolutely in that state in which I shall find myself when I am released ... in which case it is clear that I am to be divested of all my senses, even of memory (which no less than any of the senses depends on the body), and that I am to be conscious only of desires and ideas. Wherefore

I understand that if I turn to my god when I am released, I shall be happy, and happy for ever; but if I turn away from Him, unhappy. If I turn to Him, I shall understand to what it is that I turn, and how blessedly (but not without repentance, an act of the utmost affliction of mind): if I turn away, and how damnably; but I shall not know to what it is that I turn (and not without the utmost confusion of mind). For that to which I had used to turn myself was but an appearance, which will be there for me no longer once I am released from my body.[74]

These images might be said to resonate with Beckett's works in many places. *The Unnamable, All Strange Away,*[75] *Imagination Dead Imagine*[76] to name some of the more obvious (the latter two texts describing the stripping-back of sensation and images). *The Unnamable* has often been considered to perhaps describe a beyond or a hell, and, with good reason Dante has been mentioned in respect to this idea. Yet if, as critics contend, Beckett was interested in images from the visual arts, which he found in paintings and adapted to his works, why should we be surprised if he at times used the images of philosophy in a similar way, why should we not consider the Geulingian hell to be as much a point of reference or possibility in *The Unnamable* to the far more complex hell of Dante?

This description of hell occurs in the *Metaphysica Vera*, which Beckett read closely and took extensive notes to.[77] It is most clearly in the *Metaphysics* that Geulincx pays attention to the question of whether we can exist after death (without our bodies). There is at least one other description from the *Ethics*, however, which Beckett cites in his notes, which brings to mind the situation of the Unnamable. The idea that the Unnamable might inhabit an afterlife is one which occurred to the very first readers of the work. It is interesting, however, to turn to passages which Beckett cites from the *Ethics*, which shed a different light on the insistence of the Unnamable that he must go on. We have seen above how the last lines of Molloy's narrative, and the last paragraph of Moran's, can be compared to images which occur in Geulincx and appear in Beckett's notes. The same might be said of the final lines of *The Unnamable*: 'I can't go on, I'll go on'.

Beckett cites the following passage from note 36 to 'The Inspection of Self':

it is remarkable how men wish to fend off not only death itself by every possible means, but even the consciousness of death, and as it were to flee from it and evade it. The following saying vividly depicts the mood of someone who is in such an excitable and distressed state: *I see that I can be taken away, either now or at some other time.*[78]

Beckett immediately follows this with a quotation from Geulincx's annotation 38:

They are, accordingly, led by stupidity, and a certain stubbornness in acting, and by the diabolical instigation to persist with something once it has been started (for this is at the instigation of the Devil, as I shall show quite clearly in Treatise IV, in the Section concerned with the Devil).[79]

The link to the Devil and the hell he oversees is further underlined by a quotation from Geulincx's annotation 40, which immediately follows that from annotation 38:

we learn from the Inspection of Ourselves that we also are subject to sin, in fact subject to the Devil; for he is the instigator who continually inculcates into us this creed: *Continue, because you have begun* ... since something should not be continued because you have begun it but because Reason dictates it.[80]

The going on for no other reason than that one has begun could be understood to offer us an image of the situation of the Unnamable. The situation of an 'I think' which involves utter ignorance, the situation of one confronted by ignorance, suffering that ignorance, in this case apparently after death. The afterworld described is clearly, in Geulincx's terms, hell, because it is only hell which involves this kind of confusion. Heaven, as we have seen, links us at last with knowledge. In some ways this reading might seem perverse: the Unnamable tells us he wishes to end by finally saying what needs to be said to bring on silence at last. Yet there is an ignorance which blocks the way to this. One might compare this situation to that in *Play*, where the three protagonists are also stuck in a process of regurgitating their stories in an effort to end. In this play, however, it is clear that they are, in effect ignorant, and that this ignorance is such that there is a danger that it will prevent any movement to a new phase: none of the three are aware that the other two are in the same place they find themselves in, for example. Further, each of them makes comments which confirm their own arrogance, their own pride.

w2: They might even feel sorry for me, if they could see me. But never so sorry as I for them.
. . .
m: I pity them in any case, yes, compare my lot with theirs, however blessed, and – . . . Pity them.
. . .
w1: Poor creature. Poor creatures.[81]

Pride is the worst of sins for Geulincx: it is the direct opposite to the most important cardinal virtue, humility. Readings such as this, of course, are always based on conjecture, on leaping a gap.

A POST-WAR IMAGE OF THOUGHT: THE ABSENCE
OF SELF-PRESENCE

I belong to that generation of people who, when they were students, were enclosed
within an horizon marked by Marxism, phenomenology, existentialism, etc. . . . I
was like all the other students of philosophy at that time, and for me, the rupture
came with Beckett: *Waiting for Godot*, a breathtaking spectacle.[82]

The exact nature of the relationship between a work of literature and the
life of the writer who creates that work is, evidently, impossible to describe
perfectly. It does not follow, however, that the problem is therefore without interest; on the contrary, attempting to trace some elements of its
outline remains an endeavour of some importance, one that allows us to
develop our understanding not only of the works themselves but also of the
nature of the writing process.

The problem of the nature of the relationship between the writing
subject and what is written was clearly an important one in the post-
World War Two France in which Beckett wrote most of his best-known
works. I will discuss this moment and its importance to our understanding
of Beckett in more detail here. In order to begin, however, it is worth
noting how Michel Foucault's comments on this question are often mis-
interpreted. As Maurice Blanchot explains,

. . . it is accepted as a certainty that Foucault, adhering in this to a certain
conception of literary production, got rid of, purely and simply, the notion of
the subject: no more oeuvre, no more author, no more creative unity. But things
are not that simple. The subject does not disappear; rather its excessively determined unity is put in question. What arouses interest and inquiry is its disap-
pearance . . . or rather its dispersal . . .[83]

Foucault further focused on what is at stake with this problem in an
interview in 1983:

. . . someone who is a writer doesn't simply create his[84] work in his books, in what
he publishes . . . in the end it's himself writing his books. And it's this relation of
himself to his books, of his life to his books, which is the central point, the seat of
his activity and his work . . . The work is more than the work: the writing subject
is part of the work.[85]

The problem does not require the obliteration of the question of the
relationship between the writing and the writing subject, then; on the
contrary it is the complexity of this relation which is, precisely,
the problem, and which therefore requires ongoing examination.
H. Porter Abbott cites Beckett's comment that he felt, in relation to his

own work, like 'a mole in a molehill',[86] an image that conveys some of the complexity involved.

At the beginning of this chapter I discuss the notion of the image of thought in relation to writing. In Beckett, *The Unnamable* with its emphasis on the problem of the dispersal of the subject, follows, logically as well as chronologically, *Malone Dies*. *Malone Dies* examines not only the process of dying, but the relation between the writer (in this case fictionalised as Malone, and distanced from 'Samuel Beckett') and what is written. How the writer pictures his life in relation to his work is of key importance. If philosophy needs an image of thought (implicit presuppositions about what one understands it means to think) in order to begin thinking, literature needs an understanding of the subject/object relationship (the relationship between the world which is described and the narrator who describes that world). We have seen in chapter 3 how Beckett considers that art needs to begin to call this relation into question. This calling into question, however, does not make the relation disappear; on the contrary, it focuses upon it as a problem and establishes its instability, putting gaps in places where there once were clear links.

Marcel Proust developed a theory that the artistic process is one of translation: one that does not involve a transcription from life but a transformation of it. That is, elements are drawn from life and characteristics from real people, but these are put at the service of a new world, a fictional world which is created.[87] So, too, Beckett is a writer whose life and work have long been known to intersect,[88] but his work has also, as much as any other writer, problematised how we might understand this relationship. From *The Unnamable* through to *Texts for Nothing*,[89] and on into certain later short prose pieces, Beckett offers an image of the author as an absence, and an image of thought as the absence of fixed self-presence. This absence is, in fact, a recognition of groundlessness, a recognition that at the core of the self is an invincible ignorance concerning who one is or how one is. It expresses the situation discussed above, of one who is ignorant, suffering that ignorance. We have seen above how Beckett borrows aspects of this image of thought from Geulincx, but in doing so he removes the ground of God which Geulincx indicates as being affirmed through our ignorance. The turn from God as guarantor of truth, of course, is something which is generally thought to have begun with Descartes. Man is put in God's place, via the cogito (much as this simplifies and perhaps misrepresents Descartes). Beckett returns to Descartes's seventeeth century but chooses Geulincx over Descartes in developing an understanding of the basis for knowledge.

The absent author in Beckett is no longer like that described by Stephen in Joyce's *A Portrait of the Artist as a Young Man*, who, building upon the aesthetic model of Flaubert, suggests that, 'The artist, like the God of creation, remains within or behind or beyond or above his handiwork, invisible, refined out of existence, indifferent, paring his fingernails.'[90] Rather, whereas in Stephen's description the author is omnipotent and omniscient, Beckett's narrator is all-nescient, altogether ignorant. This aesthetic image of thought, which Beckett drew and reinvented from a marginalized seventeenth-century philosophical image of thought (and was the first to recognize as of crucial importance to the set of problems which presented themselves in France after World War Two), in turn passed back into a philosophical imagination. That is, I would suggest that, in developing his image of thought as a discourse which passes through and animates its participants, it is not by simple chance that Michel Foucault turns to the works of Samuel Beckett in order to illustrate his ideas. Further, as others have already demonstrated, Foucault was not alone in developing a set of ideas related to these questions of the subject in France at this time. Leslie Hill, for example, who has also written an influential study on Beckett tracing, in part, the importance of language to the constitution of the subject,[91] effectively demonstrates the proximity of the work of Blanchot, Bataille and Klossowski around this set of problems.[92]

A central concern of *The Unnamable* is the question of what it means to think; indeed, it formulates a new image of thinking for literature, one which involves a failure of thought, as the self mercilessly seeks out itself and fails to grasp it. It is an image of the absence of self-presence and, because it follows *Malone Dies*, it refers the problem of such absence back from the problem of thinking itself (in *The Unnamable*) to the problem of the interrelation between the writing and the one who writes (*Malone Dies*).

Writing about the early French critical reception of Beckett, which only began with *Molloy*, Bruno Clément reminds us that a number of very famous names are associated with this initial welcome: Georges Bataille, Maurice Blanchot and Alain Robbe-Grillet. While recognizing the diversity of these early critical texts Clément claims that they nevertheless share a common element in that 'they are written "under influence"'. He goes on to explain:

I mean ... their content is indebted, in more than one way, depending on the particular case, to the discourse used by the work itself ... the most striking example remains ... 'Où maintenant? Qui maintenant', that Maurice Blanchot produced just after the publication of *L'Innommable*. In this famous text, which was to provide the tonality of Beckettian studies for a long time, one realizes with the passing of time that the critic is, so to speak, 'ventriloquized' by the text about which it claims to be saying something.[93]

Clément goes on to categorise Beckett's writing in *L'Innommable* as posing specific difficulties to its first readers, including those famous readers cited above, because it was 'a young and original oeuvre, lacking any real external bench mark which would allow it to be effectively apprehended'.[94] The key problem, however, is 'due to the duality of narrative authorities that it proposes'.[95] That is, the reader becomes aware that there is already, in the work being read, a voice which resembles the critical voice: the voice of the commentator. This in turn renders further critical reading difficult as, to a certain extent, the task of criticism has already been performed by the work itself. Elsewhere, in *Le lecteur et son modèle*, Clément explains that the very essence of commentary is the search for identity. Commentary, Clément contends, whether it concerns the self or the Other, always poses the question of identity.[96]

In Beckett's *The Unnamable* there is a fierce scrutiny of the self by the self, very much of the kind, as we have seen, demanded by Arnold Geulincx and which he termed 'autology' and makes use of in the *Inspectio Sui*. The critical eye focuses so fiercely on the self that the self disperses and flees, yet rather than the problem of the relation of the self to the work vanishing it becomes diabolically complex.

THE ORDER OF DISCOURSE

On 2 December 1970 Michel Foucault delivered his inaugural address, *L'Ordre du discours*, to the Collège de France, an institution founded in the sixteenth century, 'which, unlike the University of Paris, had as its aim the advancement of knowledge rather than the classification of accumulated and traditional materials'.[97] In this paper Foucault discusses procedures that control and delimit discourse. At the beginning of *L'Ordre du discours* Foucault states:

I would have been pleased if there were behind me (having taken up the speech a very long time since, doubling in advance everything that I am going to say) a voice that would speak like this: 'You must go on, I can't go on, you must go on, [sic – Foucault skips some words here] you must say words, as long as there are any, until they find me, until they say me, strange pain, strange sin, you must go on, perhaps it's done already, perhaps they have said me already, perhaps they have carried me to the threshold of my story, before the door that opens on my own story, that would surprise me, if it opens.'[98]

The quotation above, of course, which is cited by Foucault without attribution, is taken from the last page of Beckett's *L'Innommable* (*The Unnamable*). Foucault continues by discussing those procedures that in some fashion exert themselves from outside the discourse and function as systems of exclusion. He isolates three: firstly, the establishment of forbidden topics – sex, for example, and other taboo areas. Secondly, the establishment of the desire to seek truth, understood as consisting of verified facts and so on – the *modus operandi* adopted by science, which has since colonised most other discourse. Finally, the demarcation of madness as an inadmissible discourse.

He then moves on to isolate a second group of internal procedures: 'since the discourses themselves exercise their own means of control'.[99] The first among these is the commentary. There is a sort of hierarchy of discourses. The Bible, for example, is a primary text supporting innumerable secondary texts that comment on it. It is a game of repetition where the perceived relations never cease to modify themselves over time.[100] Commentary may consist of a kind of restatement of the primary text, or it might consist of saying something other than the source, but it must always be tied to and referred to that source. 'The new is not in what is said, but in the event of its return'.[101] In the light of Bruno Clément's research one might gloss this further to suggest that the commentary also involves a process of identification (of the commentating text with the primary text).

The second of the internal procedures is concerned with the 'author'. 'The author, not understood, of course, as the speaking individual who has pronounced or written a text, but the author as a principle for the grouping of discourses, as the unity and origin of their significations, as seat of their coherence.'[102] With regard to literature and philosophy the author has been used as a principle of limitation since the Middle Ages.

We require that the author establish the unity of the text we file under his name; we require that he reveals, or at least carries with him the hidden sense that runs through his texts; we require that he articulate these things, through his personal life and lived experiences, through the real history/story whose birth he has witnessed. The author is that which gives to the disquieting language of fiction, its unities, its nodes of coherence, and its insertion into the real.[103]

The third internal procedure for the control and delimitation of discourse is the establishment of the discipline. A discipline carries with it the rules for the formation of the discourse pertaining to that discipline. The examples

Foucault gives relate to the sciences: there are procedures that must be followed if one's work is to be considered science at all. If you are working outside the well-established rules of a discipline and you happen to come to a conclusion which is of great relevance to the field of study straddled by that discipline, your conclusion will not, cannot, be taken into account. Foucault gives examples of breakthroughs of relevance to the disciplines of medicine and biology which were ignored because they were stumbled across outside the discursive procedures established by these disciplines.[104]

With regard to these three internal procedures Foucault concludes:

We are in the habit of seeing in the fecundity of an author, in the multiplicity of commentaries, in the development of a discipline, so many infinite resources for the creation of discourse. Perhaps, but they are no less principles of constraint; and it is probable that we cannot take into account their positivity and multiplicity, if we do not take into consideration their restrictive and constraining functions.[105]

I have found it necessary to give this summary for two reasons. Firstly, it needs to be noted that Foucault is underlining the principles of constraint here, at least in part, in order to allow us to better take into account the 'positivity' and 'multiplicity' generated by the concepts of the 'author', the 'commentary' and 'the discipline'. Rather than wishing to do away with these categories and the complex sets of interrelations they imply, then, Foucault's work seeks to better understand the complexity.

Secondly, it is important to understand the crucial shift in aesthetic understanding taking place here, which is nothing less than the overturning of one image of thought (in the field of aesthetics) by a new image. This new image of thought, or a version of it, is one to which not only Foucault and Blanchot among others might be thought to adhere, but is also one which these thinkers believe they see in the works of Samuel Beckett. In his discussion of this aspect of Foucault's works Deleuze suggests that:

Foucault echoes Blanchot in denouncing all linguistic personology and seeing the different positions for the speaking subject as located within a deep anonymous murmur. It is within this murmur without beginning or end that Foucault would like to be situated, in the place assigned to him by statements.[106]

We see this too in the work of Jacques Derrida, who said of Beckett: 'This is an author to whom I feel very close, or to whom I would like to feel myself very close'.[107]

The shift in image of thought is a shift from a notion that art needs to be understood through recognition of the individual intuition of the artist, an intuition which often cannot be contained or expressed by language, to a notion that discourse is anonymous, belonging to groups rather than individuals, and which, in passing through individuals, animates them, playing them like marionettes. Both 'images' are simplified here. The former conception was dominant from the late nineteenth until the mid-twentieth century (and, indeed, can be traced back at least to the Romantics) in part due to the influence of Henri Bergson and his concept of intuition. I have touched upon this in previous chapters and return to it in chapter 6 below. However, it is not a simple matter of overturning, as the two images in effect enter into dialogue.

Bruno Clément, in a passage cited above, has suggested that Blanchot, like most French critics of Beckett until the early 1990s, was merely ventriloquised by Beckett's texts; that, in the manner Foucault describes in *L'Ordre du discours*, Blanchot's text merely restates Beckett's text.[108] The argument is persuasive, yet, rather than simply being ventriloquised, I would suggest that an inflection occurs as Blanchot restates ideas expressed in *L'Innommable*. This inflection is subtle, and Clément's contention that critics such as Badiou and Deleuze use Beckett differently (putting him to the service of their discourse rather than being co-opted by his)[109] remains, on the whole, convincing. Yet the difference is one of degree rather than kind, as Blanchot's inflection renders his Beckett Blanchovian (while it remains recognisably Beckettian), just as Foucault's inflection renders his Beckett Foucauldian (while it remains recognisably Beckettian). In contrast to this, Clément argues that Deleuze, like Badiou and Anzieu, concentrates almost exclusively on those aspects of Beckett which fit best with their own thought.[110] This notion of inflection, in turn, might be linked with Foucault's understanding of discourse and Deleuze's and Guattari's concept of creation to provide us with a sketch for a theory of influence; one which strangely seems to mix the image of thought described by Foucault with that described by Bergson. Creation involves a process of synthesis or relay: new forms are made, but out of old forms; that is, the statements of the discursive formation do pass through the writing subject but they are also given an idiosyncratic shape by the orientation, disposition and intuition of the new writer.

Foucault's essay 'Qu'est-ce qu'un auteur?' ('What is an Author?') was delivered at the Société française de philosophie on 22 February 1969. In the discussion which followed the paper (which has not been published in English versions of the essay), Lucien Goldmann, in the course of aggressively commenting on Foucault's paper, states that:

the negation of the subject is today the central idea of a whole group of thinkers, or more exactly of a whole philosophical movement ... one might call the French school of non-genetic structuralism, which is notably comprised of the names of Lévi-Strauss, Roland Barthes, Althusser, Derrida, etc.[111]

In response to Goldmann, Foucault dissociates himself from notions of structure and structuralism and suggests these are not present in his work.[112] He also goes on to disagree with Goldmann's assessment that he has done away with the idea of subject. Still, the kind of association which Goldmann proposes is now well known and commonly accepted. While the thinkers on this list differ in many respects, one might argue that they partook of an image of thought which became extremely influential and which expressed ideas to which Beckett's works have often been compared. Those thinkers listed above and many other equally well-known names from this era shared an interest in language, or, to use Foucault's preferred term, discourse. The image of thought they helped to build (adding to foundations supplied by earlier thinkers in the fields of linguistics, sociology, psychoanalysis and philosophy) was one in which the idea of the subject as a ground or foundation for knowledge was called into question. This prior image of thought of the stable subject was, in caricature, considered to have replaced God (as the guarantor of truth) with Man. Knowledge, it was presupposed, remaining Cartesian in this, could be built upon the idea of human perception and the verifications this would allow through experimentation. So, too, scientific methodology would allow the verification of these perceptions.

The generation of thinkers which included Foucault might be seen to have contributed to further establishing a new image of thought which complicated and undermined the former view. In the place of the fixed, stable subject, for Foucault, discourse itself was established as that which now might be said to found knowledge. Discourse, as described by Foucault in *The Archaeology of Knowledge*,[113] was something which could be thought to pass through and animate groups (comprised of individuals who were aligned with groups through their allegiance to the order of the discourse produced by those groups). The word, then, discourse, became a kind of pneuma or breath, playing those subjected to it like marionettes.

The philosophical image, then, in line with the descriptions offered by Le Doeuff in *The Philosophical Imaginary*,[114] enters into a system of relays. Beckett modifies Geulincx and adds elements from other systems to his system in creating a set of ideas and images which are then his own. The image of thinking as involving an absence of self-presence which he describes is, in turn, picked up and developed by a generation of French philosophers, including Blanchot, Foucault and Derrida.

CHAPTER 6

Beckett, Berkeley, Bergson, Film: *the intuition image*

IMAGES, PHILOSOPHY, LITERATURE

As touched upon in the discussion of Le Doeuff, the supposed conflict between the knowledge (considered dubious, unworthy) offered by the senses and that offered by the light of reason alone (which alone might lead us to the truth) has long drawn a distinction between images and ideas or concepts. We see this, of course, in the celebrated image of the cave in Plato's *Republic*: the truth, the Idea, is like the light of the sun, and is only open to us through reason, whereas we are habitually caught up with the play of images which are illusory and misleading, like the shadows on the wall of the cave. Perhaps still more famously Descartes opposed the light of reason (which delivers us clear and distinct ideas or concepts) to the confused impressions we are given by the images offered to us by the senses.

Yet, if one looks slightly closer, it becomes apparent that the image and the idea are also closely linked. Nietzsche, in the *Birth of Tragedy*, points out that Plato not only attacks art and artists, casting them out of his Republic, but also provides a life-raft for art with his Dialogues.[1] So too Stephen Gaukroger has brought to light Descartes's interest in rhetoric – the vividness of images – as a way of expressing truths. Gaukroger conjectures that Descartes may have developed his notion of clear and distinct ideas from his reading of the classical rhetoric of Quintilian, who speaks of the image that is so striking that it instantly convinces us of its truth.[2] Here, then, literature and philosophy come together, the vivid image expresses truth after all and leads us to the immediate light of understanding, something which is taken up in turn by Spinoza when he speaks of the third kind of knowledge (sometimes understood to involve intuition), which alone allows us access to eternal truths. Indeed, the idea that intuition of one kind or another can guarantee truth has a long history in philosophy and has often been linked to understandings of the image.[3]

BERGSON: INTUITION AND IMAGE

Perhaps the most striking equation of the image and intuition is to be found in Henri Bergson. In 1911, Bergson delivered a paper to the Philosophical Congress in Bologna entitled 'Philosophical Intuition', where he offers the most explicit and concise outline of his concept of intuition and its importance to philosophical thought.[4]

When, after long study, we really begin to understand a philosopher's thought, he suggests, its complications lessen and its various parts fit into one another so that, in effect, 'the whole is brought together into a single point'.[5] Within this point, there is the intuition, which is that spontaneous element which began the whole process for the philosopher, and the impossibility of expressing this intuition, or the desire to express this inexpressible, is what drives the philosopher to develop his or her system. Because the 'attitude of the body' (to use Bergson's phrase) which expresses this notion seems somehow to approach attitudes expressed slightly differently by Beckett – who claimed to be striking at the same couple of nails all his creative life,[6] attacking over and again the same ideas given at the outset without managing to adequately convey what must be conveyed (*The Unnamable* offering the most striking formulation of this dilemma) – I quote from Bergson at length:

In this point is something simple, infinitely simple, so extraordinarily simple that the philosopher has never succeeded in saying it. And that is why he went on talking all his life. He could not formulate what he had in mind without feeling himself obliged to correct his formula, then to correct his correction: thus, from theory to theory, correcting when he thought he was completing, what he has accomplished ... has been to convey with an increasing approximation the simplicity of his original intuition. All the complexity of his doctrine, which would go on ad infinitum, is therefore only the incommensurability between his simple intuition and the means at his disposal of expressing it.[7]

Bergson then goes on to explain that, while, in studying the thought of the philosopher, we cannot ourselves find the intuition which eluded the philosopher, we can arrive at an approximation of it, an approximation which is, precisely, the image:

But what we shall manage to recapture and to hold is a certain intermediary image between the simplicity of the concrete intuition and the complexity of the abstractions which translate it, a receding and vanishing image[8], which haunts ... the mind of the philosopher ... and which, if it is not the intuition itself, approaches it much more closely than the conceptual expression, of necessity symbolical, to which the intuition must have recourse in order to furnish 'explanation'.[9]

Again, we see here a distinction being drawn between the image as something which immediately presents something to the mind (something which both invites and overflows interpretation) and the symbol which involves processes of representing clear points of relation. Yet one might ponder the exact nature of the relation between 'the image' Bergson describes in *Matter and Memory* and 'the image' discussed in relation to intuition in the essay 'Philosophical Intuition'. The two work in slightly different ways. The image described in *Matter and Memory* is that which is presented to the brain by the world, as we have seen in chapter 1. The image, here, however, is not this primary image; rather, it is a response generated to an immediate intuition. This secondary image, created by the individual, is in some sense suggested by the original intuition, but does not fully succeed in reproducing or expressing that intuition. If this image can be, as Bergson explains in *An Introduction to Metaphysics*,[10] superior to the concept in coming to terms with or expressing the intuition, this is partly because images can link together and cover more territory (like a panoramic photograph). This secondary image shares crucial qualities with the immediate images given to perception, however. Most importantly, they both are able to offer an excess of meaning. For this reason the secondary image is able to approximate something of the plenitude of the intuition which immediately grasps a reality in its multi-dimensional complexity. This secondary image is of great importance to our understanding of the use of the image in Beckett. Such images can be created by the mind, or found and made use of, in response to the intuition, which in turn is an immediate response to the image of being which presents itself to the individual. The secondary image, then, interprets the primary image (via the intuition) without closing down its meaning. As the narrator of *Dream of Fair to Middling Women* states:

The real presence was a pest because it did not give the imagination a break . . . the object that becomes invisible before your eyes is, so to speak, the brightest and best.[11]

There is a strong connection between the two kinds of image. The intuition image described here is not a weak reflection but has intense power, occurring to the philosopher with the immediacy and force of a real presence. It is hardly surprising that Bergson's notions of intuition and the image proved attractive to artists, as they forge a road between the direct perception, or apprehension, of artistic insight and the conceptual understandings offered by philosophy. He seems to imply that in producing an image an artist might get to a source of understanding, finding a terrain where intuition can be expressed through sensation. What concerns us here, then, is the relevance of Bergson's ideas to Beckett and Beckett's use of the image as a means of translating philosophical ideas into an artistic language.

BECKETT ON BERGSON

As noted above, the importance of Henri Bergson to what were then contemporary theories of aesthetics was recognised by a young Samuel Beckett (who, as a teacher of French literature at Trinity College Dublin, offered a lecture that set out the nature of this influence).[12] A conception of art based on notions of individual intuition remained current until immediately after World War Two, at least. This is apparent in Beckett's 1949 letter to Georges Duthuit, where he disparages the notion of 'relation' (of the artist, with his or her intuition, to the world), which a certain understanding of this conception of intuition presupposes.[13] That is, Beckett disparages the notion that 'intuition' presupposes an understanding of an inside/outside dichotomy. Importantly, he does not renounce the idea of intuition altogether; rather, he wants to understand it as being far more complex than has been thought, involving not just an understanding stemming uniquely from a self in relation to a world, but as a confused, chaotic interaction between that self and that world:

can one conceive of an expression in the absence of relations, whatever they may be, as much between the I and the not-I as within the former?

Is it necessary to specify the nature of these relations of self to self? . . . Let's say it is a matter of the happy knack of existing in several forms, in which each in a sense takes turns at certifying the others . . .

'Terebrated' [perforated] in this way . . . the artist can wallow in so-called non-figurative painting with complete peace of mind, assured of never being short of a theme, of always being in front of himself . . . And here, once more, the definition of the artist as the one who never ceases to be *in front of* prevails . . . It is not the relation with this or that order of encounter that he refuses, but the state of being quite simply in relation full stop, the state of being in front of. We have waited a long time for the artist who has enough courage, who is enough at ease among the great tornados of intuition to realise that the break with the outside implies the break with the inside, that no relations of replacement for the naive relations exist, that what we call the outside and the inside are the very same thing.[14]

Beckett does not have done with intuition; on the contrary, it is retained in his aesthetic, but in more complex form than a simple understanding of outside and inside. The problem of outside and inside does not disappear, just as the problem of author and work does not disappear in Foucault and his contemporaries; rather, it becomes complex to the point where one might wish to concede, in the language of Arnold Geulincx, that it is ineffable. Ineffability frustrates those who seek to be comforted by simple truths, so it is tempting for readers to simplify by removing one side of the dichotomy altogether, as readers who have chosen to ignore the problem of the nonrelation of the author and the work have done. Yet this is clearly unsatisfactory and distorts the ideas developed considerably. As Beckett continues from the passage cited above: 'I'm not saying that he doesn't search to reestablish correspondence. What is important is that he does not manage to.'[15]

BECKETT, BERGSON, BERKELEY

As one progresses further through Bergson's essay 'Philosophical Intuition', however, the points of correspondence with Beckett become still more striking, because when Bergson develops an example of how one might work from the 'image' one can discover in the attitude of the philosopher, he chooses one of the philosophers Beckett knew best, Bishop Berkeley. Such a discussion could only have intrigued Beckett, who not only studied Berkeley in the 1930s but also indicated a keen interest in the relation between the artist and the philosopher in discussing this reading with Thomas MacGreevy:

As I have been reading the sacré évèque I was alive to the badness of Colum's attempt in the last D. M. [*Dublin Magazine*] to relate him to the artist. Colum makes him [Berkeley] make perception an act of will. Berkeley is at pains, in the principles [*Treatise Concerning the Principles of Human Knowledge*] and Dialogues [*Three Dialogues between Hylas and Philonous*], to insist on the contrary.[16]

One might suggest that Beckett had read Berkeley's work closely, and so would have been unlikely to reduce him to the role of idealist buffoon, best brushed aside with the vigour of a Dr Johnson (whose image of kicking the stone to 'refute' Berkeley's system Beckett characterises in a letter to MacGreevy of 1934 as 'mièvre' or puerile);[17] rather, one might suggest that, in using Berkeley, as he does most famously in *Film*, Beckett would have been genuinely interested in the attitude adopted by the Bishop in formulating his *esse est percipi*, even while, as the attitude of the artist requires, wishing to express no confidence in the truth value of the formula.

Bergson too considers Berkeley worth some effort, and what is perhaps most interesting in relation to Beckett is the image which Bergson isolates as coming closest to expressing Berkeley's philosophical intuition. Berkeley's system, Bergson contends, resolves into four fundamental theses: affirming a) that matter is a cluster of ideas (idealism), b) that general ideas are merely words (nominalism), c) that minds are real and characterised by will (spiritualism) and d) through a consideration of matter that God exists (theism).[18] Bergson then goes on to show how Berkeley's idealism 'signifies ... that matter is coextensive with our representation of it',[19] that is, that matter is all surface and so is completely revealed and realised. Bergson suggests that for Berkeley the term 'idea' designates a completely realised existence, an existence which 'is indistinguishable from its seeming'[20] while the word 'thing' designates a reservoir of possibilities. It is the supposed hiddenness or unrealised nature of 'things' which Berkeley objects to, and so he prefers to call those bodies which exist 'ideas' because everything which exists is, for him, completely realised and laid out on a surface which is completely visible (at least to God). Therefore, Bergson concludes, Berkeley's idealism coincides with his nominalism, as abstract and general ideas have no real existence. This is because nothing can be abstracted or extracted from the continuous surface which is matter. Yet if the links between bodies are only words, the link between God and bodies is real, for Berkeley, who places God behind all manifestations of matter. Finally, it is God who gives us perceptions or 'ideas', yet we must gather together or move toward these ideas in being. What characterises us in this movement, then, is the 'reverse of an idea'; it is *will* which is 'constantly limited by divine will', and 'The meeting-place of these two wills is precisely what we call matter.'[21]

In this way, then, Bergson attempts to show how each of Berkeley's four theses interpenetrate one another in the manner of 'a living being'.[22] So we are being led toward the point which Bergson promised us lies at the heart of the philosophical system and is drawn from an original intuition, an intuition which we can only approach through an image which approximates it. This image is powerful in and of its own right, but it is still more interesting for our purposes because of the oblique angle at which it strikes the surface of Beckett's work *Film*, which develops images around Berkeley's *esse est percipi*. Bergson claims that the image which strikes him most from Berkeley is the following:

... that Berkeley perceives matter as a *thin transparent film* situated between man and God. It remains transparent as long as the philosophers leave it alone, and in that case God reveals Himself through it. But let the metaphysicians meddle with it, or even common sense in so far as it deals in metaphysics: immediately the film becomes dull, thick and opaque, and forms a screen because such words as

Substance, Force, abstract Extension, etc. slip behind it, settle there like a layer of dust, and hinder us from seeing God through the transparency.[23]

A THIN TRANSPARENT FILM

Images, of course, are only sometimes linked to philosophy in Beckett and are not always of the same kind, even when they might be linked with concepts. That Beckett does at times link images to philosophical concepts, however, is made explicit in the treatment to *Film* of 1963.[24] This treatment differs from the majority of Beckett's other works, for theatre, or TV, in that it includes some unusually explicit general comments about the rationale or structure of the piece.

Esse est percipi
    All extraneous perception suppressed, animal, human, divine, self-perception maintains in being.
    Search of non-being in flight from extraneous perception breaking down in inescapability of self-perception.
    No truth value attaches to above, regarded as merely of structural and dramatic convenience.[25]

Elements of the above, taken from the 'General' section of this treatment, have often been quoted with emphasis generally placed on the statement that 'no truth value' is to be ascribed.[26] While this statement is important as it indicates elements of Beckett's *modus operandi* when using materials from philosophy (that is, not to take them seriously with respect to the systems from which they are drawn but rather to use them for his own aesthetic purposes) it would be foolish to then read it as indicating that the philosophical figure – 'To be is to be perceived' – from Berkeley, and perhaps, elements of the figure of Berkeley himself[27] are no longer present. Rather, the formulation is undeniably borrowed for 'structural and dramatic' purposes: the entire work explores this idea, and it does so by describing a series of events, and a series of images, which relate directly to this idea (which is done both with rigour and without caring about whether or not the premises involved in the formulation might be true).

    There can be little doubt about the answer to the question, then, as to whether Beckett makes use of philosophical ideas in his works, even though he rarely indicates his points of reference so explicitly. There can also be little doubt that one way in which Beckett transforms these rational ideas into lived sensations is through the use of images. *Film* explores the contours of Berkeley's idea through feeling: sensations of concepts that describe a concept of sensation.

Deleuze, who draws upon the work of Bergson in isolating his concept of the movement-image in his *Cinema* books, begins his essay on Beckett's *Film* by stating that he will propose 'un découpage (ou une distinction des cas) un peu différent de celui de Beckett lui-même'.[28] That is, whereas Beckett divides his treatment into three parts – 1) The street; 2) Stairs; and 3) The room – Deleuze divides his essay into three cases: 1) The Wall and the Staircase, Action; 2) The Room, Perception; 3) The Rocking Chair, Affection. Whereas Beckett's divisions relate to changes of scene, Deleuze's relate to the shifts he perceives in types of cinematic image – the action image, the perception image, and the affection image – which he identifies in his writings on cinema as the three elemental kinds of movement-image of which the cinema is capable.[29]

Deleuze, in his reading of *Film*, pays special attention to its cinematic qualities and its relation to an understanding of the potentialities of film form. This focuses on one side of the concept of image as it occurs in Beckett's work, but it leaves aside a number of issues which concern the manner in which images interact with the philosophical concepts with which they have been drawn into relation. Deleuze's approach seems to be encouraged by the choice of title – *Film* – which leads the viewer to consider what this work has to say about film form and the functioning of the cinematic image (something which is further underlined by Beckett's decision to make this film almost completely silent).

Yet, we have seen above how Bergson, in his essay on Berkeley, has identified an image of matter as a thin transparent film situated between God and man, and this image moves us in a slightly different direction from Deleuze. In *Murphy*, Beckett begins his famous chapter on Murphy's mind with a quotation from Spinoza '… Amor intellectualis … quo Deus se ipsum amat …' ('the intellectual Love with which God loves himself')[30] but alters the quotation by replacing Spinoza's reference to God with one to Murphy, 'Amor intellectualis quo Murphy se ipsum amat' ('the intellectual Love with which Murphy loves himself').[31] So too, one might contend that Bergson's image of Berkeley might be seen to operate in Beckett's *Film*, although Beckett has altered the formulation so that the transparent film is no longer matter, but pure consciousness, which is penetrated by perception, and is no longer situated between God and man, but between O and E, the two sides of a single being. E wishes to gaze through the thin film of consciousness at being itself, whereas O wishes to cloud the film, to throw up obstacles to it so that his being may not be perceived.[32]

Further, through the attention undoubtedly still drawn to the filmic medium itself by the title, the thin transparent film might also be seen to stand between the split self O and E, and the viewer who is able to perceive the agony inherent in a consciousness of being (through being perceived). One sits in the dark in the auditorium and is not perceived in turn so the identification with the audience is of unequal force, but a similarity with the late play *Catastrophe*,[33] which ends with the protagonist staring back out at the audience (which is, precisely, the catastrophe or denouement within the play), emerges here. *Film* both begins and ends with a big close-up of the eye, an image which directly hails the viewer as complicit in the manner of Baudelaire's 'hypocrite lecteur'. It is important to note that Beckett's written treatment and the final filmed version differ in a number of ways. Certain opening scenes had to be cut due to technical difficulties and Beckett compensated for these lost scenes by inserting the image of the eye in close-up.[34]

As has often been noted Beckett chose the title *Film* after toying with the idea of calling the work 'The Eye'.[35] 'The Eye', rather than referring the viewer back to the functioning of the filmic medium, would refer the viewer back to the philosophical image, because it is the image of the eye which most succinctly encompasses Berkeley's formulation. The filmed 'eye' cannot see the audience, and the audience knows this, treating it at the same time as an object (with the shape of an 'O') to be inspected. Here, then, is a clear example of a philosophical image, one which offers a précis of the entire project. The eye as image, at once E and O, itself includes a transparent film or lens through which we feel the presence of being. The 'eye' leads us toward an obvious pun with 'I'; but one of the things which Beckett's *Film* makes us see with regard to Berkeley's formulation is that it does not allow or involve any simple connection between the eye and the I, that is, following Arthur Rimbaud's formula, another favourite of Beckett, 'Je est [sic] un autre' (I is another). One might note how O and E, who confronts him, both, with their eye patches, lack an eye. Indeed the shape of Berkeley's formulation *esse est percipi* involves reflection between two sides of being, but reflection which never allows a simple coming together into a complete subject.

The shape is circular, yet again it seems to involve a gap which causes that circle to fail to close. It is a broken hermeneutic circle: while it refers to being and perception, two key attributes of conscious beings, it estranges them from self-identity. The gap is infinitesimally small, a thin transparent film, but unbridgeable or impenetrable nonetheless, and this logic of the unbridgeable gap is already present in Berkeley's formula. The film is also a surface.

Esse (to be) is an active infinitive, yet remains incomplete in itself as its active nature depends on the passive infinitive which follows, and further it refers to no grammatical person. As for *est* (is), while it suggests immediate identification between the two sides of the formulation, it is a third-person singular, understood in an impersonal sense; as such it embodies the transparent film between the two sides E and O, being and being perceived. *Percipi* (to be perceived) is a passive infinitive, again referring to no grammatical person. Any (active) being, then, is reflected in (passively) being perceived, and this being in reflection is necessarily impersonal or detached from immediate identification with an 'I'. Importantly, Beckett calls neither element a subject in this work: O stands for Object and E for Eye;[36] any 'I' would somehow either have to emerge between these two (yet as we have seen, the 'is' which comes between also eludes the first person) or somehow escape their correspondence. The incompletable circular shape is drawn from Berkeley, then, but Beckett uses it to underline structures which reflect his own concerns.

The eye, however, is not the sole image in Beckett's *Film*, which, in the absence of any language but the whispered 'shhh!', Beckett referred to as being composed of what he intended to be 'ideograms'.[37] Deleuze claims Beckett brings the elemental movement-images of cinematic form to light by exhausting them, and in a similar way Beckett might be said to bring Berkeley's concept to light by attempting to negate it. That is, if to be is to be perceived, how does one escape being? How does one escape being perceived? In each case the exhaustion of the type of film image identified by Deleuze is connected to notions of perceivedness. Deleuze's 'action image', through which a moving camera follows a moving figure, is exhausted or negated by the fact that the figure is *fleeing from* the notion of perceivedness the pursuing camera embodies here. So too we are made conscious of the 'perception images' supplied by the various sets of eyes which watch O (the animals, the image of God, the mirror, the window) because O attempts to extinguish, remove or cover them. Finally, the 'affection image', the close-up through which emotion is conveyed, is negated because the process of perceivedness it represents itself causes the horrified emotion conveyed, a horror to which, again, one can only respond with flight or the attempt to hide.[38]

'THE AGONY OF PERCEIVEDNESS'

A number of images directly relate to Berkeley's formula, yet one which stands out is the facial expression of an 'agony of perceivedness'[39] apparent three times (once in each of Beckett's three sections) in *Film*. That is, once when E confronts O at the film's climax and twice when E confronts others: the couple in the street and the flower woman on the stairs. The flight from perception, the agony of perceivedness and the relation of self-perception to this agony of perceivedness are all tied to Berkeley though all are also clearly filtered through Beckett's own understandings. That is, the agonies of perceivedness clearly relate being to being perceived, but the trauma involved in this is not implicit in Berkeley's concept. Rather, *Film* seems to involve a refashioning of the image in line with a different intuition. The thin transparent film Bergson identifies in Berkeley no longer rests between ourselves and the wonder of God (in the manner of Kant's sublime or Schopenhauer's Idea); rather, now presented as pure consciousness instead of matter, it stands between and forever separates being and being perceived (two sides of a single self in the case of O and E but something else in the case of E and the others), revealing, as it is penetrated, horror rather than ecstasy.

Deleuze asks at the outset of his essay on Beckett's *Film* what it is that is so horrible in perceivedness. He concludes at last that the fear stems from the perception of self by self which can only be escaped in death. Yet there is something inexplicable in the horror, reminding us, perhaps, of the final words of Conrad's Kurtz in *Heart of Darkness*,[40] which also stem from a revelation which is not everyday, but may relate to the equivocal images which emerge as one confronts the endeavour to end and pursues a final recognition of the nature of one's being. While similar situations occur throughout Beckett's works, in some ways Deleuze's answer remains unsatisfactory, as the horror of perceivedness cannot be definitively related to a perception of self by self in this work. This is because it not only occurs with O and E but also with the others.

Watching *Film*, we are made aware that the process of understanding, or being confronted by, the agony, is not an everyday process; rather, it seems to be a limit experience perhaps linked with an intuition of an end to one's own being and not to being *per se*. This conjecture might explain why O checks his pulse, once on the stairs, and once in the rocking chair (which is apparent in the film itself though never mentioned in the treatment, and only in passing in Beckett's correspondence with Schneider).[41] Furthermore, while Deleuze maintains the opposite, the evidence of both the finished film and the treatment indicate that it remains unclear, as is typical with Beckett, whether or not we are supposed to think O dies at the end. It is clear, however, that a consciousness of perceivedness, and the consciousness of being it implies, is such an uncommon, and an uncommonly unpleasant, sensation that it brings with it a threat of death or non-being, not so much as an escape or solution to being perceived (as Deleuze contends)[42] but as a simple consequence of it. The question as to whether it can ever be escaped remains, as again is typical of Beckett, unanswerable.

One assumes the others (the couple in the street, the flower woman on the stairs) who confront E and feel the horror of his gaze are not looking at an image of themselves, but the perceiving side of the E/O protagonist. Just as O's horrified attempts to escape being perceived must be considered atypical or at a limit point, so too the intentness or intensity of E's perception is atypical or at a limit point, and it is this intensity which must affect the others, forcing through the film of their consciousness and penetrating their being. As Beckett stated to Schneider and others before production began, neither O nor E has a 'normal' perception, and it is E's abnormally intense gaze which horrifies the couple and the flower woman (causing harm to the latter). O's abnormality, then, inversely reflects E's abnormality, and a unity is only obtained by leaping across the gap between. As Beckett told Schneider:

the space in [the] picture is [a] function of two perceptions, both of which are diseased ... [which] enable one to deform normal vision. Unity is the quality of this apprehension.[43]

Rather than the perception of self by self alone causing horror, then, it is this process taken to a limit, a limit at which a penetration through consciousness to being is possible, coming at, or bringing on, a moment near the end of life.

'IT'S DONE I'VE DONE THE IMAGE'[44]

This is not the only unbridgeable gap that must be traversed, however. Making the image is difficult as, in being realised, images can come loose from the intuitions which brought them forth and become something else. Beckett seemed to make this point in writing to Alan Schneider about *Film* and the differences between what he imagined at the outset (and tried to circumscribe in his written treatment) and what was finally captured on film.

after the second [viewing of a rough cut of *Film*] I felt it really was something. Not quite in the way intended, but as a sheer beauty, power and strangeness of image ... In other words and generally speaking, from having been troubled by a certain failure to communicate fully by purely visual means the basic intention, I now begin to feel that this is unimportant and that the images obtained probably gain in force what they lose as ideograms and that the whole idea behind the film, while sufficiently expressed for those so minded, has been chiefly of value on the formal and structural level.[45]

What we witness, perhaps, in these comments, is a statement similar to that made by Bergson when he considers how the philosopher continually fails to express the intuition. Beckett's point seems to go further, however, as, adding complexity to the well-known discourse of 'failure' which surrounds his work because of certain points of emphasis in his aesthetic writings (and *Three Dialogues with George Duthuit* in particular), he goes on to suggest that the failure of intention loses its importance. That is, what has been created, while still linked to the intuitive intention which engendered it, takes on a life and validity of its own separate from that intuition and intention:

I described it to Barney after the first screening as an 'interesting failure'. This I now see as much too severe. It does I suppose in a sense fail with reference to a purely intellectual schema, but in so doing has acquired a dimension and a validity of its own that are worth far more than any merely efficient translation of intention.[46]

The question of 'intention' is one which, indeed, forces itself forward as one attempts to interpret *Film*, due to the strange and unequal exchange between the written treatment and the actual film. In a note to the screenplay[47] Beckett is careful to explain that the room O enters could not be his own room because 'he wouldn't have a room of this kind. He wouldn't have a room of eyes.'[48] The explanation given in the text is that this is his mother's room and that he has come here to look after her pets while she is in hospital. Yet, it is difficult to understand how a viewer who has not read the screenplay could come to an understanding of this point, which is nowhere indicated in the actual film. Rather, one might wonder why O is now behaving in this way in a room which one might, against Beckett's intentions, understand to be his own.

It is worth considering how such an 'erroneous' reading might proceed and how it might affect an understanding of the whole. O covers what had been an open window, and an uncovered mirror, tears up images, such as that of God the father and a number of pictures referring to his past, which one might assume he had not felt the need to destroy in the past, and removes or covers pets whose presence one might assume he had not found oppressive in the past. A clear reference to past practice is offered when O removes the image of God the father, as this leaves a patch on the wall which signifies it had long been in this position, directly before the rocking chair, one assumes, watching O. That is, being, and the perceivedness it implies, seems to have only just become a matter to inspire fear, rather than always having been this.

The lack of complete correspondence between intention and finished film, between the film itself and the treatment (which Beckett never changed to reflect the finished film, though the opportunity clearly presented itself) is further underlined with reference to the opening scenes, which were cut from the film due to problems in production.[49] In the treatment the others in the opening scene are described in a manner which clearly sets them apart from O, thereby underlining the abnormality of perception pertaining to both O and E.

All persons in the opening scene to be shown in some way perceiving – one another, an object, a shop window, a poster, etc., i.e. all contendedly in *percipere* [perceiving] and *percipi* [being perceived].[50]

Interestingly, the misreading of the room as belonging to O, allowed by the absence of any diegetic reference to O's mother or O's reason for visiting the room, would allow one who were to view the film alone to come to a similar understanding of O's and E's abnormality as the scenes cut from the finished film.

As Bergson suggests, there is a gap between the 'intuition' and the 'image'; a gap which is inherent in the word 'intention', through which the mind, projecting itself into a void, strives at an elusive expression of that which it is barely possible to grasp; a gap we experience in negative image in the equally perilous endeavour at understanding or re-experiencing the sensation sent out towards us; a gap which is furthermore reflected in variations between the 'intentions' expressed in the film treatment and other texts[51] and the finished film itself.

The image eludes the intuition which it never completely expressed in any case. Furthermore, once it has come into being as artistic expression, the image is no longer a mere approximation of the artist's intention (or intuition). The artist fails to fully express the intention but succeeds in creating an image. This image, in turn, carries with it an attribute shared by all images: that it does not convey a single meaning, but, rather, is open to interpretations, interpretations which might overlap with, but also exceed, or elude, the intended meanings. Each of these interpretations, however, will in turn be exceeded or eluded by the image, which offers still further potential meanings than those circumscribed by the interpretation of any given reader. A dynamic interplay, then, is set up between the image, the intentions which found the image and the interpretations which relate to the image. One place one might search for the power of artistic expression is in the series of gaps and the efforts to bridge those gaps which are implicit in any artistic image.

What *Film* in part offers is the exploration of a medium which draws its power, the power to produce sensations, through gaps, nonrelations. Images provide sparks which leap from one side to the next, like messages across synapses, thereby allowing the formation of a unity among difference: intuition and sensation, intuition and the idea, intention and reception, philosophy and literature.

The Ancient Stoics and the ontological image

'MAKE SENSE WHO MAY'

An obituary of Beckett written by Alfred Simon was published in *Le Monde* on 27 December 1989. With Beckett's French contemporaries, and perhaps Sartre in particular, in mind, Simon wrote:

> It has been generally believed that Beckett's oeuvre is a stranger to any political preoccupation. In virtue of the axiom 'to be apolitical is to be right-wing' inflexible members of the doctrinal Left even attempted to pass Beckett off as a writer of the Right. More subtle than these, Cioran was correct to see him as 'one of those who consider that history is a dimension through which man must pass'. Alas, here is yet another self-evident truth that will need to be revised! Lately we have seen him take the side of certain individuals: Arrabal, Vaclav Havel and even Jack Lang! His recent dramatic works, like *Catastrophe* and *Quoi où* [*What Where*] are the politically engaged works of an author who fled from politically engaged literature; they are the most highly political plays of the recent period.[1]

While I won't be discussing *Catastrophe* in this chapter, one might claim that, leaving aside its genesis as a work commissioned in support of the Czech playwright Vaclav Havel, who was then being held as a political prisoner,[2] it has in common with *What Where* an interest in violence and violent relationships, as both involve torture, of the body and spirit.[3] Indeed, as I hope to show in thinking about *What Where* in the context of Beckett's oeuvre (drawing upon Stoic understandings of bodies and their relationship to the image, and incorporeals),[4] politics itself, if it is understood as involving those processes which hold social bodies together, might be understood here to be coextensive with the nature of violence itself.

These claims are already alarming: how can one speak of 'politics itself' or 'violence itself' when both terms seem to encompass sets of events and practices which are heterogeneous and apparently inseparable from particular circumstances? Yet *What Where* offers us a strange sort of abstraction: an image of a being of violence, or a violent relation. That is, an image is produced of a group of individuals who have entered into a dysfunctional relationship to comprise a larger body, this relationship is held in place through force of habit, and this habit is one of violence. In order to distinguish this image from the other kinds of image described above, such an image might be called an ontological image: that is, an image of the being of a certain state or disposition.

We need to step back for a moment and attempt to connect what is at stake here with what has been discussed so far. Firstly, there is the question of relation. As we have seen in chapter 3, Beckett turns from an aesthetic of relation to one of nonrelation, and the latter is well developed by 1946. The idea of nonrelation is complex and somewhat paradoxical, with the under-mining of relations at times proceeding by drawing attention to disconti-nuities within a relation rather than severing the relation altogether. With regard to the question of relationships, as we have seen in chapter 3, from *Godot* on, where they appear, these become more and more dysfunctional. A similar set of dysfunctional relationships (where the protagonists fail to connect with or understand one another) occurs in *What Where*. However, there is another important aspect to the relationships in this play (and a number of structurally similar plays written after *Play* in 1963).[5] That is, these dysfunctional relationships are seen, through habit, to harden into circuits which repeat themselves. Habit is closely aligned with disposition: that is, a disposition might be understood to be the manifestation in some being of a habit or set of habits; a disposition is an habitual mode of being. The Latin word *habitus* (which, in his translation of Geulincx's *Ethics*, Martin Wilson translates as 'disposition') interested Arnold Geulincx, and Beckett quotes the following definition of *habitus* in his notes to Geulincx:

Disposition, or *disposability*, has two senses, custom and facility; the latter as effect, the former as cause; so that disposition is nothing other than *facility engendered by custom*.[6]

As we will see in what follows, disposition itself can be understood to be a state of being. Another way to put this would be to claim that the disposi-tion *is* a thing or an object. Indeed, as I mentioned in passing above, Beckett himself described *What Where* in the following terms: 'I don't know what it means, don't ask me what it means, it's an object.'[7]

In Berlin in 2000 I delivered an earlier version of this chapter to a Beckett conference. In question time Beckett's biographer James Knowlson stood and claimed that he could confirm that Beckett knew the works of Bréhier to which I refer here[8]. The three major Ancient Greek Stoics were Zeno of Citium[9] (334–262 BC), Cleanthes (*c*.331–232 BC) and Chrysippus

(*c.*280–*c.*206 BC). There are a number of strong links to the Greek Stoics in Beckett's works which justify a close reading of their system in relation to Beckett. Firstly, the concept of 'φαντασια' ('phantasia' or image)[10] as that which is immediately impressed on the senses like a 'signet ring in wax' offers one of the earliest and most influential definitions of the image as presentation (which we have seen to be of key importance to Beckett). Secondly, as I discuss below, the Ancient Stoics also developed an extremely influential understanding of the nature of 'sense' and the processes of making sense (something which clearly interested Beckett, and is made explicit in the penultimate line of *What Where*). Thirdly, while he refutes many of their conclusions, Arnold Geulincx was clearly influenced by the Stoics.[11]

To illustrate this, I will again cite a passage from Bréhier which might serve as a point of comparison. The following quotation is from Cicero, who reports that the Ancient Stoic Zeno of Citium described how one moves through stages of knowledge as follows:

> He would raise his hand, spread out his fingers, and say: 'This is [image]'. Then he would bend his fingers slightly and say: 'This is assent'. Then he would clinch his fist and say: 'This is perception.' Finally he would clasp his right fist to his left hand and say: 'This is wisdom which belongs only to the sage.'[12]

Beckett quotes the following passage from Geulincx in his notes to his *Ethics*: 'Diligence is a perpetual grasping at Reason, wisdom the capture of it: the diligent man grasps at Reason, the wise man captures it.'[13] The Stoic notion that wisdom can be achieved through immediate apprehension of the object (the comprehensive image) links to the following description in Geulincx (which is again quoted by Beckett), who clearly understands wisdom as involving an immediate forceful impression upon the senses:

> Wisdom [*sapientia*] is so-called from 'to taste' [*sapere*], which is when we examine with our sense of taste something corporeal. The scope of the other senses reaches only to the exterior of things, and grasps only the surface of the things towards which it is directed, but taste invades and penetrates the interior parts of the body whose interior is subjected to it. . . . It is the same with Wisdom, which is born of profound attention to Reason, invades and penetrates the object, and pronounces concerning it far otherwise than the common sense of men or the 'received intelligence' of the Scholastics.[14]

So too, for both Geulincx and the Ancient Stoics, wisdom is indeed rare, and the attempt to understand what is beyond understanding is considered to be vain by both (for Geulincx, as we have seen, attempting to understand the ineffable is impious, and for the Stoics, as we will see, the making sense of incorporeals is called into question).

While, like many of Beckett's later plays, *What Where* is only seldom performed, it is well known amongst Beckett critics for its penultimate line if nothing else. The 'make sense who may' of *What Where*[15] has, like the 'no symbols where none intended' of *Watt*,[16] taken on a life of its own outside the work, becoming a talisman to use both against the difficulties of many of Beckett's works themselves (relieving one of any critical responsibility to engage with them) and against the seemingly vain (whether tragic, heroic or comic) essays of those who foolishly choose not to use the talisman themselves. That is, it has become a commonplace in place of interpretation or a symbol of an ideal (but necessarily absent) elaboration of pure uninterpretability. What is disappointing about such commonplaces is the self-satisfied sense of safety they bring with them, when any serious apprehension of the works when they are performed or read leaves one unsettled. We are struck by some unfamiliar aspect of 'the real' here (and as underline below, I mean 'real' with the full force the Stoics gave to the term). Just as we have seen, in chapters 2 and 3, how the formula from *Watt* might be related to an understanding of the nature of the symbol, in contrast to an understanding of the nature of the image, here I will attempt to outline how the formula from *What Where* brings us back to a theory of sense, which develops a contrast between bodies (and images which are bodies) and incorporeals such as language.

There are, then, other ways of approaching the final line of *What Where* than as a self-evident signal, a 'keep out'. If one agrees with Alfred Simon that the play is political, then in what sense is it so? Moreover, how does it confront the questions of 'sense' which it explicitly points us towards, and what is the relation of politics and sense (or meaning) to violence, as violence, and the unrelieved and painful ignorance which drives this violence, appear throughout this play in the guise of the senselessness of the imperative of finding or making sense.

BAM: Well?
BOM: [*Head bowed throughout.*] Nothing.
. . .
BAM: He didn't say it?
V: Good.
BOM: No.
BAM: You gave him the works?
BOM: Yes.
BAM: And he didn't say it?
BOM: No.

BAM: He wept?
BOM: Yes.
BAM: Screamed?
BOM: Yes.
BAM: Begged for mercy?
BOM: Yes.
BAM: But didn't say it?
BOM: No.
BAM: Then why stop?
BOM: He passed out.
BAM: And you didn't revive him?
BOM: I tried.
BAM: Well?
BOM: I couldn't.
　　　[*Pause.*]
BAM: It's a lie. [*Pause.*] He said it to you. [*Pause.*] Confess he said it to you.
　　　[*Pause.*] You'll be given the works until you confess.
V: 　Good.
　　　In the end Bim appears.
[*BIM enters at E, halts at 2 head haught.*]
BAM: [*To* BIM] Are you free?
BIM: Yes.
BAM: Take him away and give him the works until he confesses.[17]

It is possible that all these questions are interinvolved: the political nature of this play perhaps stems from the fact it concerns, in a specific and unusual way, an image of violence. As noted above, the word 'image' is one of several terms which have been used to translate the Stoic term *phantasia*. Cleanthes defined this term as an 'impression on the soul' (just as a signet-ring makes a depression in wax), and, somewhat in disagreement, Chrysippus defined it as a 'modification of the soul'.[18] Yet these definitions have in common the notion of actions and bodies (as the Stoics considered the soul to be a body).[19] Chrysippus' definition is more complex, however, in that it allows for both active and passive images, whereas Cleanthes's only allows for passive images. That is, a body is acted upon by retaining the impression or images of another, for Cleanthes, while it might either be being acted upon or acting in being modified, for Chrysippus. This notion of the physical impressions or images bodies leave upon one another or upon themselves, which thereby allow us to apprehend bodies (those realities which are causes), is contrasted with the incorporeal sense we make of words and events, a sense which floats above and fails to affect the real.[20] Such a contrast allows us not only to reflect on the nature of sense, but further to apprehend the image as that which is outside sense, and which is potentially able to go beyond mere sense so as to reach genuine understanding, as, rather than involving the necessarily reductive interpretations of sense, the image is that through which we encounter causes themselves in that it presents a situation in all its complexity: it asks to be understood while resisting straightforward interpretation.

BODIES AND INCORPOREALS

In considering the question of 'sense' in *The Logic of Sense* Deleuze turns to the works of Lewis Carroll, and the Greek Stoics: Carroll because he 'provided the first great account, the first great *mise en scène* of the paradoxes of sense',[21] and the Stoics because they were the 'initiators of a new image of the philosopher which broke away from the pre-Socratics, Socratic philosophy, and Platonism. This new image is already closely linked to the paradoxical constitution of the theory of sense.'[22] One of Deleuze's major sources in piecing together a theory of sense from the fragments left by the three major Greek Stoics was Emile Bréhier, who wrote two books on the Stoics: *Chrysippe et l'ancien stoïcisme* (1910) and *La Théorie des incorporels dans l'ancien stoïcisme* (1908). As stated above, it is quite likely that Beckett knew these books. Before moving on to discuss Beckett's own interest in the paradoxes of sense and image, then, it is useful to outline some aspects of the Stoic distinction between bodies and incorporeals. The link between the idea of the image found in the Stoics and that developed by Bergson, and the early British modernists via Bergson, is something that Beckett would have recognised.

In *The Logic of Sense*, Deleuze describes how the Stoics 'split' the causal relation, thinking of bodies, including images, as causes, and events, which are incorporeal, as effects.[23] Bodies are the only real things, and we mark this reality in language by using the noun. They are causes which exist in the present and are defined as everything which is able to act or suffer an action.[24] Apart from bodies, however, there are a series of incorporeals, among which is the event, which is understood as a surface effect and expressed using the verb.[25] Also understood as incorporeals are the expressible (or language, from which we derive sense), the void, and time and place.[26]

An important proposition for the Stoics is that things must share the same nature to be able to affect one another: therefore, something which is incorporeal cannot affect a body.[27] This underlines Deleuze's point that the causal relation is effectively split by the Stoics, as, rather than following one from the other, causes (bodies) are grouped with causes and effects (incorporeals) with effects.[28] Yet it is important not to misunderstand this 'split' as involving the complete lack of relation between one and the other. There is, in fact, a relation between cause and effect, as 'the cause is that through which something comes about';[29] that is, the incorporeal effect emerges from the corporeal cause, or, to be more precise, the interrelation of one cause and another cause brings about an effect. Yet causes cannot proceed from effects, nor can one cause cause another cause. What is split, then, is the causal chain as it is habitually imagined, where causes are linked to effects which in turn become causes. This is why Bréhier states that the relation of cause and effect is absent from Stoic philosophy: bodies cannot in truth be said to cause one another; rather, if there is a relation between them it is as 'the moments or aspects of the existence of the same single being'. That is, the split might be understood as another example of nonrelation. One being is not the cause of another; rather, one causes certain things in another.[30] Only bodies exist and they only exist in the present, which is the only aspect of time which might be said to exist; in contrast the future and the past cannot be said to exist, rather, like effects, they subsist or inhere and are incorporeal.[31] Like future and past time, events do not exist in a physical form; rather, they are attributed to bodies, they are happenings or becomings which subsist in the Aion Deleuze describes, which is that time which is not yet here and only just past, the 'split' moment (without any specific mark of division) that evades the fixed present moment.[32]

Using a famous Stoic example, we might say a body cuts another body,[33] yet the *event of being cut* could not itself be thought of as a body: the event is *attributed to* bodies but could not be thought of as a *quality of* one or the other. Sambursky translates Sextus Empiricus' explanation of the Stoic position as follows: 'Every cause is a body which is the cause to a body of something incorporeal happening to it'.[34] Effects do happen, then, but they do not exist in the manner of a body; they have *something* but it is not quite being;[35] they have what Deleuze calls an 'extra-being'.[36] There is, in a physical sense, an interaction of bodies: one cause acts upon another, which suffers the action . . . it is a matter of the juxtaposition and interpenetration of bodies. The effect, however, is that which happens on the surface, and is attributed to bodies. The effect, the event, insofar as it is 'something' (an incorporeal, an extra-being rather than a being) might be considered *a kind of making sense of* the actions of bodies.

A similar point might be made concerning words themselves. Words, in that they pass as vibrations through the air, are bodies, but their *meaning* is incorporeal;[37] the sense does not have a physical presence; rather, it is attributed to the bodies of the words. As Bréhier explains, for the Stoics, 'thought was a body and sound was a body. A body has its own independent nature, its unity. The fact of being signified by a word must, therefore, be added to it as an incorporeal attribute which in no way changes it.'[38] The problem of the isolation of the word from the world, a problem which Beckett meditates upon most thoroughly in *The Unnamable*, can be put another way in relation to Stoic understandings of the expressible as an incorporeal:

Let us consider the complex status of sense or of that which is expressed. On the one hand, it does not exist outside the proposition which expresses it; what is expressed does not exist outside its expression. This is why we cannot say that sense exists, but rather that it inheres or subsists.[39]

The expressible, then, and the event, and becoming, occupy the same terrain, the time of Aion. As Deleuze points out: 'The event is coextensive with becoming, and becoming is itself coextensive with language.'[40] To put this another way, incorporeals share the same nature in that they each contribute to the making of sense: the expressible, or language, is where sense habitually lives, but we have seen here how events are already interpretations; so too 'becoming' might be understood as another way of describing what has just happened or is just about to happen; that is, of making sense of the mixture of bodies. The story of the individual is intimately aligned with the making sense of processes of change (one thinks, for example, of Malone's becomings).

Any act, then, is always an interaction of bodies, yet, as we have seen, the effect is abstracted from bodies. When we think of a violent 'act', however, we usually mean the event. When we speak of what someone does to someone else, we pay attention to the event, not to the bodies which have entered into relation. This, in the light of Stoic logic, is a misunderstanding.

SENSELESS VIOLENCE

The problem of sense was already intimately aligned with questions of violence in Beckett's works well before *What Where*. In his prose works immediately after World War Two numerous events of apparently random or senseless violence are described: Mercier and Camier kill a policeman[41] Molloy assaults a charcoal burner he meets in the woods,[42] and Moran kills the stranger who intrudes into his camp in *Molloy*;[43] Malone is attacked by a stranger who appears at his bedside,[44] and Lemuel kills the philanthropists in *Malone Dies*.[45] All of these events might be interpreted as stemming from a turbulence which develops along a front between order and chaos (with order imposing itself on chaos, and chaos resisting order), yet such meaning is never fully confirmed by the text, as the first-person narrators pass over these incidents without attempting to come to terms with their meaning.

Elsewhere in *Malone Dies*, in recounting the story of Sapo and the Lamberts, the narrator does comment in passing on a violent eruption which seems similar in its nature (although directed at inanimate objects rather than other humans), yet here it is to underline the apparent meaninglessness of such events:

> She sat down, emptied out the lentils on the table and began to sort them. So that soon there were two heaps on the table, one big heap getting smaller and one small heap getting bigger. But suddenly with a furious gesture she swept the two together, annihilating thus in less than a second the work of two or three minutes ... To stop in the middle of a tedious and perhaps futile task was something that Sapo could readily understand .... the moment comes when one desists, because it is the wisest thing to do, discouraged, but not to the extent of undoing all that has been done. But what if her purpose, in sorting the lentils, were not to rid them of all that was not lentil, but only the greater part, what then? I don't know. Whereas there are other tasks, other days, of which one may fairly safely say that they are finished, though I do not see which.[46]

Here the violent gesture is meaningless, as it undoes what has been done already: in effect the eruption negates the task which was on the way to being performed, but this interpretation of meaninglessness itself is put in question as the task itself is shown to be just as meaningless as the eruption which negates it. Violent events, then, seem in part to involve the perhaps meaningless negation of a process which is in train.

What is of further interest here is the dim outline of an idea which these events of negation allow us to see: the senseless act of violence emerges from a sea of equally senseless, though apparently less violent, events; it stands out in its apparent difference, yet it is clearly made of the same stuff from which it emerges. Events, as we have seen, are already interpretations; they are attributed to bodies as that which those bodies do; they are that which makes sense of the actions of bodies, yet, for the Stoics at least, there was always the conclusion to be drawn from this that in being incorporeal such events and such expressibles were always detached from the real, always unable to bring us to a real understanding of things, and so these producers of meaning might paradoxically be considered to be ultimately meaningless.[47]

Such an insight led the Stoics to 'follow nature', so as to live like the sage, and we are in a better position now to see what this means. It is not a naive slogan; rather, it involves an understanding of what nature is, how it is composed of bodies, and only *made sense of* via incorporeals. If one wishes to truly understand, to understand the real, then one must look for understanding outside language; one must look for understanding through the images of bodies themselves, images which themselves are bodies. Is this the secret of the sage, who, like Molloy, lives 'far from words',[48] if, unlike Molloy, in the hope of finding the real? Or the secret of the torment of the Unnamable, who cannot escape from words?

The violent events of Beckett's immediate post-war works might be said in part to offer us descriptions of senseless violence emerging from the senseless interpretations which societies impose. How might we understand the blow of the one who strikes Malone, if not as a desperate effort of the social body to impose meaning on one who is moving away from that 'sense' toward pure image, sensation, not sense? As ever, though, the identification is not neat in Beckett, and the process of negation is more thorough still. That is, if sense is questioned and negated in his works, so too, in other places, is the image or imagination.[49] Beckett tries a number of, at times opposing, strategies of negation, but what is of interest here is the use, rather than the negation, of the image. How might we understand Mercier's and Camier's killing of the policeman, or Lemuel's murders, if not as attempts to avoid clear interpretation, to offer an object which asks to be understood but which frustrates easy interpretation, and Molloy's attack on the charcoal burner if not as an effort to avoid being 'known'? While this may be the case, it might be argued that after these works, in one or two places at least, Beckett returned to the question of violence, yet this time from a different perspective.

BEINGS OF VIOLENCE

If the earlier works describe violent events (incorporeals), then some of the works after this time might be said to describe violent relations rather than violent events. As we have seen in chapter 3, one might understand the interactions which hold Clov and Hamm together in *Endgame* as a violent relation or dysfunctional relationship; indeed, the prototype of such (non)-relations emerges from that of Pozzo and Lucky in *Godot*.[50] Such violent (non)relations might also be seen in *Enough*,[51] *Happy Days*,[52] *How It Is*[53] and various other works, yet I feel a new aspect is added to them in works such as *Play, Come and Go*,[54] *The Lost Ones*,[55] *What Where* and *Quad*,[56] so that these interactions cease being simply relations (or nonrelations) of bodies and become bodies themselves.

A. A. Long notes with regard to the Stoics' physics of bodies:

The Stoics distinguished three kinds of bodies, or perhaps more accurately, four kinds, the fourth being a subdivision of the third: bodies composed of 'separated' parts, such as an army; bodies composed of 'contiguous' parts, such as a house or a ship; 'unified' bodies, such as stones and logs; and fourthly, or a subdivision of the last category, bodies unified and 'grown together', namely, living things.[57]

What leads me to want to think of the above-mentioned works by Beckett as the image of bodies is the manner in which related elements move and interact tightly. The most obvious example of this is *Quad*, where the movements of the participants[58] resemble the movements of particles within a molecule. This movement is rendered diagrammatically by Beckett as follows:[59]

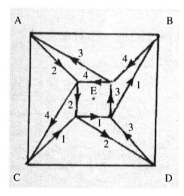

A similar movement occurs in *What Where*; first without words, and then with words as the participants move from position to position.[60] So too *Come and Go* describes such an abstracted movement, which also involves the working through of possible permutations.[61] With regard to Beckett's shorter fiction, the participants in *The Lost Ones* are similarly abstracted, and while the 'molecular' structure outlined by their movements is far more complex (and therefore open to a potentially enormous series of permutations) they too might be thought of as comprising a body.[62] *Play*, which is the earliest of all these works, lacks this air of complete abstraction because of the element of differentiation allowed by the different, though interconnected, stories of each character, yet it should be noted that the three faces are 'so lost to age and aspect as to seem almost part of the urns',[63] and the repetition, as in *What Where* and *Quad*, adds to the feeling that this relation of actions repeated (perhaps to infinity) is discrete; is, that is, an individual thing, or, as Beckett states, an 'object'.

The reading of these works as including images of dysfunctional relations as bodies rests perhaps more on a Spinozian or Epicurean understanding of the body (which considers the body to be formed from elements or atoms which have entered into relations)[64] than the Stoic bodies described by Long, as the Stoic body is not thought of as being made of elements.[65] In effect, for the Stoics there is only one body which exists yet, again paradoxically, it is infinitely divisible. I would suggest, however, that through the repetition and the similarity of the participants, the relations described by Beckett do seem so strongly related as to have 'grown together'. One might ask, then, to what purpose?

While Beckett is best known for the quality of humour in many of his works it is always a humour which hides or reveals a seriousness. When Beckett suggests he will show us *how it is*, then, there is no reason why we should not take him literally; that is, to recognise that at a certain degree of abstraction he is offering us 'the real'. Perhaps the insight this strange description of bodies of relation allows is an understanding, which I am suggesting he shares with the Stoics, of how, on the level of causes and bodies, actions proceed from states of affairs or dispositions. If it is possible to think, using Stoic terminology, that certain of the post-war works such as the 'Trilogy' and *Mercier and Camier* at times represent events, and violent events among other things, then one might claim that certain of Beckett's later works show us not incorporeal events or becomings, but ontological images: images of bodies, dispositions, states of affairs.

Rather than being shown a violent event (which reveals its own meaninglessness at the same time as the meaninglessness of the milieu from which it emerges) these later works might be thought of as developing images of beings, which are at times beings of violence (although certainly not only this). This is not to suggest that *Quad, Come and Go, What Where, Play* and *The Lost Ones* are identical in purpose: on the contrary, each of these shows us images of different states of affairs, different dispositions, and if the latter three at least are in part concerned with violence, then it is a different order of violence in each case (political in *What Where*, interpersonal in *Play* and somehow involving the human condition in *The Lost Ones*). However, each has in common that they present us with the image of a kind of being rather than representing a kind of event. In the case of *What Where* that image is a being of violence, or more specifically a being of political violence, a violence based on ignorance allied with an insatiable desire for that unknowable knowledge that might render infallible control possible.

This process might be understood more fully through reference to the reading of the Stoics offered by Josiah Gould. We have seen how four categories of being were attributed to the Stoics, and these were, in order of priority: substance (of which all being partakes as each individual is a substance), quality (it is a quality which distinguishes one being from another), disposition and relative disposition. Gould goes on to state that in one fragment Chrysippus shows that the emotions correspond to a state or disposition of the soul.[66] On this point, one might also refer to Long, who quotes Aetius to the effect that an image 'is an affection in the soul, which reveals itself and its cause'.[67] Relating this logic to the above arguments one might claim that in *What Where* Beckett creates an ontological image of a being of violence, with violence understood as a disposition or state of affairs, a state of affairs which is not interpreted through events or the sense of language but which, rather, impresses an image upon us which reveals itself and the cause which it is.

Understanding the kind of violence in *What Where* as a state of affairs, as the image of a being or object, rather than an event or a series of events, is further illuminating if one follows Gould's line of thought a little further. He suggests that for Chrysippus:

a cause 'has being and is a body' but that of which it is a cause has neither being nor body (II 336). Zeno had held that that of which the cause is a cause is an 'accident' or a 'predicate'; the cause is that through which something comes about; for example, through wisdom 'being wise' comes into being; through the soul, 'living' comes into being; and through self-control, being self-controlled comes into existence.[68]

If we take these notions and Beckett's images seriously the implications are profound: that is, 'being violent', for example, comes into being through 'violence', not understood as an abstract attribute or an event, but as a thing, a body, a quality which exists as the disposition of a forceful relation between parts (the interrelation of participants) and which projects an image which is impressed upon us. In *What Where*, then, rather than showing us violent events which could only ever be fully understood as being senseless, Beckett shows us an object from the inside, as if we were tasting that object, a being of violence, and thereby allows us to witness how violence, sense and the twin-faced companion to sense in politics, ignorance and the desire to know (to know, that is, the secrets which will give one power over others), are all interrelated and self-perpetuating. If *What Where* offers the image of a being of violence, perhaps it also sheds light on the nature of politics. That is, politics now understood as a human interaction based on inadequate knowledge which leads to violent acts as a means of drawing definitive interpretations (judgements), or a reaction against an inability to draw definitive interpretations, about the other.

It is even possible to read back from this to Beckett's earlier works. If the violent events emerge from a senseless set of events, these events might now, in hindsight, and in the light of the later works, be understood as simply involving incorporeal interpretations of a violent being: the violent being, of, for example, the tedious interrelation of meaningless tasks in the life of Mrs Lambert.

This said it is always useful to keep in mind Beckett's admonitions not to make identifications too neat, and his understanding that writers of fiction might treat philosophy without the utmost seriousness, in mind.[69] Long says that what constitutes the body that has grown together is pneuma, the soul,[70] and here Beckett's philosophical scepticism emerges, as the ancients were never keen to admit true being to something which was in itself necessarily imperfect. The bodies of violence Beckett creates are nothing if not imperfect: indeed, they offer us imperfection in essence. Further, like Spinoza, the Stoics considered self-preservation to be an important aspect of the being of a body,[71] that is, such bodies would have the desire to continue, but these all grow fainter, and betray within themselves a desire to have done.

One also needs to consider the exact nature of the bodies which exist in Beckett's works. In *What Where*, for example, they explicitly state: 'We are the last five./In the present as were we still.'[72] Further, Beckett himself suggested that 'v' (a megaphone in the original version, which he replaced in a German TV version with a distorted larger image of Bam's face) is a being beyond death as it represents 'The image of Bam in the beyond or beyond the grave or whatever you want to call it'.[73] So too, Beckett referred to the lit playing area in this production as the 'field of memory'.[74] None of these things, however, prevent us from considering them to be bodies. A memory is still an image,[75] which in turn are bodies for the Stoics. So too, even if v, who remembers, is read as an image of a 'soul', for the Stoics, the soul is itself also a body, though at a different level of tension,[76] and can continue to exist after it has been separated from the rest of the body. Therefore, to underline the point made above, understanding the work as offering the image of the 'field of memory' of that Bam beyond the grave (v) does not militate against considering this piece as the image of a disposition or state of affairs. Even if it has been internalised by the dead Bam as a field of memory it might still be understood as the disposition of his soul in a determinate state. It is a state which, like the reality of the present discussed above, involves duration, as 'v' leads us through permutations which begin in 'Spring'[77] and end in 'Winter',[78] yet one always remains in 'the present as were we still' (the domain of bodies and the real).

THE IMAGE AND THE REAL

Bréhier shows how the Stoics considered that certain kinds of truth were momentary and subject to change: such changeable truths might be related to the facts of events. Such events are constantly undergoing change, becoming, and so too certain truths are true only at certain times and places; like the events they describe such truths are insubstantial, concerned with the order of incorporeals. Above such truth, then, the Stoics placed 'the real': the real which is related to bodies, and, as everything is an aspect of the one body, this reality is ultimately unchangeable.[79]

We are not limited through Stoic conceptions, however, to thinking of the real in this ultimate state; we are able to conceive of individual bodies, which are individual in relation to those specific qualities which pertain to them.[80] Yet such a distinction, between the true and the real, is important for our purposes here, as it allows us to better understand the difference between the sense or meaning which pertains to the expressible and incorporeals, and the images, or presentations, which pertain to bodies. That is, sense is concerned with relative and constantly shifting truths which play about the surface of things but do not in reality touch those things, whereas images or presentations involve the modification of bodies. Images, indeed, cannot be understood as being apart from bodies. According to Gould, 'A presentation is not something apart from the soul, but is a determinate condition of it . . . a presentation in the soul is, in fact, a modification of it . . . it *is* the soul in a determinate state.'[81] The soul, then, does not make sense of an image; rather the image is that soul in a certain state. As Gould puts it, 'the soul or mind is described as not standing over against a passion but as itself transformed into the passion'.[82] A violent disposition or state of affairs is a body.

In digesting this point, it is important to return to one touched on above: that is, not all images are equally valid. Bréhier, indeed, shows how only comprehensive images are truly real.[83] It is possible, then, that one might be deceived by a false image, or conceive a passion through ignorance, and indeed the notion of 'assent' in Stoic philosophy involves the process of agreeing or not to the validity of images.[84]

One might argue, then, that this has important implications for art, or at least art of a certain type. Art, that is, which concerns itself with states of affairs or dispositions rather than events. To suggest that *What Where* shows us a being of violence is to suggest that it shows us an image of a being formed by a composition of parts which comprises a body whose individuating quality is, precisely, violence. Further, in this case it is clear that this being of violence involves ignorance; that, indeed, this being of violence is composed of ignorance and the vain desire to overcome it.

BAM: Well?
BIM: Nothing.
BAM: He didn't say where?
V: Good.
BIM: Where?
V: Ah!
BAM: Where.
BIM: No.
BAM: You gave him the works?
BIM: Yes.
BAM: And he didn't say where?
BIM: No.
BAM: He wept?
BIM: Yes.
BAM: Screamed?
BIM: Yes.
BAM: Begged for mercy?
BIM: Yes.
BAM: But didn't say where?
BIM: No.
BAM: Then why stop?
BIM: He passed out.
BAM: And you didn't revive him?
BIM: I tried.
BAM: Well?
BIM: I couldn't.
[*Pause.*]
BAM: It's a lie. [*Pause.*] He said where to you. [*Pause.*] Confess he said where to you. [*Pause.*] You'll be given the works until you confess.[85]

In this passage we see how the torture is driven, on the one hand, by the apparent desire to know, to know or make sense of something which cannot be known or made sense of. Further, however, it is clearly also a rigged game, as Bam asks Bim 'where' when, in the instructions he offers before this passage, Bim is only required to get Bom to confess that 'he said it to him'.[86] 'Where' is never mentioned, the question is never asked of Bom and so could never be revealed to Bim. Knowledge here, even potentially, is always only inadequate or partial knowledge.

Following the implications of the earlier discussion, then, such a being of violence paradoxically mixes bodies and incorporeals in showing us how a being of violence emerges from ignorant questioning. That is, the being of ignorance is composed through a desire to fix incorporeals by making sense of things ('what': the event; 'where': the place and the time), which, by their nature cannot be fixed.

Bréhier concludes *La Théorie des incorporels dans l'ancien stoïcisme* by describing how the Stoics abandon the incorporeal realm as a means of understanding the real.[87] In *Chrysippe et l'ancien stoïcisme* he shows how they developed the idea of the 'comprehensive image' as a way around this problem.[88]

In *What is Philosophy?* Deleuze and Guattari talk of works of art as 'beings of sensation' which affect the viewer or reader directly, drawing them into the compound of sensations which is the work of art.[89] In creating an image of a body rather than describing the event, Beckett moves to a different category of being (having moved from the vagaries of the 'something' to the reality of being). One might argue, in relation to his oeuvre as a whole, that the attempt to understand the nature of things through language alone had led him to the impasse of *The Unnamable*. An image of bodies rather than a description of events, then, might be thought of as a possible way around this impasse.

For the Stoics we experience the real via images, impressions, and if we were to come to understand a work of art as a being of sensation, we would be able to experience that thing directly, the work would be able, one might argue, to act directly on and to enter into compound with our souls.

Bam's admonition, 'make sense who may', might be understood as involving a process which is different to such an apprehension of images. Paradoxically the making of sense would move us further from rather than closer to the real. One might see how, strangely, the two forms of understanding (through making sense and apprehending images), while still somehow interinvolved, might be thought *not* to come into contact through Bam's imperative. This is because whoever attempts to make sense will be drawn into a being of violence, entering into this body, as this body is composed of those who are drawn out of their real existence and into the incorporeals of extra-being. In striving only to make sense, then, one misses the truth one seeks by entering into the body of the greater ignorance which, perhaps, and again paradoxically, involves the meaning of our being.

Conclusion

The idea of the image, its nature and its power, both with regard to perception *per se* and perception and apprehension through art, was of key importance to early twentieth-century modernism, and the aesthetic understandings developed by many major English-language writers. The importance of Bergson and his aesthetic theories, which include his theories of the image, is now, after a fairly long eclipse, again being recognised. In part, this study adds to the work of underlining the importance of this recognition.

Yet, through the new impetus and the altered direction given to Bergsonian ideas by the work of Gilles Deleuze, the idea of the image has begun to re-emerge as a key concept in contemporary theories of aesthetics. Deleuze has outlined certain problems which remain pressing in the field of aesthetics, and many of these relate to his understandings of the image, which, while passing through Bergson, are no longer Bergsonian, no longer 'modernist' understandings, but again contemporary. In part, then, this study also contributes to the process of seeking to understand the relevance of the image to contemporary theories of aesthetics.

So too, while his aesthetic understandings were clearly informed by modernism, and the Bergsonian ideas which strongly inflected English-language modernist writing, Beckett has developed the idea of the image more fully than any other writer. That is, he emerged from the modernist moment, bringing key aesthetic assumptions from modernism with him, but he also developed his own practice beyond that moment. The implications of what he has shown images can do have only just begun to be considered. In this sense, although he passed away in 1989, Beckett remains not only our contemporary, but also a writer from the future. Beckett's later plays and prose pieces have still not been fully understood, even while they have long had a strong impact on any audiences fortunate enough to witness them. The implications of what they have done not only to words, but also to images, are only just beginning to be digested. The critic has a role in this slow process. This study, in part, seeks to add to this ongoing endeavour.

WHAT IS AN IMAGE?

One of the goals of this study is the attempt to outline the nature of the image, which has a key role to play in the theories of perception developed by Bergson and Deleuze and in the aesthetic method developed by Beckett. Images are projected from bodies and then 'screened' by the brain in two senses. Firstly, they are projected onto the brain as if it were a cinema screen. Secondly, they are filtered or 'screened' by the brain, so that material considered not of interest is ignored, while material considered of immediate interest is brought into focus. There is a key distinction between the first and second process here, which is crucial to the claims made in this study. The first process involves material which has yet to be interpreted. This material, and the images which comprise it, are understood to be a 'presentation'. The second process already involves interpretation: we interpret images by editing out that which is not of interest and focusing on that which is. This process of editing is equated, by Bergson, with the production of the representation, and I argue that the interplay between the presentation and the representation is crucial to our understanding of artistic practice.

KINDS OF PHILOSOPHICAL IMAGES

Four kinds of philosophical images are sketched in this study. The image of the rocking-chair, which Beckett adapts from Arnold Geulincx, is an example of the first kind. This is the conceptual image: an image used by a philosopher to explain a concept. Michèle Le Doeuff describes how philosophers often use images when their arguments have reached a point of aporia: such images, in effect, paper over the cracks of their argument. I argue that, when Beckett adapts Geulincx's image, the Beckettian image retains an anxiety which is already present in Geulincx's thought. Further, I indicate how kinds of occlusion develop through the process of relay or borrowing, and that, when a source for an image is identified, a new power of that image to affect us is released.

Secondly, I consider the concept of the 'image of thought' and how this might apply to literature. Works of literature do not only comprise ways of thinking, they also, at times, picture what it means to think. I argue that Beckett develops an 'image of thought' in *The Unnamable* which describes an understanding of the self as an absence of self-presence. Beckett again adapts this image from Arnold Geulincx and the description of the cogito he offers, which emphasises the overwhelming ignorance at the centre of human beings. I argue that this Beckettian image resonated profoundly with the post-World War Two intellectual milieu in which it first appeared and that, in turn, it was adapted and made use of by a number of philosophers.

The example of this image of thought displays how images are transportable and translatable between media and disciplines. There is a process of exchange which can be two-way. That is, images are not only drawn from philosophy by writers like Beckett but can be, and are, borrowed in turn by philosophers from literature. Such processes of relay offer examples of how interdisciplinarity can function in practice, and how literature and philosophy might come into contact.

Thirdly, I describe another kind of image which is identified by Henri Bergson: the image which expresses an intuition. Bergson claims that while the original intuition, which gives rise to a philosophical system, is always out of reach, we can approximate it via the image. In *Film*, Beckett responds to Bishop Berkeley's conceptual formulation *esse est percipi*. In doing this, he produces a number of images which might be thought to confront, using the methods of art rather than philosophy, the problem of this formulation. That is, Beckett produces images which examine how this understanding of being might *feel*.

Finally, I discuss the ontological image, the image of being or embodied being. The images developed here are not so much borrowed from philosophy as generated in response to an ontological position described by philosophy. The Ancient Stoics saw emotional states or dispositions as, themselves, embodied. They considered that the image, which impresses itself upon the soul like a signet ring in wax, also comprises a modification of the soul. That is, they believed that such images can carry with them, or themselves comprise, dispositions or kinds of being. I examine the relevance of this to Samuel Beckett by linking a close reading of *What Where*, which I argue creates an image of a being of violence, with a discussion of Stoic understandings of bodies and incorporeals.

While this discussion of the use of the image and its relation to philosophy in the work of Samuel Beckett does not exhaust the use of philosophical images in Beckett, let alone his use of the image *per se*, it is, nevertheless, important to our understanding of it. We have seen how Beckett borrows images not just from the visual arts, but also from philosophical sources. Steps have also been taken toward a fuller understanding of the nature of the image in Beckett's works and its potentials in art more generally.

Notes

INTRODUCTION

1 Emile Bréhier, *The History of Philosophy Vol. 1: The Hellenic Age*, tr. Joseph Thomas (Chicago: University of Chicago Press, 1965), on Aristotle.
2 H. Porter Abbott, "Samuel Beckett and the Arts of Time: Painting, Music, Narrative," in Lois Oppenheim (ed.), *Samuel Beckett and the Arts* (New York: Garland, 1999); Lois Oppenheim, *The Painted Word: Samuel Beckett's Dialogue with Art* (Ann Arbor: University of Michigan Press, 2000); Linda Ben-Zvi (ed.), *Drawing on Beckett: Portraits, Performances, and Cultural Contexts* (Tel Aviv: Assaph Books, 2003).
3 James Knowlson, *Damned to Fame: The Life of Samuel Beckett* (London: Bloomsbury, 1996), pp. 256–8.
4 Owen Jander, 'The Eroica Reading List', [review of *Beethoven: The Music and the Life*, by Lewis Lockwood], *Times Literary Supplement* (4 July 2003), p. 30.
5 Jander states that twentieth-century critics are not happy to think of 'extra musical forces' in relation to Beethoven's music, though Lockwood does look at how the image might help us understand the music. I discuss the process of occlusion in images in chapter 4.
6 Henri Bergson, *An Introduction to Metaphysics*, tr. T. E. Hulme (New York and London: G. Putnam and Sons, 1912).
7 Paul Douglas, *Bergson, Eliot, and American Literature* (Lexington: University of Kentucky Press, 1986); Hilary L. Fink, *Bergson and Russian Modernism 1900–1930* (Evanston: Northwestern University Press, 1999); Robert Ferguson, *The Short Sharp Life of T. E. Hulme* (London: Penguin, 2002); Mary Ann Gillies, *Henri Bergson and British Modernism* (Montreal and Kingston: McGill-Queen's University Press, 1996); Donald R. Maxwell, *The Abacus and the Rainbow: Bergson, Proust, and the Digital-Analogic Opposition* (New York: Peter Lang, 1999); Joyce N. Megay, *Bergson et Proust: Essai de mise au point de la question de l'influence de Bergson sur Proust* (Paris: J. Vrin, 1976).
8 Gilles Deleuze, 'The Exhausted', tr. Anthony Uhlmann, in Daniel W. Smith and Michael A. Greco (eds.), *Essays Critical and Clinical* (Minneapolis: University of Minnesota Press, 1997), pp. 152–74. Gilles Deleuze, 'The

Greatest Irish Film', in *Essays Critical and Clinical*, tr. Daniel W. Smith and Michael A. Greco (Minneapolis: University of Minnesota Press, 1997), pp. 23–6. Another work also draws parallels between the use of image in Beckett and Bacon: Gilles Deleuze, *Francis Bacon: logique de la sensation* (Paris: Editions de la différence, 1996).

9 Henri Bergson, *Matter and Memory*, tr. N. M. Paul and W. S. Palmer (New York: Zone Books, 1991).

10 Gilles Deleuze, *Cinema 1: The Movement-Image*, tr. Hugh Tomlinson and Barbara Habberjam, (Minneapolis: University of Minnesota Press, 1986); Gilles Deleuze, *Cinema 2: The Time-Image*, tr. Hugh Tomlinson and Robert Galeta (Minneapolis: University of Minnesota Press, 1989).

11 For other discussions of Deleuze's use of Bergson, see François Zourabichvili, 'The Eye of Montage: Dziga Vertov and Bergsonian Materialism', in Gregory Flaxman (ed.), *The Brain is the Screen: Deleuze and the Philosophy of Cinema* (Minneapolis, University of Minnesota Press, 2000), pp. 141–52; and Jean-Clet Martin, 'Of Images and Worlds: Toward a Geology of the Cinema', in *The Brain is the Screen: Deleuze and the Philosophy of Cinema*, Gregory Flaxman (ed.), (Minneapolis: University of Minnesota Press, 2000), pp. 61–86.

12 Samuel Beckett, *Disjecta: Miscellaneous Writings and a Dramatic Fragment*, ed. Ruby Cohn (London: John Calder, 1983), pps. 28, 90, 94, 123, 130.

13 Samuel Beckett, *The Complete Short Prose*, ed. Stanley Gontarski (New York: Grove Press, 1995), pp. 182–5.

14 Beckett, *Complete Short Prose*, pp. 169–81.

15 Beckett, *Complete Short Prose*.

16 Samuel Beckett, *How It Is* (New York: Grove Press, 1964), p. 31.

17 Samuel Beckett, *The Complete Dramatic Works* (London: Faber and Faber, 1990).

18 Beckett, *Complete Dramatic Works*.

19 Samuel Beckett, 1933 typescript, Letter 57, 'To Thomas MacGreevy, 6/12/33, 6 Clare St. Dublin', TCD MS 10402, Manuscripts Department, Trinity College Library Dublin, Republic of Ireland.

20 Samuel Beckett, 1936 typescript, 'Notes to Arnold Geulincx, *Ethica, Metaphysica Vera* and *Questiones Quodlibeticae*', TCD MS 10971/6, Manuscripts Department, Trinity College Library Dublin, Republic of Ireland.

21 As I write this edition is in the process of being completed. The work has been translated by Martin Wilson for an edition to be edited by myself and Han van Ruler. The standard Latin edition, which Beckett consulted is: Arnold Geulincx, *A. Geulincx Antverpiensis Opera philosophica*, 3 vols., ed. J. P. N. Land (The Hague: Martin Nijhoff, 1891–3).

22 Samuel Beckett, *Film: complete scenario, illustrations, production shots*, With the essay, 'On Directing *Film*' by Alan Schneider, (New York: Grove, 1969).

23 Beckett, *Complete Dramatic Works*.

1 REPRESENTATION AND PRESENTATION: DELEUZE,
BERGSON, PEIRCE AND 'THE IMAGE'

1 Henri Bergson, *Matter and Memory*, tr. N. M. Paul and W. S. Palmer (New York: Zone Books, 1991), 125.
2 Samuel Beckett, *The Complete Short Prose*, ed. Stanley Gontarski (New York: Grove Press, 1995), p. 168.
3 Michael Hardt, *Gilles Deleuze: An Apprenticeship in Philosophy* (London: University College London Press, 1993), pp. xvii–xxi.
4 Ibid., pp. xviii–xix.
5 Stephen Gaukroger, *Descartes: An Intellectual Biography* (Oxford: Clarendon Press, 1995), pp. 119–23.
6 See Paul Douglas, *Bergson, Eliot, and American Literature* (Lexington: University of Kentucky Press, 1986); Hilary L. Fink, *Bergson and Russian Modernism 1900–1930.* (Evanston: Northwestern University Press, 1999); Robert Ferguson, *The Short Sharp Life of T. E. Hulme* (London: Penguin, 2002); Mary Ann Gillies, *Henri Bergson and British Modernism* (Montreal and Kingston: McGill-Queen's University Press, 1996); Donald R. Maxwell, *The Abacus and the Rainbow: Bergson, Proust, and the Digital-Analogic Opposition* (New York: Peter Lang, 1999); Joyce N. Megay, *Bergson et Proust: Essai de mise au point de la question de l'influence de Bergson sur Proust* (Paris: J. Vrin, 1976).
7 Notably D. N. Rodowick, *Gilles Deleuze's Time Machine* (Durham: Duke University Press, 1997); and Gregory Flaxman (ed.), *The Brain is the Screen: Deleuze and the Philosophy of Cinema* (Minneapolis: University of Minnesota Press, 2000).
8 Paul Redding, *The Logic of Affect* (New York: Cornell University Press, 1999), p. 38.
9 Ibid., pp. 90–123.
10 Ibid., p. 56.
11 A number of philosophers, however, have demonstrated how important the image is within philosophical thinking. See Friedrich Nietzsche, *The Birth of Tragedy: Out of the Spirit of Music* (London: Penguin, 1993); Henri Bergson, 'Philosophical Intuition', in *The Creative Mind* (New York: Philosophical Library, 1946), pp. 126–52; and Michèle Le Doeuff, *The Philosophical Imaginary*, tr. Colin Gordon (London: The Athlone Press, 1989).
12 Bergson, *Matter and Memory*, p. 9.
13 Ibid., p. 37.
14 Ibid., p. 17.
15 Ibid., p. 19.
16 Ibid., p. 47.
17 Ibid., p. 30.
18 Ibid., pp. 19–22.
19 Ibid., pp. 19–22, 74.
20 Ibid., pp. 35–6.

21 This complex process, implied in Bergson's theories, is discussed elsewhere in Deleuze's work in relation to Spinoza. See 'On the Difference between the Ethics and Morality', in Gilles Deleuze, *Spinoza: Practical Philosophy*, tr. Robert Hurley (San Francisco: City Lights Books, 1988).

22 Bergson, *Matter and Memory*, p. 39.

23 Gilles Deleuze, *Cinema 2: The Time-Image*, tr. Hugh Tomlinson and Robert Galeta (Minneapolis: University of Minnesota Press, 1989), pp. 274–5, my italics.

24 Ibid., p. 272.

25 Ibid., p. 272.

26 See Bergson, *Matter and Memory*, pp. 44–5, 84.

27 Gustave Flaubert, *Dictionnaire des idées reçues: suivi du Catalogue des idées chic* (Paris: Aubier, 1978).

28 Vicktor Shklovsky, 'The Resurrection of the Word' in *Russian Formalism: A Collection of Articles and Texts in Translation*, ed. Stephen Bann and John E. Bowlt (Edinburgh: Scottish Academic Press, 1973), pp. 41–7.

29 Marcel Proust, *À la recherche du temps perdu*, vol. I, ed. Jean-Yves Tadié (Paris: Gallimard, 1987).

30 Samuel Beckett, *Proust and Three Dialogues with Georges Duthuit* (London: John Calder, 1987).

31 Gilles Deleuze, *Cinema 1: The Movement-Image*, tr. Hugh Tomlinson and Barbara Habberjam (Minneapolis: University of Minnesota Press, 1986), p. 215.

32 Deleuze, *Cinema 1*, p. 215.

33 Gilles Deleuze, *Francis Bacon: logique de la sensation*, (Paris: Editions de la différence, 1996), p. 9.

34 Bergson, *Matter and Memory*, pp. 153–4.

35 Ezra Pound, *Make It New* (London: Faber and Faber, 1934).

36 Shklovsky, 'Resurrection of the Word'.

37 Gilles Deleuze, 'The Brain is the Screen: An Interview with Gilles Deleuze', tr. Marie Therese Guirgis, in Gregory Flaxman (ed.), *The Brain is the Screen: Deleuze and the Philosophy of Cinema* (Minneapolis: University of Minnesota Press, 2000), p. 371.

38 Bréhier states that this can be translated as 'representation or image', and, somewhat confusingly for our purposes Bréhier chooses 'representation'. The term, however, clearly refers to the image as it has been defined here, as it designates, 'the impression made on the soul by the real object and which is analogous according to Zeno to the impression of a seal on wax' (see Emile Bréhier, *The History of Philosophy Vol. 2: The Hellenistic and Roman Age*, tr. Wade Baskin (Chicago: University of Chicago Press, 1965), p. 38), which corresponds with the notion of presentation defined by the Direct Realists. For further translations of this term see note 9, chapter 7, below.

39 Emile Bréhier, *The History of Philosophy Vol. 1: The Hellenic Age*, tr. Joseph Thomas (Chicago: University of Chicago Press, 1965), p. 40.

40 See Steven Connor, *Samuel Beckett: Repetition, Theory and Text* (Oxford: Basil Blackwell, 1988).

41 Samuel Beckett, *Eleutheria*, tr. Barbara Wright, (London: Faber, 1996).

42 Dougald McMillan and Martha Fehsenfeld, *Beckett in the Theatre: The Author as Practical Playwright and Director* (London: John Calder, 1988), pp. 30–1.

43 Deleuze, *Cinema 1*, pp. 210–11.

44 Samuel Beckett, *The Complete Dramatic Works* (London: Faber and Faber, 1990).

45 Charles Sanders Peirce, *Peirce on Signs*, ed. James Hoopes (Chapel Hill: University of North Carolina Press, 1991), p. 239.

46 Ibid., p. 252.

47 Deleuze, *Cinema 2*, p. 31.

48 The affection-image, the action-image and the relation-image, which correspond to Peirce's categories of Firstness, Secondness and Thirdness. Ibid., p. 31.

49 Ibid., p. 31.

50 Peirce, *Peirce on Signs*, pp. 188–9.

51 Ibid., p. 141.

52 Bergson, *Matter and Memory*, p. 9.

53 See Peirce, *Peirce on Signs*, p. 189.

54 This process of reflex recognition is related to systems that are socially determined and belong to groups (such as language) developed through experience or work directly through stimulus response as true reflex.

55 Bergson, *Matter and Memory*, pp. 44–5, 84.

56 Peirce, *Peirce on Signs*, p. 189.

57 Peirce spends a good deal of time critiquing the notion of 'intuition', arguing that it is impossible (ibid., pp. 34–53). It should be noted that he is not directly confronting Bergson here; rather, he is critiquing a notion of intuition which considers it to offer a direct kind of conceptual knowledge, such as Descartes's 'clear and distinct' idea, which Peirce sees as being put forth as occurring without any prior interpretation. I would argue that Bergson's intuition is a more complex concept, one which does not give one immediate access to clear ideas; rather, the intuition is felt and carries with it the imperative that one seeks to express it, but it can never be adequately contained either by concepts or images (see Henri Bergson, 'Philosophical Intuition', in *The Creative Mind* (New York: Philosophical Library, 1946), pp. 126–52). From this point of view Peirce's critiques might be said to be directed at a different conception of intuition than that found in Bergson. This is not, by any means, to claim they would have been in complete agreement.

58 Bergson, *Matter and Memory*, p. 125.

59 Bergson, *An Introduction to Metaphysics*, tr. T. E. Hulme (New York and London: G. Putnam and Sons, 1912), pp. 43–45.

60 Ibid., pp. 43–5.

61 Ibid., pp. 5–6.

62 Ibid., pp. 3–4.

63 Peirce, *Peirce on Signs*, p. 189.
64 Bergson, *Introduction to Metaphysics*, p. 16.

2 BECKETT'S AESTHETIC WRITINGS AND 'THE IMAGE'

1 Samuel Beckett, *Disjecta: Miscellaneous Writings and a Dramatic Fragment*, ed. Ruby Cohn (London: John Calder, 1983), p. 90.
2 Samuel Beckett, *Watt* (London: Picador, 1988), p. 255.
3 Ibid., p. 137.
4 See ibid.
5 Ibid., p. 135: 'The first attack directed at the seized object, independently of its qualities, in its indifference, its inertia, its latency'. (My translations throughout.)
6 Ibid., p. 136: 'they are only one [thing] in this, in that they are all things, the thing, thingness'.
7 Bergson's discussion of Bishop Berkeley's understanding of the term 'thing' is of relevance here. According to Bergson, Berkeley, objects to the word 'thing' because it designates a resevoir of possibilities; that is, because it has not been completely understood or interpreted. Henri Bergson, 'Philosophical Intuition', in *The Creative Mind* (New York: Philosophical Library, 1946), p. 137. I discuss this further in chapter 6 below.
8 Beckett, *Disjecta*, p. 136: 'Because what remains representable if the essence of the object is to elude the representation?'
9 Ibid.: 'What remains is to represent the conditions of this evasion'.
10 Ibid.: 'I cannot see the object, so as to represent it, because it is what it is.'
11 Ibid.: 'I cannot see the object, so as to represent it, because I am what I am.'
12 'Letter to Georges Duthuit, 9–10 March 1949', tr. Walter Redfern, in S. E. Gontarski and Anthony Uhlmann (eds.), *Beckett after Beckett* (Gainesville: University Press of Florida, 2006), pp. 15–21.
13 Beckett, *Disjecta*.
14 Ibid., p. 26.
15 See ibid.
16 Henri Bergson, *An Introduction to Metaphysics*, tr. T. E. Hulme (New York and London: G. Putnam and Sons, 1912), pp. 5–6.
17 Beckett, *Disjecta*, p. 27.
18 Gilles Deleuze and Félix Guattari, *What is Philosophy?*, tr. Hugh Tomlinson and Graham Burchell (New York: Columbia University Press, 1994), p. 175.
19 James Joyce, *Stephen Hero* (London: Grafton Books, 1986), p. 154.
20 I have discussed the distinction between perception and apprehension in detail elsewhere. Perception is understood with reference to Bergson's understanding of the representation which involves substraction, whereas 'apprehension' is related to the presentation which appears as a whole. See Anthony Uhlmann, *Beckett and Poststructuralism* (Cambridge: Cambridge University Press, 1999), chapter 2.
21 Beckett, *Disjecta*, p. 28.

22 Samuel Beckett, *Proust and Three Dialogues with Georges Duthuit* (London: John Calder, 1987), p. 23; cited below.

23 Beckett, *Disjecta*, p. 70.

24 Ibid., p. 94.

25 Ibid., p. 94.

26 Ibid., p. 94.

27 See Paul Douglas, *Bergson, Eliot, and American Literature* (Lexington: University of Kentucky Press, 1986); Mary Ann Gillies, *Henri Bergson and British Modernism* (Montreal and Kingston: McGill-Queen's University Press, 1996); Robert Ferguson, *The Short Sharp Life of T. E. Hulme* (London: Penguin, 2002).

28 See Joyce N. Megay, *Bergson et Proust: Essai de mise au point de la question de l'influence de Bergson sur Proust* (Paris: J. Vrin, 1976); Donald R. Maxwell, *The Abacus and the Rainbow: Bergson, Proust, and the Digital-Analogic Opposition* (New York: Peter Lang, 1999).

29 Gilles Deleuze, 'The Brain is the Screen: An Interview with Gilles Deleuze' tr. Marie Therese Guirgis, in Gregory Flaxman (ed.), *The Brain is the Screen: Deleuze and the Philosophy of Cinema*, (Minneapolis: University of Minnesota Press, 2000), p. 367.

30 A similar point is made by the Stoics, who will be discussed in detail in chapter 7. 'The [image] of a thing is produced in the soul by the thing itself, but what can be expressed is what the soul represents to itself with respect to the thing and not what the thing produces in the soul.' See Emile Bréhier, *The History of Philosophy Vol. 1: The Hellenic Age*, tr. Joseph Thomas (Chicago: University of Chicago Press, 1965).

31 Rachel Burrows, 1931 ms. 'Notes to lectures by Samuel Beckett on Gide and Racine at Trinity College Dublin', TCD MIC 60, Manuscripts Department, Trinity College Library Dublin, Republic of Ireland, pp. 4–5.

32 Beckett, *Disjecta*, p. 75.

33 Ibid., p. 78.

34 Quoted in Robert Ferguson, *The Short Sharp Life of T. E. Hulme* (London: Penguin, 2002), p. 64.

35 Ferguson, *The Short Sharp Life of T. E. Hulme*, p. 64.

36 Ferguson, *The Short Sharp Life of T. E. Hulme*, p. 64.

37 Samuel Beckett, 1938 typescript, Letter 155, 'To Thomas MacGreevy, 31/1/38 [Hotel] Liberia [Paris]', TCD MS 10402, Manuscripts Department, Trinity College Library Dublin, Republic of Ireland.

38 Samuel Beckett, *Dream of Fair to Middling Women* (New York: Arcade/Riverrun, 1993).

39 Gilles Deleuze, 'The Exhausted', tr. Anthony Uhlmann, in Daniel W. Smith and Michael A. Greco (eds.), *Essays Critical and Clinical* (Minneapolis: University of Minnesota Press, 1997), pp. 152–74.

40 Though Deleuze does not cite the following letter, which to date remains unpublished, in support of this thesis, Beckett told Thomas MacGreevy in 1948 that '*Molloy* is a long book, the second last [sic] of the series begun with

Murphy, if it can be said to be a series. The last is begun and then I hope I'll hear no more of him' (Samuel Beckett, 1948 typescript, Letter 175, "To Thomas MacGreevy, 4/1/48 Paris", TCD MS 10402, Manuscripts Department, Trinity College Library Dublin, Republic of Ireland).

41 Samuel Beckett, *The Complete Short Prose*, ed. Stanley Gontarski (New York: Grove Press, 1995), p. 168.
42 Beckett, *Disjecta*.
43 Deleuze, 'The Exhausted', p. 159.
44 Ibid., p. 160.
45 Ibid., p. 160.
46 Ibid., p. 161.
47 Ibid., p. 161.
48 Gilles Deleuze, 'The Greatest Irish Film', in *Essays Critical and Clinical*, tr. Daniel W. Smith and Michael A. Greco (Minneapolis: University of Minnesota Press, 1997), pp. 23–6.
49 Gilles Deleuze, *Francis Bacon: logique de la sensation* (Paris: Editions de la différence, 1996).
50 Ibid., p. 30.
51 Samuel Beckett, *The Complete Dramatic Works* (London: Faber and Faber, 1990), p. 334.
52 Deleuze, *Francis Bacon*, pp. 16, 25.
53 Ibid., pp. 25–6.
54 Beckett, *Complete Short Prose*.
55 'What a relief the Mont Ste. Victoire after all the anthropomorphized landscape – van Goyen, Avercamp, the Ruysdaels, Hobbema, even Glaude, Wilson & Crome Yellow Esq., or paranthropomorphised by Watteau so that the Débarquement seems an illustration of 'poursuivre ta pente pourvu qu'elle soit en montant', or hyperanthropomorphized by Rubens – Tellus in record travail, or castrated by Corot; after all the landscape 'promoted' to the emotions of the hiker, postulated as <u>concerned</u> with the hiker (what an impertinence, worse than Aesop & the animals), alive the way a lap or a <u>fist</u> is alive. Cézanne seems to have been the first to see landscape & state it as material of a strictly peculiar order, incommensurable with all human expressions whatsoever. Atomistic landscape with no velleities of vitalism, landscape with personality à la rigueur, but personality in its own terms'. Samuel Beckett, 1934 typescript, Letter 63, 'To Thomas MacGreevy, 8/9/34, 34 Gertrude St, S.W. 10.', TCD MS 10402, Manuscripts Department, Trinity College Library Dublin, Republic of Ireland.
56 'You develop the Watteau indication very differently from the way it was in my mind, less philosophically and emphatically and probably more justly, certainly in a way that is justified by what leads up to and away from it as my idea of "inorganic juxtaposition" and "non-anthropomorphised humanity" would not have been.' Samuel Beckett, 1938 typescript, Letter 155, 'To Thomas MacGreevy, 31/1/38 [Hotel] Liberia [Paris]'.
57 Deleuze, *Francis Bacon*, p. 9.

58 Ibid., p. 10.
59 Beckett, *Complete Dramatic Works*.
60 Note Beckett's reticence to tell actors what his works might mean, and his preference to simply offer situations.
61 Deleuze, *Francis Bacon*, p. 14.
62 Beckett comes to strikingly similar conclusions in 'Peintres de l'Empêchement', see, in particular, the bottom of page 135, Beckett, *Disjecta*.
63 Deleuze, *Francis Bacon*, pp. 28, 70.
64 Ibid., p. 71.
65 Ibid., p. 27.
66 Ibid., p. 27, my translation.
67 Deleuze, 'The Exhausted', p. 158.
68 Beckett, *Proust*, p. 23.

3 RELATION AND NONRELATION

1 Samuel Beckett, *Proust and Three Dialogues with Georges Duthuit* (London: John Calder, 1987).
2 Judith E. Dearlove, *Accommodating the Chaos: Samuel Beckett's Nonrelational Art* (Durham: Duke University Press, 1982).
3 Samuel Beckett, *Dream of Fair to Middling Women* (New York: Arcade/ Riverrun, 1993).
4 Ibid., pp. 10–11, 55, 182–3.
5 Ibid., pp. 10–11.
6 Samuel Beckett, *Murphy* (New York: Grove Press, 1957).
7 Beckett, *Dream of Fair to Middling Women*, pp. 27–8.
8 Ibid., pp. 9–11.
9 Ibid., p. 182–3.
10 Samuel Beckett, 'Letter to Georges Duthuit, 9–10 March 1949', tr. Walter Redfern, in S. E. Gontarski and Anthony Uhlmann (eds.), *Beckett after Beckett* (Gainesville: University Press of Florida, 2006), p. 19; for the French original, see p. 16.
11 Beckett, *Dream of Fair to Middling Women*, p. 11.
12 Samuel Beckett, *The Complete Dramatic Works* (London: Faber and Faber, 1990).
13 Beckett, *Dream of Fair to Middling Women*, p. 141.
14 Samuel Beckett, *More Pricks Than Kicks* (London: Picador, 1974).
15 Samuel Beckett, *Watt* (London: Picador, 1988).
16 C. J. Ackerley, *Demented Particulars: The Annotated Murphy* (Talahassee: Journal of Beckett Studies Books, 1998).
17 Samuel Beckett, *Beckett's Dream Notebook*, edited, annotated and with an introductory essay by John Pilling (Reading: Beckett International Foundation, 1999).
18 Beckett, *Dream of Fair to Middling Women*, p. 138–9.
19 Beckett, *More Pricks Than Kicks*, p. 55.
20 Beckett, *Dream of Fair to Middling Women*, p. 211.

21 Beckett, *More Pricks Than Kicks*, p. 128.
22 Ibid., p. 170.
23 Ibid., p. 170.
24 Ibid.
25 The drawing of a pun, the use of symbols and the reference to a source are clearly connected, as is apparent in the word 'allusion', the main meanings of which include, 'a play upon words, a word-play, a pun'; 'a symbolical reference or likening; a metaphor, parable, allegory'; and 'a covert, implied, or indirect reference; a passing or incidental reference' (*The Compact Oxford English Dictionary*).
26 Beckett, *More Pricks Than Kicks*, p. 120.
27 Samuel Beckett, *Molloy* (New York: Grove, 1955), p. 41.
28 Beckett, *Murphy*, p. 63.
29 Ackerley, *Demented Particulars*, p. 90.
30 Beckett, *Murphy*, p. 93.
31 Ibid., p. 214.
32 Ibid., p. 225.
33 Ibid., pp. 234–5.
34 Ibid., p. 232.
35 Beckett, *Watt*, p. 247.
36 Ibid., p. 27.
37 Ibid., p. 27.
38 Ibid., pp. 114–15; see also pp. 132–5.
39 Gilles Deleuze, 'The Exhausted', tr. Anthony Uhlmann, in Daniel W. Smith and Michael A. Greco (eds.), *Essays Critical and Clinical* (Minneapolis: University of Minnesota Press, 1997), p. 153.
40 Ibid., p. 154.
41 Samuel Beckett, *The Unnamable* (New York: Grove, 1958).
42 Samuel Beckett, *The Complete Short Prose*, ed. Stanley Gontarski (New York: Grove Press, 1995).
43 Beckett, *Complete Dramatic Works*.
44 Beckett, *Watt*, p. 82.
45 Samuel Beckett, *Mercier and Camier* (London: Picador, 1988), p. 58.
46 Beckett, *Complete Dramatic Works*.
47 Beckett, *Mercier and Camier*, pp. 61–2.
48 Beckett, *Molloy*, p. 68.
49 Samuel Beckett, *How It Is* (New York: Grove Press, 1964), p. 30.
50 Beckett, *How It Is*, p. 30.
51 Beckett, *The Unnamable*, p. 39.
52 Beckett, *Molloy*, p. 117.
53 Beckett, *Complete Dramatic Works*, p. 150.
54 Beckett, *Molloy*, p. 54.
55 Ibid., pp. 52–3.
56 Beckett, *The Unnamable*, p. 51.
57 Beckett, *Complete Dramatic Works*.

58 James Knowlson, *Damned to Fame: The Life of Samuel Beckett* (London: Bloomsbury, 1996), p. 516.

59 See C. J. Ackerley and S. E. Gontarski, *The Grove Companion to Samuel Beckett* (New York: Grove Press, 2004), p. 47.

60 Gilles Deleuze, *Proust and Signs*, tr. Richard Howard (Minneapolis: University of Minnesota Press, 2000), p. 97.

61 Beckett, *Complete Dramatic Works*.

62 These comments from Beckett are cited in the Addenda on the DVD for the *Beckett on Film* production of *What Where*. *Beckett on Film, 19 Films by 19 Directors*, produced by Michael Colgan and Alan Moloney (Dublin: Blue Angel Films, 2001).

63 Beckett, *Complete Short Prose*.

64 Ibid.

65 Ibid.

66 Ibid.

67 Ibid.

68 Ibid.

69 Ibid.

70 Ibid.

71 Ibid.

72 Ibid.

73 Samuel Beckett, *Nohow On: Company, Ill Seen Ill Said, Worstward Ho* (London: John Calder, 1991).

74 *First Love*, 'The Expelled', 'The Calmative', 'The End', in Beckett, *Complete Short Prose*.

75 Samuel Beckett, *Malone Dies* (New York: Grove Press, 1956).

76 Beckett, *Complete Short Prose*, p. 35.

77 Beckett cited in Gontarski, 'Introduction', in Beckett, *Complete Short Prose*, p. xvi.

78 Beckett cited in ibid., p. xvi.

79 Beckett, *Mercier and Camier*, p. 7.

80 Beckett, *Dream of Fair to Middling Women*, pp. 9–10.

81 Beckett, *More Pricks Than Kicks*, p. 35.

82 Beckett, *Malone Dies*, pp. 48–50.

83 Beckett, *Complete Dramatic Works*.

84 Ibid.

85 Ibid.

86 Ibid.

87 Deleuze, 'The Exhausted', p. 159.

88 See Deleuze's comments on 'the indefinite' in ibid., p. 158.

89 Samuel Beckett, *Disjecta: Miscellaneous Writings and a Dramatic Fragment*, ed. Ruby Cohn (London: John Calder, 1983), p. 172.

90 'What is tedious about the language of words is the way in which it is burdened with calculations, memories and stories: it cannot avoid them' (Deleuze, 'The Exhausted', p. 159).

91 Ezra Pound, 'In a Station of the Metro', in Alexander W. Allison et al. (eds.), *The Norton Anthology of Poetry*, 3rd edn (New York: Norton, 1983), p. 963.

92 Beckett, *Dream of Fair to Middling Women*, p. 1.

93 Israel Shenker, '"Moody Man of Letters". Interview with Samuel Beckett', *The New York Times*, section 2 (6 May 1956), p. 3.

94 'Intention' of course, is a word which fell upon hard times in the twentieth century. The term 'intentional fallacy' has long hardened into dogma among those resistant to thought.

95 Beckett, 'Letter to Georges Duthuit', p. 19.

96 Tom F. Driver, 'Beckett by the Madeleine', *Columbia University Forum* (Summer, 1961), pp. 21–5.

97 Ibid., p. 23.

98 Gary Saul Morson and Caryl Emerson, *Mikhail Bakhtin: Creation of a Prosaics* (Stanford: Stanford University Press, 1990), p. 286. My thanks go to Stephen McLaren for directing me to this source.

99 Ibid., p. 286.

100 Beckett, *Dream of Fair to Middling Women*, p. 12.

101 Where, in a review of Jack Yeats, 'two values are related to a third' (Beckett, *Disjecta*, p. 90).

102 Beckett, *Watt*, p. 70.

103 Ibid., p. 71–2.

104 Ibid., p. 126–7.

105 Ibid., p. 128.

106 'One result of the analysis of interpretation in the nineteenth century was the recognition of the "hermeneutic circle," first developed by Schleiermacher. The circularity of interpretation concerns the relation of parts to the whole: the interpretation of each part is dependent on the interpretation of the whole. But interpretation is circular in a stronger sense: if every interpretation is itself based on interpretation, then the circle of interpretation, even if it is not vicious, cannot be escaped.' James Bohman, 'Hermeneutics', in *The Cambridge Dictionary of Philosophy*, ed. Robert Audi (Cambridge: Cambridge University Press, 1995), pp. 323–4.

107 Beckett, *Complete Short Prose*, p. 17.

108 Ibid., p. 27.

109 Ibid., pp. 36, 37.

110 Ibid., p. 62.

111 Ibid., p. 33.

112 Ibid., pp. 69–70.

113 Ibid., p. 17.

114 Ibid., p. 19.

115 Ibid., pp. 35–6.

116 All works cited in Beckett, *Complete Dramatic Works*.

117 All works cited in ibid.

118 All works cited in ibid.

119 Beckett, *Complete Dramatic Works*.

120 Ibid.
121 All works in Beckett, *Complete Short Prose*.
122 Ibid.
123 Both in Beckett, *Complete Dramatic Works*.
124 Beckett, *Watt*, p. 226–7.

4 THE PHILOSOPHICAL IMAGINARY

1 Michèle Le Doeuff, *The Philosophical Imaginary*, tr. Colin Gordon (London: The Athlone Press, 1989).
2 Ibid., p. 1.
3 Ibid., p. 19.
4 Ibid., pp. 8–9.
5 Ibid., p. 11.
6 Samuel Beckett, *Disjecta: Miscellaneous Writings and a Dramatic Fragment*, ed. Ruby Cohn (London: John Calder, 1983).
7 Le Doeuff, *The Philosophical Imaginary*, p. 3.
8 Ibid., p. 3.
9 Ibid., p. 4.
10 Ibid., p. 4.
11 Ibid., pp. 9–19.
12 Ibid., p. 19.
13 Ibid., p. 9, see also pp. 57–99.
14 Beckett, *Disjecta*, p. 136.
15 Gilles Deleuze and Félix Guattari, *What is Philosophy?*, tr. Hugh Tomlinson and Graham Burchell (New York: Columbia University Press, 1994), p. 184.
16 The major part of the work (Tractate 1 and extensive Annotations) was already published in Geulincx's life under name of *De Virtute et primis ejus Proprietatibus*, and in Dutch as *Van de hoofddeugden*. See H. J. De Vleeschauwer, *Le 'De Virtute et primis ejus Proprietatibus' d'Arnout Geulincx et sa traduction flammande 'Van de Hoofdeuchden'. Introduction et Textes* (Pretoria: Van Schaik, 1961); and Arnold Geulincx, *Van de hoofddeugden. De eerste tuchtverhandeling*, ed. with an introduction and notes by Cornelis Verhoeven (Baarn: Ambo, 1986).
17 H. J. De Vleeschauwer, *Three Centuries of Geulincx Research* (Pretoria: Communications of the University of South Africa, 1957), pp. 13–30.
18 Victor Vander Haeghen, *Geulincx. Etude sur sa vie, sa philosophie et ses ouvrages* (Paris: Gand, 1886), p. 186.
19 D. J. McCracken, *Thinking and Valuing: An Introduction, Partly Historical, to the Study of the Philosophy of Value* (London: Macmillan, 1950).
20 De Vleeschauwer, *Three Centuries of Geulincx Research*.
21 G. Nuchelmans, *Geulincx's Containment Theory of Logic* (Amsterdam, 1988).
22 Steven Nadler, 'Occasionalism and the Mind-Body Problem', in M. A. Stewart (ed.), *Studies in Seventeenth-Century European Philosophy*

(New York: Clarendon, 1997); Steven Nadler, *Spinoza: A Life* (Cambridge: Cambridge University Press, 1999).

23 Han van Ruler, 'Minds, Forms, and Spirits: the Nature of Cartesian Disenchantment' *Journal of the History of Ideas*, vol. 61 (2000), pp. 381–95; Han van Ruler, 'Arnout Geulincx', in Wiep van Bunge, Henri Krop, Han van Ruler and Paul Schuurman (eds.), *The Dictionary of Seventeenth and Eighteenth-Century Dutch Philosophers* (London: Thoemmes Continuum, 2004).

24 E. Terraillon, *La Morale de Geulincx* (Paris: Félix Alcan, 1912).

25 H. J. De Vleeschauwer, 'Les Antécédents du Transcendentalisme kantien. Geulincx et Kant', *Kantstudien* (1953–4), pp. 245–73; H. J. De Vleeschauwer, 'L'Occasionalisme et la condition humaine chez A. Geulincx', *Kantstudien* (1958), pp. 109–24; De Vleeschauwer, *Le "De Virtute et primis ejus Proprietatibus" d'Arnout Geulincx*; H. J. De Vleeschauwer, *Les Plans d'études au XVIIe siècle. I: Le Plan de Descartes; II: Le Plan d'A. Geulincx* (Pretoria: Communications of the University of South Africa, 1962 and 1964); H. J. De Vleeschauwer, *Le Problème du suicide dans la morale de Geulincx* (Pretoria: Communications of the University of South Africa, 1965).

26 Alain de Lattre, *L'Occasionalisme d'Arnold Geulincx: étude sur la constitution de la doctrine* (Paris: Editions de Minuit, 1967); Alain de Lattre, *Arnold Geulincx: présentation, choix de textes et traduction* (Paris: Seghers, 1970).

27 Bernard Rousset, *Geulincx: Entre Descartes et Spinoza* (Paris: Vrin, 1999).

28 A handful of studies in other languages, particularly German, and translations into Spanish and Italian, have also appeared. See De Vleeschauwer, *Three Centuries of Geulincx Research*.

29 Martin Wilson's translation of *Metaphysica Vera* was published in 1999. Wilson has just completed a translation of Geulincx's *Ethica* for an edition edited by Han van Ruler, Wilson and myself which will be published by Brill Press in late 2006 or early 2007.

30 This has often been translated as 'Where one is worth nothing, one should want nothing'. The Latin, *valeo*, carries the meaning both of 'to be able to, to have force' and 'to be worth'. Beckett makes use of both, in what seem to be translations of this: 'worth nothing' in *Murphy* and 'can do nothing' in *The Unnamable* (Samuel Beckett, *The Unnamable* (New York: Grove Press, 1958), p. 165). I have chosen to use 'can do' as this is most consistent with Geulincx's system.

31 Sighle Kennedy, *Murphy's Bed: A Study of Real Sources and Sur-real Associations in Samuel Beckett's First Novel* (Lewisburg: Bucknell University Press, 1971).

32 Beckett, *Disjecta*, p. 113.

33 James Knowlson, *Damned to Fame: The Life of Samuel Beckett* (London: Bloomsbury, 1996), p. 219.

34 Samuel Beckett, 1936 typescript, 'Notes to Arnold Geulincx, *Ethica*, *Metaphysica Vera* and *Questiones Quodlibeticae*', TCD MS 10971/6, Manuscripts Department, Trinity College Library Dublin, Republic of Ireland.

35 C. J. Ackerley, *Demented Particulars: The Annotated Murphy* (Talahassee: Journal of Beckett Studies Books, 1998).

36 Rupert Wood, 'Murphy, Beckett, Geulincx, God', *The Journal of Beckett Studies*, vol. 2 (1993), pp. 27–51.

37 See James Acheson, *Samuel Beckett's Artistic Theory and Practice* (London: Macmillan, 1997), pp. 50–5; Lance St John Butler, *Samuel Beckett and the Meaning of Being* (St Martin's Press: New York, 1984), pp. 156–8; Hugh Kenner, *Samuel Beckett: A Critical Study* (Berkeley: University of California Press, 1968), pp. 83–5; John Pilling, *Samuel Beckett* (London: Routledge and Kegan Paul, 1976), pp. 114–16; John Pilling, *Beckett before Godot* (Cambridge: Cambridge University Press, 1997), pp. 145–7; Pascale Casanova, *Beckett l'abstracteur* (Paris: Seuil, 1997), pp. 89–92; Steven J. Rosen, *Samuel Beckett and the Pessimistic Tradition* (New Brunswick: Rutgers University Press, 1976), p. 182.

38 Knowlson, *Damned to Fame*, p. 219.

39 Samuel Beckett, 1936 typescript, Letter 91, 'To Thomas MacGreevy, 5.3.36 Cooldrinagh', TCD MS 10402, Manuscripts Department, Trinity College Library Dublin, Republic of Ireland.

40 Geulincx, *Van de hoofddeugden*.

41 Steven Nadler, *Spinoza: A Life* (Cambridge: Cambridge University Press, 1999).

42 See J. P. N. Land, 'Arnold Geulincx and His Works', *Mind: A Quarterly Review of Psychology and Philosophy*, vol. 16 (1891), pp. 223–42; E. Terraillon, *La Morale de Geulincx* (Paris: Felix Alcan, 1912), pp. 216–21; van Ruler, 'Arnout Geulincx'.

43 Arnold Geulincx, *Metaphysics*, tr. Martin Wilson (Wisbech: Christoffel Press, 1999), p. 69.

44 David Rabouin, 'Spinoza en liberté', *Magazine Littéraire*, 370 (November 1998), p. 21.

45 Stephen Gaukroger, *Descartes: An Intellectual Biography* (Oxford: Clarendon Press, 1995), p. 16.

46 Quoting from Francis Bacon and Immanuel Kant, who cites Bacon at the beginning of his *Critique of Pure Reason*. Immanuel Kant, *Critique of Pure Reason*, tr. and ed. Paul Guyer and Allen W. Wood (Cambridge: Cambridge University Press, 1997), p. 91.

47 Beckett, *The Unnamable*, p. 58.

48 Samuel Beckett, 'Interview with Gabriel d'Aubarède', tr. C. Waters, in L. Graver and R. Federman (eds.), *Samuel Beckett, the Critical Heritage* (London: Routledge and Kegan Paul, 1979), p. 217. Interview first published in *Nouvelles littéraires*, 16 February 1961, 1:7, quoted in Wood, 'Murphy, Beckett, Geulincx, God', p. 29.

49 Ibid., p. 27.

50 Ibid., p. 44.

51 Ibid., pp. 43, 44.

52 Ibid., p. 40.

53 Ibid., p. 43.

54 Beckett, *Disjecta*, p. 22.
55 Deleuze and Guattari, *What is Philosophy?*, p. 217.
56 see Anthony Uhlmann, *Beckett and Poststructuralism* (Cambridge: Cambridge University Press, 1999), pp. 24–30.
57 P. N. Medvedev and M. M. Bakhtin, *The Formal Method in Literary Scholarship*, tr. Albert J. Wehrle (Baltimore: Johns Hopkins University Press, 1991), p. 19. See also pp. 17–23 on the 'inclusiveness' of literature.
58 Beckett might be said here to be ignoring the stipulations he expressed in 'Dante . . . Bruno. Vico. . Joyce' not to take philosophy seriously (Beckett, *Disjecta*, p. 22).
59 Samuel Beckett, *Murphy* (New York: Grove Press, 1957), pp. 192–3.
60 Beckett, *Disjecta*, p. 102.
61 See Wood on this point.
62 Samuel Beckett, *Molloy* (New York: Grove Press, 1955), p. 68.
63 See Uhlmann, *Beckett and Poststructuralism*, p. 54.
64 Samuel Beckett, 1984 Manuscript, 'Letter to Dr. E. Franzen, 17/2/54', cited in 'Babel 3, 1984', [magazine], Ms 2993: The Samuel Beckett Collection, University of Reading, UK.
65 Beckett, *The Unnamable*, pp. 68, 72, 148.
66 On this image see De Vleeschauwer, *Three Centuries of Geulincx Research*, pp. 45–56, and de Lattre, *L'Occasionalisme d'Arnold Geulincx*, pp. 553–66. The full passage cited by Beckett in his notes to Geulincx, which also includes a discussion of the mother or nurse rocking the cradle, which I develop further below, is as follows: from note 19. to Tr. 1 Cap. 2 Sec. 2, No. 2 [Inspectio Sui, page 33, in the Land Edition]. The note itself appears on page 211–12, in Arnold Geulincx, *A. Geulincx Antverpiensis Opera philosophica*, 3 vols., ed. J. P. N. Land (The Hague: Martin Nijhoff, 1891–3).

'Non . . . pedes isti moventur, quia ego ire volo, sed quia alius id me volente vult. Sicut pusio in cunis suis conditus, si eas agitari vult, saepe agitantur, non quia ipse hoc vult, sed quia mater vel nutrix, quae assidit; quaeque [. . .] id praestare potest, id etiam ipso volente praestare vult . . . Imo voluntas mea mon movet motorem, ut moveat membra mea; sed qui motum indidit materiae et leges ei dixit, is idem voluntatem meam formavit, itaque has res diversissimas (motum materiae et arbitrium voluntatis meae) inter se devinxit, ut, cum voluntas mea vellet, motus talis adesset qualem vellet, et contra cum motus adesset, voluntas eum vellet, sine ulla alterius in alterm causalitate vel influxu. Sicut duobus horologis rite inter se et ad solis diurnum cursum quadratis, altero quidem sonante, et horas nobis loquente, alterum itidem sonat, et totidem nobis indicat horas; idque absque ulla causalitate quia alterum hoc in altero causat, sed propter meram dependentiam, qua utrumque ab eadem arte et simili industria constitutum est; sic v.g. motus linguae comitatur voluntatem nostram loquendi, et haec voluntas illum motum; nec haec ab illo, nec ille ab hac dependet, sed uterque ab eodem illo summo artifice, qui haec inter se tam ineffabiliter copulavit atque devinxit.' (Beckett, 1936 typescript, 'Notes to Arnold Geulincx', 15 Verso)

('Accordingly . . . these feet are not moved because I wish to go on my way, but because another wishes what I wish. It is just like a baby laid in his cradle: if he wishes the cradle to rock it sometimes rocks, though not because he wishes it, but because his mother or nurse, sitting beside it, wills it, and because she . . . can fulfil it and also wishes to fulfil what he wishes . . . Furthermore, my will does not move the Mover to move my organs; rather, He who imparts motion to matter and has given laws to it is the same one who has formed my will, and yoked together these diverse things (the motion of matter and the decision of my will) in such a way that when my will wishes, such motion as it wishes appears; and on the other hand when motion appears my will wishes it, without either causing or influencing the other. It is the same as if two clocks agree precisely with each other and with the daily course of the Sun: when one chimes and tells the hours, the other also chimes and indicates such and such an hour; and all that without any causality in the sense of one having a causal effect on the other, but rather on account of mere dependence, inasmuch as both of them have been constructed with the same art and similar industry. So, for example, motion of the tongue accompanies our will to speak, and this will accompanies the motion, without either the latter depending on the former, or the former depending on the latter, but rather both depending on that same supreme artificer who has joined and yoked them together so ineffably.')

This translation, and those which follow, is by Martin Wilson, from his forthcoming edition (edited by Han van Ruler, Martin Wilson, and Anthony Uhlmann) of Geulincx's *Ethics*. In future references I will, for the most part, only cite the English translation while referring to the page in Land's Latin edition of Geulincx. When a particularly important passage is cited, I may also include the Latin original.

67 Samuel Beckett, *The Complete Dramatic Works* (London: Faber, 1990), pp. 321–34.

68 Ibid., pp. 431–42.

69 Geulincx, *A. Geulincx Antverpiensis Opera philosophica*, III, p. 39. Translation by Martin Wilson.

70 De Vleeschauwer has written on Geulincx's interest in the question of suicide, suggesting that he returns to this question obsessively, as if, being no stranger to ill fortune, it was a temptation he had to constantly confront. H. J. De Vleeschauwer, *Le Problème du suicide dans la morale de Geulincx*.

71 Beckett copies the following excerpt from this passage: 'Ego tantum velle hic possum, et cum volo, Deus saepe motum illum impartitur, quem volo; non quia ego volo, sed quia ipse vult me volente motum illum fieri. Ut si pusio cunas suas, in quas conditus est, agitari velit, saepe agitantur, non quia ipse hoc vult, sed quia mater vel nutrix, quae assidet, quaeque id praestare potest, id etiam ipso volente praestare vult.' Beckett, 1936 typescript, "Notes to Arnold Geulincx', 26.

('I can only will it, and when I will it, God usually imparts the motion that I will; not because I will it, but because He wills that the motion that I will should be imparted. For example, if a baby wants the cradle in which he has been laid to be rocked, it is usually rocked; though not because *he* wants it, but because his mother or nursemaid, who is sitting by the cradle and who can actually rock it, also wants to do what he wants.') Translation by Martin Wilson.

72 I have already cited one of these mentions above, in relation to an additional discussion of the 'two clocks'. I will cite the final passage below, in indicating a point of occlusion in Geulincx's use of the image of the cradle.

73 Most readers will be familiar with the lullaby I mean: 'Rockaby baby on the tree top/when the wind blows the cradle will rock/when the bough breaks the cradle will fall/down will come cradle, baby and all.'

74 Beckett, *Complete Dramatic Works*, p. 434.

75 Ibid., p. 433.

76 'Bercer v.tr. . . . est dérivé de l'ancien français *bers* (v. 1150, berz) '*berceau*', lequel est issu d'un latin populaire *bertium*, indirectement attesté par son diminutif *berciolum* qui a donné l'ancien français *berçuel* . . . *Bertium* . . . a évincé le représentant du latin *cunae* . . . Berceuse n.f. tardif (1835) . . . désignait la nourrice chargée de bercer l'enfant . . . une chanson au moyen de laquelle on endort un enfant et un siège sur lequel on peut se balancer (1867)' (*Dictionnaire historique de la langue Française*, general editor Alain Rey (Paris: Dictionnares le Robert, 1992), p. 208).

77 Beckett, *Complete Dramatic Works*, pp. 441–442.

78 Beckett, 1936 typescript, 'Notes to Arnold Geulincx', 15 verso.

79 Beckett, *Murphy*, p. 2.

80 Ibid., p. 2.

81 Ibid., p. 66.

82 Beckett, *Complete Dramatic Works*, p. 327.

83 Ibid., pp. 333–4.

84 Ibid., p. 329.

85 De Vleeschauwer, *Le Problème du suicide dans la morale de Geulincx*.

86 Geulincx, *A. Geulincx Antverpiensis Opera philosophica*, III, p. 228; Beckett, 1936 typescript, 'Notes to Arnold Geulincx', p. 26. Translation by Martin Wilson.

5 COGITO NESCIO

1 Samuel Beckett, *The Unnamable* (New York: Grove Press, 1958), p. 22.

2 Gilles Deleuze, *Negotiations, 1972–1990*, tr. Martin Joughin (New York: Columbia University Press, 1995), pp. 147–8.

3 See Paul Patton, *Deleuze and the Political* (London: Routledge, 2000) on this point, pp. 18–23.

4 Deleuze, *Negotiations*, p. 148.

5 Gilles Deleuze and Félix Guattari, *What is Philosophy?*, tr. Hugh Tomlinson and Graham Burchell (New York: Columbia University Press, 1994). This

'already-thought' is seen in Plato's 'Ideas', which pre-exist particular things and offer the forms for them, but also in Plato's notion of 'recollection' as that which makes achieving genuine understanding possible. According to Plato's myth, which outlines this understanding, our souls have encountered the truth of the forms or ideas in the life which comes before and after this life (a life above), yet when we enter our mortal bodies (which we ourselves, or our souls, choose in that life above) we forget everything we so clearly knew (including that we have taken the choice to live a given life). In our mortal lives, then, we are struck by the truth of an idea because we recognise it: we have seen it before in the life above and now that we see it again, manifested as a particular example of a universal idea, we remember it and assent to its truth. See Emile Bréhier, *The History of Philosophy Vol. 1: The Hellenic Age*, tr. Joseph Thomas (Chicago: University of Chicago Press, 1965), pp. 106–7.

6 Though, as we will see below, Deleuze confirms this in relation to literary and philosophical images of thought in *Proust and Signs*.

7 Emile Bréhier, *Chrysippe et l'ancien stoïcisme* (Paris: Félix Alcan, 1910), pp. 86–98; Emile Bréhier, *The History of Philosophy Vol. 2: The Hellenistic and Roman Age*, tr. Wade Baskin (Chicago: University of Chicago Press, 1965), pp. 38–9. In *Chrysippe*, Bréhier translates this alternatively as 'la représentation compréhensive' and 'l'image compréhensive' (86–98).

8 Bréhier, *Chrysippe*, p. 97.

9 Ibid., p. 87.

10 Gilles Deleuze, *Proust and Signs*, tr. Richard Howard (Minneapolis: University of Minnesota Press, 2000), p. 94.

11 Ibid., pp. 94–5.

12 Ibid., p. 95.

13 Ibid., p. 97.

14 Proust, quoted in ibid., p. 95.

15 Paul Redding, *The Logic of Affect* (New York: Cornell University Press, 1999), p. 56.

16 Proust, quoted in Deleuze, *Proust and Signs*, p. 97.

17 Ibid., p. 95.

18 Ibid., p. 100.

19 Ibid., p. 101.

20 Such as when Beckett glosses the use of the name 'Philaretus' in English, 'Geulincx's fictitious apostrophe, virtuous but hasty', at Samuel Beckett, 1936 typescript, 'Notes to Arnold Geulincx, *Ethica*, *Metaphysica Vera* and *Questiones Quodlibeticae*', TCDMS 10971/6, Manuscripts Department, Trinity College Library Dublin, Republic of Ireland, p. 11 verso, or adds the general description in English, 'Humility no virtue for the ancients' at ibid., p. 7.

21 Arnold Geulincx, *A. Geulincx Antverpiensis Opera philosophica*, 3 vols., ed. J. P. N. Land (The Hague: Martin Nijhoff, 1891–3), p. 6.

22 I will proceed here by citing the page reference to the Latin edition of Geulincx, followed by the page number to Beckett's typescript notes in

Trinity College. All translations are by Martin Wilson. Geulincx, *Opera philosophica*, p. 167; Beckett, 1936 typescript, 'Notes to Arnold Geulincx', p. 9.

23 Geulincx, *Opera philosophica*, pp. 214–15; Beckett, 1936 typescript, 'Notes to Arnold Geulincx', p. 23.

24 Geulincx, *Opera philosophica*, p. 149.

25 Beckett, *The Unnamable*, p. 83.

26 Geulincx, *Opera philosophica*, p. 182; Beckett, 1936 typescript, 'Notes to Arnold Geulincx', p. 11.

27 Geulincx, *Opera philosophica*, p. 181; Beckett, 1936 typescript, 'Notes to Arnold Geulincx', p. 11.

28 Samuel Beckett, *Molloy* (New York: Grove Press, 1955), p. 241.

29 Geulincx, *Opera philosophica*, p. 23; Beckett, 1936 typescript, 'Notes to Arnold Geulincx', p. 12.

30 Geulincx, *Opera philosophica*, p. 57; Beckett, 1936 typescript, 'Notes to Arnold Geulincx', p. 32.

31 Beckett, *The Unnamable*, p. 27.

32 Geulincx, *Opera philosophica*, p. 40; Beckett, 1936 typescript, 'Notes to Arnold Geulincx', p. 27.

33 Geulincx, *Opera philosophica*, p. 40; Beckett, 1936 typescript, 'Notes to Arnold Geulincx', p. 27.

34 Geulincx, *Opera philosophica*, p. 40; Beckett, 1936 typescript, 'Notes to Arnold Geulincx', p. 27.

35 Beckett, *Molloy*, p. 181.

36 René Descartes, 'Principles of Philosophy' in *The Philosophical Writings of Descartes*, vol. I, trs. John Cottingham, Robert Stoothoff and Dugald Murdoch (Cambridge: Cambridge University Press, 1985), p. 194.

37 Ibid., pp. 197–200.

38 Ibid., p. 203.

39 Ibid.

40 René Descartes, *Discourse on Method and the Meditations*, tr. with an introduction by F. E. Sutcliffe (London: Penguin, 1968).

41 René Descartes, 'Discourse on Method', in *The Philosophical Writings of Descartes*, vol. I, trs. John Cottingham, Robert Stoothoff and Dugald Murdoch (Cambridge: Cambridge University Press, 1985), 111–51.

42 Geulincx's importance as an original thinker has been outlined by a few critics, and most convincingly by de Lattre (the most comprehensive study yet made), Terraillon (who carefully outlines points of divergence and similarity between Geulincx and Descartes), De Vleeschauwer (in particular for his comparisons with Kant and the notion of the thing in itself in Geulincx but also for his interesting essay on suicide and his bibliographic essay), Nuchelmans (with regard to the originality of Geulincx's logic), Rousset (for the forceful argument concerning Geulincx's relation to Spinoza which I draw upon below) and McCracken (who draws on and develops Terraillon's comparisons of Descartes and Geulincx, in applying Geulincx's ideas to a theory of value). Recently Steven Nadler and Han van Ruler have begun to develop interesting

new insights into Geulincx's works. See Alain de Lattre, *L'Occasionalisme d'Arnold Geulincx: étude sur la constitution de la doctrine* (Paris: Editions de Minuit, 1967); E. Terraillon, *La Morale de Geulincx* (Paris: Félix Alcan, 1912); H. J. De Vleeschauwer, 'Les Antécédents du Transcendentalisme kantien. Geulincx et Kant', *Kantstudien* (1953–4), pp. 245–73; H. J. De Vleeschauwer, *Three Centuries of Geulincx Research* (Pretoria: Communications of the University of South Africa, 1957); H. J. De Vleeschauwer, 'L'Occasionalisme et la condition humanine chez A. Geulincx', *Kantstudien* (1958), pp. 109–24. H. J. De Vleeschauwer, *Le 'De Virtute et primis ejus Proprietatibus' d'Arnout Geulincx et sa traduction flammande 'Van de Hoofdeuchden'. Introduction et Textes* (Pretoria: Van Schaik, 1961); H. J. De Vleeschauwer, *Les Plans d'études au XVIIe siècle. I: Le Plan de Descartes; II: Le Plan d'A. Geulincx.* (Pretoria: University of South Africa, 1962 and 1964); H. J. De Vleeschauwer, *Le Problème du suicide dans la morale de Geulincx* (Pretoria: Communications of the University of South Africa, 1965); G. Nuchelmans, *Geulincx's Containment Theory of Logic* (Amsterdam, 1988); Bernard Rousset, *Geulincx: Entre Descartes et Spinoza* (Paris: Vrin, 1999); Steven Nadler, 'Occasionalism and the Mind-Body Problem', in M. A. Stewart (ed.), *Studies in Seventeenth-Century European Philosophy* (New York: Clarendon, 1997); Steven Nadler, 'Knowledge, Volitional Agency and Causation in Malebranche and Geulincx', *British Journal for the History of Philosophy*, vol. 7, no. 2 (1999), pp. 263–74; Han van Ruler, 'Minds, Forms, and Spirits: the Nature of Cartesian Disenchantment', *Journal of the History of Ideas*, vol. 61 (2000), pp. 381–95; Han van Ruler, 'Arnout Geulincx', in Wiep van Bunge, Henri Krop, Han van Ruler and Paul Schuurman (eds.), *The Dictionary of Seventeenth and Eighteenth-Century Dutch Philosophers* (London: Thoemmes Continuum, 2004).

43 Rousset, *Geulincx*, p. 20.

44 Ibid. The outlines of these arguments are drawn largely on pp. 7–34 and 178–88. Rousset died while working on this book, and so the final sections of it, outlining some of his understanding of Geulincx's importance, exist only in note and point form. He undertook the project having been diagnosed with a terminal illness as he considered its subject to be of the utmost importance to the history of philosophy (these ideas had occurred to him many years before, but it was only the illness which made him recognise the urgency of at last beginning this task). See the Postface by Pierre-François Moreau, pp. 174–7.

45 Ibid., p. 55.

46 Tom F. Driver, 'Beckett by the Madeleine', *Columbia University Forum* (Summer, 1961), p. 23.

47 Stephen Gaukroger, *Descartes: An Intellectual Biography* (Oxford: Clarendon Press, 1995), pp. 362, 375.

48 Geulincx begins this third book of the *Metaphysics* with what might be read as a direct confrontation with Spinoza, who begins his *Ethics* with his first part, 'On God'. Geulincx argues that, 'If we want to philosophise rigorously, we must begin with the idea of God; but given our inadequacies, in practice it is

more convenient to begin with His attributes, and proceed to knowledge of God a posteriori: in contrast, an angelic mind could begin with the idea' (Arnold Geulincx, *Metaphysics*, tr. Martin Wilson (Wisbech: Christoffel Press, 1999), p. 93). Spinoza builds his system in beginning with an immediate, intuitive, adequate understanding of the being of God or Nature while Geulincx works towards a recognition of the prime knowledge (the immediate understanding of our being which will enable us to recognise the priority of God's being) through, in the first instance, the fundamental supposition ('that one should start to behave as though everything were false', ibid., p. 21). While sure knowledge (knowledge of eternal truths; that is, knowledge based upon prime knowledge) is most closely aligned with metaphysics for Geulincx, it is also closely linked to geometry, arithmetic and logic 'and perhaps also Ethics' (ibid., p. 20), but physics, for him, has a less exact affinity with prime knowledge, one which draws both on eternal truths and supposition. Theology, however, unlike those sciences which make use of the application of a priori reason to knowledge of eternal truths, must begin a posteriori, yet as Rousset explains this does not mean it is empirical (Rousset, *Geulincx*, p. 82). Importantly, then, the keystone to any adequate knowledge of things, for Geulincx, is always that (theology) which one knows and can know the least about. In contrast, if, as Gaukroger argues, Descartes's *Physics* haunt his metaphysics, then their emphasis would have to be read as involving an understanding not of the inadequacy of our knowledge but its adequacy to a task such as the development of a definitive natural philosophy.

49 As he also does, indeed, for Geulincx, who in no way refutes the truth of science based on eternal truths which exist in the mind of God (Geulincx, *Metaphysics*, p. 96).

50 Ibid., p. 98.

51 See Benedictus de Spinoza, *Ethics*, tr. Andrew Boyle and revised with an introduction by G. H. R. Parkinson (London: Everyman, 1992), Book 3.

52 See Geulincx, *Metaphysics*, pp. 35, 105–6.

53 Ibid., p. 106.

54 Geulincx, *Opera philosophica*, p. 32. Beckett cites much of this passage in his notes.

55 See Israel Shenker, '"Moody Man of Letters". Interview with Samuel Beckett', *The New York Times*, section 2 (6 May 1956), pp. 1, 3.

56 There is a real challenge to Spinoza here: the idea of somehow achieving adequate knowledge and thereby becoming eternal is key to his system and if this is not possible the conclusions of his system must veer toward those of Geulincx.

57 Geulincx, *Metaphysics*, p. 35.

58 Beckett, *The Unnamable*, p. 82.

59 Ibid., p. 21.

60 Geulincx, *Opera philosophica*, III, p. 206; Beckett, 1936 typescript, 'Notes to Arnold Geulincx', p. 14.

61 Geulincx, *Metaphysics*, pp. 113–15.

62 Ibid., pp. 94–5.
63 See Descartes, 'Principles of Philosophy', Part I.
64 Beckett, *The Unnamable*, p. 22.
65 Geulincx, *Metaphysics*, p. 45.
66 See Rousset, *Geulincx*, p. 133.
67 Beckett, *The Unnamable*, p. 165.
68 Geulincx, *Opera philosophica*, p. 204; Beckett, 1936 typescript, 'Notes to Arnold Geulincx', p. 14.
69 Descartes, 'Principles of Philosophy', p. 204.
70 Ibid., p. 202.
71 Geulincx, *Opera philosophica*, pp. 111–12.
72 See Rousset, *Geulincx*, pp. 130–5.
73 Geulincx, *Metaphysics*, pp. 45–6.
74 Ibid., pp. 45–6.
75 Samuel Beckett, *The Complete Short Prose*, ed. Stanley Gontarski (New York: Grove Press, 1995).
76 Ibid.
77 See Beckett, 1936 typescript, 'Notes to Arnold Geulincx', pp. 1–6.
78 Geulincx, *Opera philosophica*, p. 217; see Beckett, 1936 typescript, 'Notes to Arnold Geulincx', p. 24.
79 Geulincx, *Opera philosophica*, p. 218; see Beckett, 1936 typescript, 'Notes to Arnold Geulincx', p. 24.
80 Geulincx, *Opera philosophica*, p. 218; see Beckett, 1936 typescript, 'Notes to Arnold Geulincx', p. 24.
81 Samuel Beckett, *The Complete Dramatic Works* (London: Faber and Faber, 1990), pp. 315–16.
82 Michel Foucault, 'Archéologie d'une passion' (interview with Charles Ruas), *Magazine littéraire*, number 221 (July–August 1985), p. 105. All translations from this source are mine.
83 Maurice Blanchot, 'Michel Foucault as I Imagine Him', tr. Jeffrey Mehlman, *Foucault/Blanchot* (New York: Zone, 1990), p. 76.
84 I have chosen to translate the pronoun as masculine here as Foucault is specifically discussing the work of Raymond Roussel.
85 Foucault, 'Archéologie d'une passion', p. 104.
86 H. Porter Abbott, *Beckett Writing Beckett: The Author in the Autograph* (Ithaca and London: Cornell University Press, 1996), p. xi.
87 See Jean-Yves Tadié, *Marcel Proust: a Life*, tr. Euan Cameron (London: Penguin, 2001), pp. 311, 345–50, 368–9.
88 See James Knowlson, *Damned to Fame: The Life of Samuel Beckett* (London: Bloomsbury, 1996); Anthony Cronin, *Samuel Beckett: The Last Modernist* (London: HarperCollins, 1996); Deirdre Bair, *Samuel Beckett: A Biography* (London: Vintage, 1990); Lawrence E. Harvey, *Samuel Beckett Poet and Critic* (Princeton: Princeton University Press, 1970); Eoin O'Brien, *The Beckett Country: Samuel Beckett's Ireland* (Dublin: Black Cat, 1986); Angela B. Moorjani, *Abysmal Games in the Novels of Samuel Beckett*

(Chapel Hill: University of North Carolina Press, 1982); Abbott, *Beckett Writing Beckett*.

89 Beckett, *Complete Short Prose*.
90 James Joyce, *A Portrait of the Artist as a Young Man* (London: Grafton Books, 1977), pp. 194–5.
91 Leslie Hill, *Beckett's Fiction in Different Words* (Cambridge: Cambridge University Press, 1990), p. x.
92 See Leslie Hill, *Bataille, Klossowski, Blanchot: Writing at the Limit* (Oxford: Oxford University Press, 2001).
93 Bruno Clément, 'What the Philosophers Do with Samuel Beckett', tr. Anthony Uhlmann, in S. E. Gontarski and Anthony Uhlmann (eds.), *Beckett after Beckett* (Gainesville: University Press of Florida, 2006), p. 118.
94 Ibid., p. 119.
95 Ibid., p. 119.
96 Bruno Clément, *Le Lecteur et son modèle: Voltaire, Pascal, Hugo, Shakespeare, Sartre, Flaubert* (Paris: Presses Universitaires de France, 1999), p. 14.
97 Emile Bréhier, *The History of Philosophy Vol. 3: The Middle Ages and the Renaissance*, tr. Wade Baskin (Chicago: University of Chicago Press, 1967), p. 215.
98 Michel Foucault, *L'Ordre du discours: Leçon inaugurale au Collège de France prononcée le 2 décembre 1970* (Paris: Gallimard, 1971), translations from this source are mine, p. 8.
99 Ibid., p. 23.
100 Ibid., p. 26.
101 Ibid., p. 28.
102 Ibid., p. 28.
103 Ibid., p. 30.
104 Ibid., pp. 32–8.
105 Ibid., p. 38.
106 Gilles Deleuze, *Foucault*, tr. and ed. Sean Hand (London: Athlone, 1988), p. 7.
107 Jacques Derrida, '"This Strange Institution Called Literature": An Interview with Jacques Derrida' (with Derek Attridge), tr. Geoffrey Bennington and Rachel Bowlby, in Derek Attridge (ed.), *Acts of Literature* (New York: Routledge, 1992), p. 60.
108 Clément, 'What the Philosophers Do with Samuel Beckett', p. 116–19.
109 Ibid., p. 120.
110 Ibid., p. 121.
111 Michel Foucault, 'Qu'est-ce qu'un auteur?', *Bulletin de le Société française de Philosophie*, vol. 63, no. 3 (February 1969), p. 97, my translation.
112 Ibid., p. 100.
113 Michel Foucault, *The Archaeology of Knowledge*, tr. A. M. Sheridan Smith (London: Routledge, 1989).
114 Michèle Le Doeuff, *The Philosophical Imaginary*, tr. Colin Gordon (London: The Athlone Press, 1989).

6 BECKETT, BERKELEY, BERGSON, *FILM*: THE
INTUITION IMAGE

1 Friedrich Nietzsche, *The Birth of Tragedy: Out of the Spirit of Music* (London: Penguin, 1993), p. 69.

2 Stephen Gaukroger, *Descartes: An Intellectual Biography* (Oxford: Clarendon Press, 1995), pp. 119–23. It is possible that Quintilian, in turn, drew this idea from the Stoic conception of the 'comprehensive image' which has also been touched upon above.

3 See, for example, Emile Bréhier, *The History of Philosophy Vol. 1: The Hellenic Age*, tr. Joseph Thomas (Chicago: University of Chicago Press, 1965), on Plato, pp. 105, 121–2, and Aristotle, pp. 180, 214.

4 Henri Bergson, 'Philosophical Intuition', in *The Creative Mind* (New York: Philosophical Library, 1946), pp. 126–52.

5 Ibid., p. 128.

6 Beckett makes this statement in a letter to L. E. Harvey: Samuel Beckett, 1967 manuscript, 'Letter to L. E. Harvey "Ussy, 20.2.67."' Beckett collection, Rare Books Library, Dartmouth College, Hanover, NH, USA.

7 Bergson, 'Philosophical Intuition', p. 128.

8 This aspect of the nature of the image brings to mind Deleuze's description of Beckett's use of the image in 'The Exhausted' which I discuss in chapter 2: 'What counts in the image is not its meager content, but the energy – mad and ready to explode – that it has harnessed, which is why images never last long' (Gilles Deleuze, 'The Exhausted', tr. Anthony Uhlmann, in Daniel W. Smith and Michael A. Greco (eds.), *Essays Critical and Clinical* (Minneapolis: University of Minnesota Press, 1997), pp. 160–1). Deleuze, of course, takes Bergson as one of his points of departure.

9 Bergson, 'Philosophical Intuition', pp. 128–9.

10 Henri Bergson, *An Introduction to Metaphysics*, tr. T. E. Hulme (New York and London: G. Putnam and Sons, 1912).

11 Samuel Beckett, *Dream of Fair to Middling Women* (New York: Arcade/Riverrun, 1993), p. 12.

12 Rachel Burrows, 1931 manuscript, 'Notes to lectures by Samuel Beckett on Gide and Racine at Trinity College Dublin', TCD MIC 60, Manuscripts Department, Trinity College Library Dublin, Republic of Ireland.

13 Samuel Beckett, 'Letter to Georges Duthuit, 9–10 March 1949', tr. Walter Redfern, in S. E. Gontarski and Anthony Uhlmann (eds.), *Beckett after Beckett* (Gainesville: University Press of Florida, 2006), pp. 15–21.

14 Ibid., pp. 18–19.

15 Ibid., p. 19.

16 Samuel Beckett, 1936 typescript, Letter 85, 'To Thomas MacGreevy, 9/1/36 [written as 35 in error] Cooldrinagh', TCD MS 10402, Manuscripts Department, Trinity College Library Dublin, Republic of Ireland.

17 Samuel Beckett, 1934 typescript, Letter 63, 'To Thomas MacGreevy, 8/9/34, 34 Gertrude St, S. W. 10.', TCD MS 10402, Manuscripts Department, Trinity College Library Dublin, Republic of Ireland.

18 Bergson, 'Philosophical Intuition', p. 134.
19 Ibid., p. 136.
20 Ibid., p. 137.
21 Ibid., p. 139.
22 Ibid., p. 139.
23 Ibid., p. 140.
24 Samuel Beckett, *The Complete Dramatic Works* (London: Faber and Faber, 1990), pp. 323–34; Samuel Beckett, *Film: Complete Scenario, Illustrations, Production Shots*, with the essay 'On Directing *Film*' by Alan Schneider (New York: Grove Press, 1969), pp. 9–61.
25 Beckett, *Complete Dramatic Works*, p. 323.
26 See, for example, Sylvie Debevec Henning, '"Film": a Dialogue between Beckett and Berkeley', *Journal of Beckett Studies*, no. 7 (spring 1982), pp. 89–100.
27 See Gilles Deleuze, 'The Greatest Irish Film', in *Essays Critical and Clinical*, tr. Daniel W. Smith and Michael A. Greco (Minneapolis: University of Minnesota Press, 1997), p. 23.
28 Gilles Deleuze, *Critique et Clinique* (Paris: Editions de Minuit, 1993), p. 36. The translation of Smith and Greco – 'a cutting of the film (or a distinction of cases) that differs slightly from the one proposed by Beckett himself' (Gilles Deleuze, 'The Greatest Irish Film', p. 23) – renders this point slightly confusing by inserting the phrase 'of the film' in translating 'découpage', thereby giving one the impression that Deleuze is proposing a reading of the completed film, *Film*, whose form has been changed from that given to us by Beckett and Schneider. We should, rather, understand this comment to refer to the structure of Deleuze's essay and its points of emphasis, in relation to the structure of Beckett's written treatment.
29 See Deleuze, Gilles Deleuze, *Cinema 1: The Movement-Image*, tr. Hugh Tomlinson and Barbara Habberjam (Minneapolis: University of Minnesota Press, 1986), pp. 66–70, and Deleuze, 'The Greatest Irish Film', 23–6.
30 Benedictus de Spinoza, *Opera*, J. ed. Van Vloten and J. P. N. Land, vol. I (Hagae Comitum: Martinum Nijhoff, 1882), p. 272.
31 Samuel Beckett, *Murphy* (New York: Grove Press, 1957), p. 107.
32 See Beckett, *Complete Dramatic Works*, pp. 323–4.
33 See ibid.
34 See the chapter on *Film* in Alan Schneider, *Entrances: An American Director's Journey* (New York: Limelight Editions, 1987), and Schneider's essay in Beckett, *Film*, pp. 63–94, on which that chapter is based.
35 Schneider, *Entrances*, p. 355.
36 Beckett, *Complete Dramatic Works*, p. 323.
37 Samuel Beckett and Alan Schneider, *No Author Better Served: the Correspondence of Samuel Beckett and Alan Schneider*, ed. Maurice Harmon (Cambridge, MA: Harvard University Press, 1998), p. 166.
38 See Deleuze, 'The Greatest Irish Film'.
39 Beckett, *Complete Dramatic Works*, p. 325.

40 'The horror, the horror' (Joseph Conrad, *Heart of Darkness* (London: Penguin, 1989), p. 121).

41 Beckett and Schneider, *No Author Better Served*, p. 161.

42 See Deleuze, 'The Greatest Irish Film'.

43 Quoted in Stanley Gontarski, 'Appendix A: Beckett on *Film*', in *The Intent of Undoing in Samuel Beckett's Dramatic Texts* (Bloomington: Indiana University Press, 1985), p. 187, see also p. 191.

44 From 'The Image', in Beckett, *Complete Dramatic Works*, p. 168.

45 Beckett and Schneider, *No Author Better Served*, p. 166.

46 Ibid., p. 166.

47 Beckett, *Complete Dramatic Works*, p. 332.

48 Beckett, quoted in Gontarski, 'Appendix A: Beckett on *Film*', p. 190.

49 See Schneider, in Beckett, *Film*, p. 77.

50 Beckett, *Complete Dramatic Works*, p. 324.

51 See ibid.; Beckett, *Film*; Schneider, *Entrances*; and Gontarski, 'Appendix A: Beckett on *Film*'.

7 THE ANCIENT STOICS AND THE ONTOLOGICAL IMAGE

1 Alfred Simon, 'Le mort de Samuel Beckett: L'auteur d' "En attendant Godot" est décédé vendredi 22 décembre à Paris', *Le Monde* (27 December 1989), p. 10.

2 See Michel Cournot, 'Avignon: Une nuit de l'Aida – Nous pensons beaucoup à vous, Vaclav Havel', *Le Monde* (24 July 1982), p. 14; Pierre Marcabru, 'Avignon, La nuit de l'Aida – Le poisson noyé – Communisme: l'Innommable', *Le Figaro* (23 July 1982), p. 19.

3 See Samuel Beckett, *The Complete Dramatic Works* (London: Faber and Faber, 1990).

4 The only Beckett critic to discuss Beckett's work in relation to the Stoics in any detail is Steven J. Rosen, yet his comments mostly concern the later, Roman, Stoics and the sage tradition; see Steven J. Rosen, *Samuel Beckett and the Pessimistic Tradition* (New Brunswick: Rutgers University Press, 1976), pp. 26–9, 86–90. Here, however, I will be largely concerned with aspects of the physics of the Ancient Greek Stoics, whose work survives only in fragments but whose system has been shown to be remarkably consistent in numerous works of commentary. I hope to show, in part (and by concentrating on their theory of incorporeals and bodies – and the image which brings us into direct contact with these bodies), that the precept 'follow nature', which Rosen cites in relation to the Roman Stoics (p. 86), is not the naive slogan it might at first appear, but is rather built on the sophisticated and (to our ears) unusual understanding of the physical world which was elaborated by the Greek Stoics.

5 See Beckett, *Complete Dramatic Works*.

6 Arnold Geulincx, *A. Geulincx Antverpiensis Opera philosophica*, 3 vols., ed. J. P. N. Land (The Hague: Martin Nijhoff, 1891–3), III, p. 170; Samuel Beckett, 1936 typescript, 'Notes to Arnold Geulincx, *Ethica, Metaphysica Vera*

and *Questiones Quodlibeticae'*, TCD MS 10971/6, Manuscripts Department, Trinity College Library Dublin, Republic of Ireland, p. 10. Translation by Martin Wilson.

7 These comments from Beckett are cited in the Addenda on the DVD for the Beckett on Film production of *What Where. Beckett on Film, 19 Films by 19 Directors*, produced by Michael Colgan and Alan Moloney (Dublin: Blue Angel Films, 2001).

8 I wrote to Knowlson in late 2003 asking him if he could indicate the source of this information. He replied that he was, at that time, not able to find the source he referred to in 2000. In his biography of Beckett, Knowlson quotes a letter from 1930 in which Beckett tells Tom MacGreevy how Beckett's friend Jean Beaufret, who was particularly interested in Greek philosophy, was bringing him books from the library and speaking 'abstractions' 'every second day' (James Knowlson, *Damned to Fame: The Life of Samuel Beckett* (London: Bloomsbury, 1996), pp. 96–7). It is unlikely that a young French scholar, such as Beaufret, with his particular interest in the Greeks, did not study the Stoics, who were a major strand of Greek thought, and therefore the works of Bréhier (1876–1952), who was the foremost authority on the Stoics in Paris at this time (the books discussed here were originally published in 1908 and 1910) and who taught at the nearby Sorbonne.

9 Not to be confused with Zeno the Eleatic, whom Beckett mentions in a number of texts.

10 See Emile Bréhier, *The History of Philosophy Vol. 2: The Hellenistic and Roman Age*, tr. Wade Baskin (Chicago: University of Chicago Press, 1965), p. 38; Emile Bréhier, *Chrysippe et l'ancien stoïcisme* (Paris: Félix Alcan, 1910), pp. 80–6. Other translations of this term are 'impression', 'imaging' (see A. A. Long, *Stoic Studies* (Cambridge: Cambridge University Press, 1996), p. 246, footnote 41), or 'presentation' (see Josiah B. Gould, *The Philosophy of Chrysippus* (Leiden: E. J. Brill, 1970), pp. 130–1; S. Sandbach, *The Stoics* (London: Chatto and Windus, 1975), pp. 85–91; and S. Sambursky, *Physics of the Stoics* (London: Routledge and Kegan Paul, 1959), p. 25), and 'representation' (see Long, *Stoic Studies*, pp. 264–85; Emile Bréhier, *Chrysippe*, pp. 81–5). The various translations can cause confusion, but the terms 'image' and 'presentation' are most justifiable as the impression of the image is direct and unmediated rather than being re-presented.

11 See Bernard Rousset, *Geulincx: Entre Descartes et Spinoza* (Paris: Vrin, 1999), p. 133.

12 Bréhier, *The History of Philosophy Vol. 2*, p. 40.

13 Geulincx, *Opera philosophica*, p. 179; Beckett, 1936 typescript, 'Notes to Arnold Geulincx', p. 11.

14 Geulincx, *Opera philosophica*, p. 179; Beckett, 1936 typescript, 'Notes to Arnold Geulincx', p. 11.

15 Beckett, *Complete Dramatic Works*, p. 476.

16 Samuel Beckett, *Watt* (London: Picador, 1988), p. 255.

17 Beckett, *Complete Dramatic Works*, pp. 472–3.

18 Sambursky, *Physics of the Stoics*, p. 25.

19 See Long, *Stoic Studies*, pp. 233–6.

20 On the distinction between the *lekta* (or sense) and comprehensive image see Bréhier, *Chrysippe*, pp. 59–107, and Émile Bréhier, *La Théorie des incorporels dans l'ancien stoïcisme* (Paris: Librairie philosophique J. Vrin, 1997) (1st edn 1908), pp. 60–3; on the *lekta* see ibid., pp. 14–36; Michael Frede, 'Principles of Stoic Grammar', in John M. Rist (ed.), *The Stoics* (Berkeley and Los Angeles: University of California Press, 1978), pp. 29–32; and Andreas Graeser, 'The Stoic Theory of Meaning', in Rist (ed.), *The Stoics*, p. 87.

21 Gilles Deleuze, *The Logic of Sense*, tr. Mark Lester with Charles Stivale, ed. Constantin V. Boundas (New York: Columbia University Press, 1990), p. xiii.

22 Ibid., p. xiv. While I have referred to Deleuze's readings from time to time here, I have not attempted to offer a reading of his development of Stoic concepts. Interestingly, although building upon an initial reading of Bréhier, Deleuze takes us in quite a different direction to him, by, for example, affirming the incorporeal in ways not found in Bréhier or the other interpretations of the Stoics I have consulted here. Deleuze's readings are compelling; my purpose here, however, is to endeavour to trace the system of the Stoics through commentators rather than to examine Deleuze's creative development of their concepts.

23 Ibid., pp. 4–11.

24 Bréhier, *La Théorie des incorporels dans l'ancien stoïcisme*, p. 6.

25 Ibid., p. 12.

26 See ibid., pp. 4–11.

27 Ibid., p. 50.

28 Deleuze, *The Logic of Sense*, p. 6.

29 See Gould, *The Philosophy of Chrysippus*, pp. 107–8.

30 Bréhier, *La Théorie des incorporels dans l'ancien stoïcisme*, p. 11. No doubt, it is still more complex than this. See Long, *Stoic Studies*, on the problem of the possibilities of the incorporeal *lekta* in some way influencing the corporeal (pp. 244–9, 284).

31 Bréhier, *La Théorie des incorporels dans l'ancien stoïcisme*, pp. 57–8. Bréhier's understanding of the Stoic notion of time is extremely complex. He suggests that, while there is a present continuity or duration, there is no present moment. That is, time, being a continuity, is infinitely divisible (in the manner of bodies, see Gould, *The Philosophy of Chrysippus*, p. 117) so that 'through division there is no present time. One can only speak of time in a certain extension' (Bréhier, *La Théorie des incorporels dans l'ancien stoïcisme*, p. 57). There is, then, no more limit between the past and the future than there is between one body and another: that is, 'in present time one part is future the other past' (ibid., p. 58). The present, which alone exists, is elusive (ibid., pp. 63–4), slipping now into the past and now pushing into the future. There is, then, as Bréhier concludes, a tendency here to deny the reality of time (ibid., p. 59) as it directly applies only to verbs and events and is incorporeal (what has happened, what will happen), yet, paradoxically, it is in the present that

'one accomplishes an act' (ibid., p. 58), and only bodies are able to act or be acted upon.

32 Deleuze, *Logic of Sense*, pp. 63–4.

33 See Bréhier, *La Théorie des incorporels dans l'ancien stoïcisme*, pp. 11–13; Gould, *The Philosophy of Chrysippus*, p. 101.

34 Samburskey, *Physics of the Stoics*, p. 53.

35 There are four categories of being for the Stoics: substance, quality, disposition and relative disposition, and above these there is a higher notion which encompasses all four, called 'the something', and it is to this category that incorporeals belong (see ibid., p. 17; Gould, *The Philosophy of Chrysippus*, p. 107; and Deleuze, *Logic of Sense*, p. 7).

36 Ibid., p. 7.

37 See Long, *Stoic Studies*, p. 247.

38 Bréhier, *La Théorie des incorporels dans l'ancien stoïcisme*, p. 15.

39 Deleuze, *Logic of Sense*, p. 21.

40 Ibid., p. 8.

41 Samuel Beckett, *Mercier and Camier* (London: Picador, 1988), pp. 92–4.

42 Samuel Beckett, *Molloy* (New York: Grove Press, 1955), pp. 112–14.

43 Ibid., pp. 206–9.

44 Samuel Beckett, *Malone Dies* (New York: Grove Press, 1956), pp. 99–104.

45 Ibid., pp. 118–19.

46 Ibid., p. 39.

47 See Bréhier, *La Théorie des incorporels dans l'ancien stoïcisme*, pp. 60–3.

48 Beckett, *Molloy*, p. 41.

49 See *Imagination Dead Imagine* and *All Strange Away*: Samuel Beckett, *The Complete Short Prose*, ed. Stanley Gontarski (New York: Grove Press, 1995).

50 See Beckett, *Complete Dramatic Works*.

51 Beckett, *Complete Short Prose*.

52 Beckett, *Complete Dramatic Works*.

53 Samuel Beckett, *How It Is* (New York: Grove Press, 1964).

54 Beckett, *Complete Dramatic Works*.

55 Beckett, *Complete Short Prose*.

56 Beckett, *Complete Dramatic Works*.

57 Long, *Stoic Studies*, p. 229.

58 They are no longer characters, and are now, as in *What Where*, barely individuated at all, with only differences of colour or position or percussive sound allowing us to tell them apart, and this growing together of the participants further leads one to think of them as one body (see Beckett, *Complete Dramatic Works*, pp. 451–3, 469).

59 Ibid., p. 453.

60 Ibid., pp. 470–6. As I touch upon below, Beckett has stated that *What Where* involves a 'field of memory' (see Stanley Gontarski, 'Notes to *What Where*: The Revised Text*, by Samuel Beckett', *Journal of Beckett Studies*, vol. 2, no. 1. (1992), pp. 1–25), but even so, according to A. A. Long, the Stoics, 'classify all

occurrent sensations and feelings, recollections, imaginations, and all transient thoughts' as images (*Stoic Studies*, p. 271).

61 For a reading of how *Quad* and the TV plays involve the exhaustion of possibilities see Gilles Deleuze, 'The Exhausted', tr. Anthony Uhlmann, in Daniel W. Smith and Michael A. Greco (eds.), *Essays Critical and Clinical* (Minneapolis: University of Minnesota Press, 1997), pp. 152–74.

62 See Beckett, *Complete Short Prose*.

63 Beckett, *Complete Dramatic Works*, p. 308.

64 See S. Sambursky, *The Physical World of the Greeks* (London: Routledge and Kegan Paul, 1956), pp. 123–6.

65 Gould, *The Philosophy of Chrysippus*, p. 117; Sambursky, *Physics of the Stoics*, pp. 7–17.

66 Gould, *The Philosophy of Chrysippus*, p. 107.

67 Long, *Stoic Studies*, p. 271; see also pp. 269–71.

68 Gould, *The Philosophy of Chrysippus*, pp. 107–8.

69 See Samuel Beckett, *Disjecta: Miscellaneous Writings and a Dramatic Fragment*, ed. Ruby Cohn (London: John Calder, 1983), p. 22.

70 Long, *Stoic Studies*, pp. 229–30.

71 Bréhier, *The History of Philosophy Vol. 2*, p. 56.

72 Beckett, *Complete Dramatic Works*, p. 470.

73 Beckett, quoted in Gontarski, 'Notes to *What Where: The Revised Text*', p. 11.

74 Ibid., p. 12.

75 Long, *Stoic Studies*, p. 271.

76 See Ibid., p. 226.

77 Beckett, *Complete Dramatic Works*, p. 470.

78 Ibid., p. 476.

79 Bréhier, *Chrysippe*, pp. 80–100.

80 Ibid., p. 110; Gould, *The Philosophy of Chrysippus*, p. 103

81 Ibid., pp. 130–1.

82 Ibid., p. 131.

83 Bréhier, *Chrysippe*, pp. 86–98.

84 See ibid., pp. 98–100; Long, *Stoic Studies*, p. 274.

85 Beckett, *Complete Dramatic Works*, pp. 474–5.

86 Ibid., p. 473.

87 Bréhier, *La Théorie des incorporels dans l'ancien stoïcisme*, pp. 60–3.

88 Bréhier, *Chrysippe*, pp. 86–98.

89 Gilles Deleuze and Félix Guattari, *What is Philosophy?*, tr. Hugh Tomlinson and Graham Burchell (New York: Columbia University Press, 1994), pp. 163–99.

Works cited

Abbott, H. Porter, *Beckett Writing Beckett: The Author in the Autograph* (Ithaca and London: Cornell University Press, 1996).

'Samuel Beckett and the Arts of Time: Painting, Music, Narrative', in Lois Oppenheim (ed.), *Samuel Beckett and the Arts* (New York: Garland, 1999), pp. 7–24.

Acheson, James, *Samuel Beckett's Artistic Theory and Practice* (London: Macmillan, 1997).

Ackerley, C. J., *Demented Particulars: The Annotated Murphy* (Talahassee: Journal of Beckett Studies Books, 1998).

and S. E. Gontarski, *The Grove Companion to Samuel Beckett* (New York: Grove Press, 2004).

Bair, Deirdre, *Samuel Beckett: A Biography* (London: Vintage, 1990).

Beckett on Film, 19 Films by 19 Directors, produced by Michael Colgan and Alan Moloney (Dublin: Blue Angel Films, 2001).

Beckett, Samuel, 1933 typescript, Letter 57, 'To Thomas MacGreevy, 6/12/33, 6 Clare St. Dublin', TCD MS 10402, Manuscripts Department, Trinity College Library Dublin, Republic of Ireland.

1934 typescript, Letter 63, 'To Thomas MacGreevy, 8/9/34, 34 Gertrude St, S.W. 10.', TCD MS 10402, Manuscripts Department, Trinity College Library Dublin, Republic of Ireland.

1936 typescript, Letter 85, 'To Thomas MacGreevy, 9/1/36 [written as 35 in error] Cooldrinagh', TCD MS 10402, Manuscripts Department, Trinity College Library Dublin, Republic of Ireland.

1936 typescript, 'Notes to Arnold Geulincx, *Ethica, Metaphysica Vera* and *Questiones Quodlibeticae*', TCD MS 10971/6, Manuscripts Department, Trinity College Library Dublin, Republic of Ireland.

1936 typescript, Letter 91, 'To Thomas MacGreevy, 5.3.36 Cooldrinagh', TCD MS 10402, Manuscripts Department, Trinity College Library Dublin, Republic of Ireland.

1938 typescript, Letter 155, 'To Thomas MacGreevy, 31/1/38 [Hotel] Liberia [Paris]', TCD MS 10402, Manuscripts Department, Trinity College Library Dublin, Republic of Ireland.

1948 typescript, Letter 175, 'To Thomas MacGreevy, 4/1/48 Paris', TCD MS 10402, Manuscripts Department, Trinity College Library Dublin, Republic of Ireland.

L'Innommable (Paris: Editions de Minuit, 1953).

Molloy (New York: Grove Press, 1955).

Malone Dies (New York: Grove Press, 1956).

Murphy (New York: Grove Press, 1957).

The Unnamable (New York: Grove Press, 1958).

How It Is (New York: Grove Press, 1964).

1967 manuscript, 'Letter to L. E. Harvey "Ussy, 20.2.67."' Beckett collection, Rare Books Library, Dartmouth College, Hanover, NH, USA.

Film: Complete Scenario, Illustrations, Production Shots, with the essay 'On Directing *Film*' by Alan Schneider (New York: Grove Press, 1969).

More Pricks Than Kicks (London: Picador, 1974).

'Interview with Gabriel d'Aubarède', tr. C. Waters, in L. Graver and R. Federman (eds.), *Samuel Beckett, the Critical Heritage* (London: Routledge and Kegan Paul, 1979), p. 217.

Disjecta: Miscellaneous Writings and a Dramatic Fragment, ed. Ruby Cohn (London: John Calder, 1983).

1984 manuscript, 'Letter to Dr. E. Franzen, 17/2/54', cited in 'Babel 3, 1984' [magazine], Ms 2993, The Samuel Beckett Collection, University of Reading, UK.

Proust and Three Dialogues with Georges Duthuit (London: John Calder, 1987).

Mercier and Camier (London: Picador, 1988).

Watt (London: Picador, 1988).

The Complete Dramatic Works (London: Faber and Faber, 1990).

Nohow On: Company, Ill Seen Ill Said, Worstward H. (London: John Calder, 1991).

Dream of Fair to Middling Women (New York: Arcade/Riverrun, 1993).

The Complete Short Prose, ed. Stanley Gontarski (New York: Grove Press, 1995).

Beckett's Dream Notebook, edited, annotated and with an introductory essay by John Pilling (Reading: Beckett International Foundation, 1999).

'Letter to Georges Duthuit, 9–10 March 1949', tr. Walter Redfern, in S. E. Gontarski and Anthony Uhlmann (eds.), *Beckett after Beckett* (Gainesville: University Press of Florida, 2006), pp. 15–21.

Beckett, Samuel, and Alan Schneider, *No Author Better Served: the Correspondence of Samuel Beckett and Alan Schneider*, ed. Maurice Harmon (Cambridge, MA: Harvard University Press, 1998).

Ben-Zvi, Linda (ed.), *Drawing on Beckett: Portraits, Performances, and Cultural Contexts* (Tel Aviv: Assaph Books, 2003).

Bergson, Henri, *An Introduction to Metaphysics*, tr. T. E. Hulme (New York and London: G. Putnam and Sons, 1912).

'Philosophical Intuition', in *The Creative Mind* (New York: Philosophical Library, 1946), pp. 126–52.

Matter and Memory, tr. N. M. Paul and W. S. Palmer (New York: Zone Books, 1991).

Blanchot, Maurice, 'Where Now? Who Now?' in *On Beckett, Essays and Criticism*, ed. S. E. Gontarski (New York: Grove Press, 1986), pp. 141–9.

'Michel Foucault as I Imagine Him', tr. Jeffrey Mehlman, *Foucault/Blanchot* (New York: Zone, 1990), pp. 61–109.

Bohman, James, 'Hermeneutics', in Robert Audi (ed.), *The Cambridge Dictionary of Philosophy* (Cambridge: Cambridge University Press, 1995), pp. 323–4.

Bréhier, Emile, *Chrysippe et l'ancien stoïcisme* (Paris: Félix Alcan, 1910).

The History of Philosophy Vol. 1: The Hellenic Age, tr. Joseph Thomas, (Chicago: University of Chicago Press, 1965).

The History of Philosophy Vol. 2: The Hellenistic and Roman Age, tr. Wade Baskin (Chicago: University of Chicago Press, 1965).

The History of Philosophy Vol. 3: The Middle Ages and the Renaissance, tr. Wade Baskin (Chicago: University of Chicago Press, 1967).

La Théorie des incorporels dans l'ancien stoïcisme (Paris: Librairie philosophique J. Vrin, 1997) (1st edn 1908).

Butler, Lance St John, *Samuel Beckett and the Meaning of Being* (St Martin's Press: New York, 1984).

Burrows, Rachel, 1931 manuscript, 'Notes to lectures by Samuel Beckett on Gide and Racine at Trinity College Dublin', TCD MIC 60, Manuscripts Department, Trinity College Library Dublin, Republic of Ireland.

Casanova, Pascale, *Beckett l'abstracteur* (Paris: Seuil, 1997).

Clément, Bruno, *Le Lecteur et son modèle: Voltaire, Pascal, Hugo, Shakespeare, Sartre, Flaubert* (Paris: Presses Universitaires de France, 1999).

'What the Philosophers Do with Samuel Beckett', tr. Anthony Uhlmann, in S. E. Gontarski and Anthony Uhlmann (eds.), *Beckett after Beckett* (Gainesville: University Press of Florida, 2006), pp. 116–37.

Connor, Steven, *Samuel Beckett: Repetition, Theory and Text* (Oxford: Basil Blackwell, 1988).

Conrad, Joseph, *Heart of Darkness* (London: Penguin, 1989).

Cournot, Michel, 'Avignon: Une nuit de l'Aida – Nous pensons beaucoup à vous, Vaclav Havel', *Le Monde* (24 July 1982), p. 14.

Cronin, Anthony, *Samuel Beckett: The Last Modernist* (London: Harper Collins, 1996).

Dearlove, Judith E., *Accommodating the Chaos: Samuel Beckett's Nonrelational Art* (Durham: Duke University Press, 1982).

Defoe, Daniel, *Robinson Crusoe* (London: Penguin Books, 2004).

de Lattre, Alain, *L'Occasionalisme d'Arnold Geulincx: étude sur la constitution de la doctrine* (Paris: Editions de Minuit, 1967).

Arnold Geulincx: présentation, choix de textes et traduction (Paris: Seghers, 1970).

Deleuze, Gilles, *Cinema 1: The Movement-Image*, tr. Hugh Tomlinson and Barbara Habberjam (Minneapolis: University of Minnesota Press, 1986).

Spinoza: Practical Philosophy, tr. Robert Hurley (San Francisco: City Lights Books, 1988).

Foucault, tr. and ed. Sean Hand (London: Athlone, 1988).

Cinema 2: The Time-Image, tr. Hugh Tomlinson and Robert Galeta (Minneapolis: University of Minnesota Press, 1989).

The Logic of Sense, tr. Mark Lester with Charles Stivale, ed. Constantin V. Boundas (New York: Columbia University Press, 1990).

Critique et Clinique (Paris: Editions de Minuit, 1993).

The Fold: Leibniz and the Baroque, tr. Tom Conley (Minneapolis: University of Minnesota Press, 1993).

Difference and Repetition, tr. Paul Patton (New York: Columbia University Press, 1994).

Negotiations, 1972–1990, tr. Martin Joughin (New York: Columbia University Press, 1995).

Francis Bacon: logique de la sensation (Paris: Editions de la différence, 1996).

'The Exhausted', tr. Anthony Uhlmann, in Daniel W. Smith and Michael A. Greco (eds.), *Essays Critical and Clinical* (Minneapolis: University of Minnesota Press, 1997), pp. 152–74.

'The Greatest Irish Film', in *Essays Critical and Clinical*, tr. Daniel W. Smith and Michael A. Greco (Minneapolis: University of Minnesota Press, 1997), pp. 23–6.

'The Brain is the Screen: An Interview with Gilles Deleuze', tr. Marie Therese Guirgis, in Gregory Flaxman (ed.), *The Brain is the Screen: Deleuze and the Philosophy of Cinema* (Minneapolis, University of Minnesota Press, 2000), pp. 365–74.

Proust and Signs, tr. Richard Howard (Minneapolis: University of Minnesota Press, 2000).

and Félix Guattari, *A Thousand Plateaus*, tr. Brian Massumi (Minneapolis: University of Minnesota Press, 1987).

What is Philosophy?, tr. Hugh Tomlinson and Graham Burchell (New York: Columbia University Press, 1994).

Derrida, Jacques, ' "This Strange Institution Called Literature": An Interview with Jacques Derrida' (with Derek Attridge), tr. Geoffrey Bennington and Rachel Bowlby, in Derek Attridge (ed.), *Acts of Literature* (New York: Routledge, 1992), pp. 33–75.

Descartes, René, *Discourse on Method and the Meditations*, tr. with an introduction by F. E. Sutcliffe (London: Penguin, 1968).

'Discourse on Method', in *The Philosophical Writings of Descartes*, vol. I, trs. John Cottingham, Robert Stoothoff and Dugald Murdoch (Cambridge: Cambridge University Press, 1985), pp. 111–51.

'Principles of Philosophy' in *The Philosophical Writings of Descartes*, vol. I, trs. John Cottingham, Robert Stoothoff and Dugald Murdoch (Cambridge: Cambridge University Press, 1985), pp. 177–291.

De Vleeschauwer, H. J., 'Les Antécédents du Transcendentalisme kantien. Geulincx et Kant', *Kantstudien* (1953–4), pp. 245–73.

Three Centuries of Geulincx Research (Pretoria: Communications of the University of South Africa, 1957).

'L'Occasionalisme et la condition humanine chez A. Geulincx', *Kantstudien* (1958), pp. 109–24.

Le *'De Virtute et primis ejus Proprietatibus' d'Arnout Geulincx et sa traduction flammande 'Van de Hoofdeuchden'. Introduction et Textes* (Pretoria: Van Schaik, 1961).

Les Plans d'études au XVIIe siècle. I: Le Plan de Descartes; II: Le Plan d'A. Geulincx. (Pretoria: Communications of the University of South Africa, 1962 and 1964).

Le Problème du suicide dans la morale de Geulincx (Pretoria: Communications of the University of South Africa, 1965).

Dictionnaire historique de la langue Française, general editor Alain Rey (Paris: Dictionnares le Robert, 1992).

Douglas, Paul, *Bergson, Eliot, and American Literature* (Lexington: University of Kentucky Press, 1986).

Driver, Tom F., 'Beckett by the Madeleine', *Columbia University Forum* (summer, 1961), pp. 21–5.

Ferguson, Robert, *The Short Sharp Life of T. E. Hulme* (London: Penguin, 2002).

Fink, Hilary L., *Bergson and Russian Modernism 1900–1930* (Evanston: Northwestern University Press, 1999).

Flaubert, Gustave, *Dictionnaire des idées reçues: suivi du Catalogue des idées chic* (Paris: Aubier, 1978).

Flaxman, Gregory (ed.), *The Brain is the Screen: Deleuze and the Philosophy of Cinema* (Minneapolis: University of Minnesota Press, 2000).

Foucault, Michel, 'Qu'est-ce qu'un auteur?', *Bulletin de le Société française de Philosophie*, vol. 63, no. 3 (February 1969), pp. 73–104.

L'Ordre du discours: Leçon inaugurale au Collège de France prononcée le 2 décembre 1970 (Paris: Gallimard, 1971).

'What is an Author?', in *Language, Counter-Memory, Practice. Selected Essays and Interviews*, ed. Donald F. Bouchard, trs. Donald F. Bouchard and Sherry Simon (Ithaca: Cornell University Press, 1977), pp. 124–7.

'Archéologie d'une passion' (interview with Charles Ruas), *Magazine littéraire*, number 221 (July–August 1985), pp. 100–5.

The Archaeology of Knowledge, tr. A. M. Sheridan Smith (London: Routledge, 1989).

Frede, Michael, 'Principles of Stoic Grammar', in John M. Rist (ed.), *The Stoics* (Berkeley and Los Angeles: University of California Press, 1978), pp. 27–76.

Gaukroger, Stephen, *Descartes: An Intellectual Biography* (Oxford: Clarendon Press, 1995).

Geulincx, Arnold, *A. Geulincx Antverpiensis Opera philosophica*, 3 vols., ed. J. P. N. Land, (The Hague: Martin Nijhoff, 1891–3).

Van de hoofddeugden. De eerste tuchtverhandeling, ed. with an introduction and notes by Cornelis Verhoeven (Baarn: Ambo, 1986).

Metaphysics, tr. Martin Wilson (Wisbech: Christoffel Press, 1999).

Gillies, Mary Ann, *Henri Bergson and British Modernism* (Montreal and Kingston: McGill-Queen's University Press, 1996).

Gontarski, Stanley, 'Appendix A: Beckett on *Film*', in *The Intent of Undoing in Samuel Beckett's Dramatic Texts* (Bloomington: Indiana University Press, 1985), pp. 187–92.

'Notes to *What Where: The Revised Text*, by Samuel Beckett', *Journal of Beckett Studies*, vol. 2, no. 1. (1992), pp. 1–25.

Gould, Josiah B., *The Philosophy of Chrysippus* (Leiden: E. J. Brill, 1970).

Graeser, Andreas, 'The Stoic Theory of Meaning', in John M. Rist (ed.), *The Stoics* (Berkeley and Los Angeles: University of California Press, 1978), pp. 77–100.

Hardt, Michael, *Gilles Deleuze: An Apprenticeship in Philosophy* (London: University College London Press, 1993).

Harvey, Lawrence E., *Samuel Beckett Poet and Critic* (Princeton: Princeton University Press, 1970).

Henning, Sylvie Debevec, '"Film": a Dialogue between Beckett and Berkeley', *Journal of Beckett Studies*, no. 7 (spring 1982), pp. 89–100.

Hill, Leslie, *Beckett's Fiction in Different Words* (Cambridge: Cambridge University Press, 1990).

Bataille, Klossowski, Blanchot: Writing at the Limit (Oxford: Oxford University Press, 2001).

Jander, Owen, 'The Eroica Reading List' [review of *Beethoven: The Music and the Life*, by Lewis Lockwood], *Times Literary Supplement* (4 July 2003), p. 30.

Joyce, James, *A Portrait of the Artist as a Young Man* (London: Grafton Books, 1977).

Stephen Hero (London: Grafton Books, 1986).

Kant, Immanuel, *Critique of Pure Reason*, tr. and ed. Paul Guyer and Allen W. Wood (Cambridge: Cambridge University Press, 1997).

Kennedy, Sighle, *Murphy's Bed: A Study of Real Sources and Sur-real Associations in Samuel Beckett's First Novel* (Lewisburg: Bucknell University Press, 1971).

Kenner, Hugh, *Samuel Beckett: A Critical Study* (Berkeley: University of California Press, 1968).

Knowlson, James, *Damned to Fame: The Life of Samuel Beckett* (London: Bloomsbury, 1996).

Land, J. P. N., 'Arnold Geulincx and His Works', *Mind: A Quarterly Review of Psychology and Philosophy*, vol. 16 (1891), pp. 223–42.

Le Doeuff, Michèle, *The Philosophical Imaginary*, tr. Colin Gordon (London: The Athlone Press, 1989).

Long, A. A., *Stoic Studies* (Cambridge: Cambridge University Press, 1996).

Marcabru, Pierre, 'Avignon, La nuit de l'Aida – Le poisson noyé – Communisme: l'Innommable', *Le Figaro* (23 July 1982), p. 19.

'Le Mort de Beckett', *Le Figaro* (27 December 1989) p. 1.

Martin, Jean-Clet, 'Of Images and Worlds: Toward a Geology of the Cinema', in Gregory Flaxman (ed.), *The Brain is the Screen: Deleuze and the Philosophy of Cinema* (Minneapolis: University of Minnesota Press, 2000), pp. 61–86.

Maxwell, Donald R., *The Abacus and the Rainbow: Bergson, Proust, and the Digital-Analogic Opposition* (New York: Peter Lang, 1999).

McCracken, D. J., *Thinking and Valuing: An Introduction, Partly Historical, to the Study of the Philosophy of Value* (London: Macmillan, 1950).

McMillan, Dougald, and Martha Fehsenfeld, *Beckett in the Theatre: The Author as Practical Playwright and Director* (London: John Calder, 1988).

Medvedev, P. N., and M. M. Bakhtin, *The Formal Method in Literary Scholarship*, tr. Albert J. Wehrle (Baltimore: Johns Hopkins University Press, 1991).

Megay, Joyce N., *Bergson et Proust: Essai de mise au point de la question de l'influence de Bergson sur Proust* (Paris: J. Vrin, 1976).

Moorjani, Angela B., *Abysmal Games in the Novels of Samuel Beckett* (Chapel Hill: University of North Carolina Press, 1982).

Morson, Gary Saul, and Caryl Emerson, *Mikhail Bakhtin: Creation of a Prosaics* (Stanford: Stanford University Press, 1990).

Nadler, Steven, 'Occasionalism and the Mind-Body Problem', in M. A. Stewart (ed.), *Studies in Seventeenth-Century European Philosophy* (New York: Clarendon, 1997), pp. 75–95.

'Knowledge, Volitional Agency and Causation in Malebranche and Geulincx', *British Journal for the History of Philosophy*, vol. 7, no. 2 (1999), pp. 263–74.

Spinoza: A Life (Cambridge: Cambridge University Press, 1999).

Nietzsche, Friedrich, *The Birth of Tragedy: Out of the Spirit of Music* (London: Penguin, 1993).

Nuchelmans, G., *Geulincx's Containment Theory of Logic* (Amsterdam, 1988).

O'Brien, Eoin, *The Beckett Country: Samuel Beckett's Ireland* (Dublin: Black Cat, 1986).

Oppenheim, Lois, *The Painted Word: Samuel Beckett's Dialogue with Art* (Ann Arbor: University of Michigan Press, 2000).

Patton, Paul, *Deleuze and the Political* (London: Routledge, 2000).

Peirce, Charles Sanders, *Peirce on Signs*, ed. James Hoopes (Chapel Hill: University of North Carolina Press, 1991).

Pilling, John, *Samuel Beckett* (London: Routledge and Kegan Paul, 1976).

Beckett before Godot (Cambridge: Cambridge University Press, 1997).

Plato, *The Collected Dialogues, Including the Letters*, ed. Edith Hamilton and Huntington Cairns (Princeton: Princeton University Press, 1996).

Pound, Ezra, *Make It New* (London: Faber and Faber, 1934).

'In a Station of the Metro', in Alexander W. Allison et al. (eds.), *The Norton Anthology of Poetry*, 3rd edn (New York: Norton, 1983), p. 963.

Proust, Marcel, *A la recherche du temps perdu*, vol. I, ed. Jean-Yves Tadié (Paris: Gallimard, 1987).

Rabouin, David, 'Spinoza en liberté', *Magazine Littéraire*, 370 (November 1998), p. 20.

Redding, Paul, *The Logic of Affect* (New York: Cornell University Press, 1999).

Rodowick, D. N., *Gilles Deleuze's Time Machine* (Durham: Duke University Press, 1997).

Rosen, Steven J., *Samuel Beckett and the Pessimistic Tradition* (New Brunswick: Rutgers University Press, 1976).

Rousset, Bernard, *Geulincx: Entre Descartes et Spinoza* (Paris: Vrin, 1999).

Sambursky, S., *The Physical World of the Greeks* (London: Routledge and Kegan Paul, 1956).

Physics of the Stoics (London: Routledge and Kegan Paul, 1959).

Sandbach, F. H., *The Stoics* (London: Chatto and Windus, 1975).

Schneider, Alan, *Entrances: An American Director's Journey* (New York: Limelight Editions, 1987).

Shenker, Israel, '"Moody Man of Letters". Interview with Samuel Beckett', *The New York Times*, section 2 (6 May 1956), pp. 1, 3.

Shklovsky, Vicktor, 'The Resurrection of the Word' in *Russian Formalism: A Collection of Articles and Texts in Translation*, ed. Stephen Bann and John E. Bowlt (Edinburgh: Scottish Academic Press, 1973), pp. 41–7.

Simon, Alfred, 'Le mort de Samuel Beckett: L'auteur d' "En attendant Godot" est décédé vendredi 22 décembre à Paris', *Le Monde* (27 December 1989), pp. 1, 10.

Spinoza, Benedictus de, *Opera*, ed. J. Van Vloten and J. P. N. Land, Vol. 1 (Hagae Comitum: Martinum Nijhoff, 1882).

Ethics, tr. Andrew Boyle and revised with an introduction by G. H. R. Parkinson (London: Everyman, 1992).

Tadié, Jean-Yves, *Marcel Proust: a Life*, tr. Euan Cameron (London: Penguin, 2001).

Terraillon, E., *La Morale de Geulincx* (Paris: Félix Alcan, 1912).

Uhlmann, Anthony, *Beckett and Poststructuralism* (Cambridge: Cambridge University Press, 1999).

Vander Haeghen, Victor, *Geulincx. Etude sur sa vie, sa philosophie et ses ouvrages* (Paris: Gand, 1886).

van Ruler, Han, 'Minds, Forms, and Spirits: the Nature of Cartesian Disenchantment', *Journal of the History of Ideas*, vol. 61 (2000), pp. 381–95.

'Arnout Geulincx', in Wiep van Bunge, Henri Krop, Han van Ruler and Paul Schuurman (eds.), *The Dictionary of Seventeenth- and Eighteenth-Century Dutch Philosophers* (London: Thoemmes Continuum, 2004).

Wood, Rupert, 'Murphy, Beckett, Geulincx, God' *The Journal of Beckett Studies*, vol. 2 (1993), pp. 27–51.

Zourabichvili, François, 'The Eye of Montage: Dziga Vertov and Bergsonian Materialism', in Gregory Flaxman (ed.), *The Brain is the Screen: Deleuze and the Philosophy of Cinema* (Minneapolis: University of Minnesota Press, 2000), pp. 141–52.

Index